Messiah's Calendar Book 2

The Feasts of the Lord

and how to observe them in a way that glorifies Jesus

Messiah's Calendar Book 2

The Feasts of the Lord

and how to observe them in a way that glorifies Jesus

James T. and Lisa M. Cummins

Messiah's Calendar Book 2: The Feasts of the Lord
and how to observe them in a way that glorifies Jesus
Copyright © 2019 by James T. and Lisa M. Cummins
First printing 2019

Published by James T. and Lisa M. Cummins
Fruitland Park, Florida 34731 USA

This publication may be freely reproduced in hardcopy on paper, in whole or in part, by any individual or organization, provided that (a) the contents are not altered in any way and (b) any resulting paper reproductions are never sold or made available to others in exchange for payment or reimbursement of any kind (i.e., hardcopies may be made for purely educational purposes, not for commercial use). Electronic copies may <u>not</u> be distributed to others, in whole or in part, by means of electronic distribution systems or networks of any kind, including but not limited to the internet, social networking, cellular networks, file sharing systems or any other means. (Electronic images of the book <u>may</u> be displayed on a projection device within a classroom, meeting room or auditorium for educational purposes.) Brief excerpts of this book may be quoted within the context of articles/reviews, whether in electronic format or in hardcopy.

Interior design by Lisa M. Cummins

Cover design by Lisa M. Cummins

*Give me understanding, and I will keep Your Torah (instruction).
Yes, I will obey it with my whole heart.*

Psalm 119:34

*For most certainly, I tell you, until heaven and earth pass away,
not even one smallest letter or one tiny pen stroke shall in any way
pass away from the law, until all things are accomplished.
Whoever, therefore, shall break one of these least commandments,
and teach others to do so, shall be called least in the Kingdom of Heaven;
but whoever shall do and teach them shall be called
great in the Kingdom of Heaven.*

Matthew 5:18-19

*In this mountain, the L*ORD *of Armies will make for all peoples a feast of rich foods, a banquet of aged wines, of choicest meats, of well refined wines of the finest vintage. He will destroy in this mountain the face of the enveloping shroud that hangs over all peoples, and the veil that is spread over all nations. He has swallowed up death forever! Adonai the L*ORD *will wipe away tears from off all faces. He will take the reproach of His people away from off all the earth, for the L*ORD *has spoken it.*

Isaiah 25:6-8

Table of Contents

The Signs on the Door, painting by James Jacques Joseph Tissot, c. 1896-1902

Introduction 15
Why people might read this book 15
How this book is arranged 16
Observing the feasts... is it mandatory? 17
Hebrew and Greek terms made easy 17

**Overview of the Biblical Year
and God's Appointed Times** 19
Biblical Year Graphic 20
Seven major "appointed times" of the Lord 22
The prophetic significance of the seven major appointed times . 23
Appointed Times Graphic 24

Passover: Messiah's Death 27
From bondage to freedom 29
Spiritual freedom in the Old Testament 29
Spiritual freedom in the New Testament 30
The Passover Lamb in the Old and New Testaments 30
Applying the blood in the Old and New Testaments 31
Jesus is the door of salvation 31
A feast without leaven (Old and New Testaments) 32
Passover/Unleavened Bread as a unit 33
A memorial forever 34
Passover isn't just for Jews 35
A memorial forever – the New Testament 35
Do "this" in remembrance of Me 36
The "cup after the meal" 36
Other powerful seder symbols 37

Observance of Passover 39
The Seder Plate 41
The Four Cups 42
The Bread of Affliction 43
The Four Questions 44
Favorite Passover Recipes 45

The Search for the Leaven, etching by Bernard Picart, circa 1733.

Unleavened Bread: Messiah's Burial...........47
What is leaven? 49
Scriptural terms for *leaven*..49
Scriptural terms for *unleavened*...50
God's Feast of Unleavened Bread 50
Repetitions of the commandment 52
Unleavened Bread's prophetic significance 53
Leaven in the New Testament...54
Unleavened Bread in the New Testament.............................55
Bedikat Chametz – the traditional search for leaven and
its Messianic symbolism...56

Observance of the Feast of Unleavened Bread 59
Bedikat Chametz..60
Matzah-Based Recipes 61

Firstfruits: Messiah's Resurrection 63
The commandment of the feast 65
God's timing of the Feast of Firstfruits 66
Scriptural terms for *firstfruits*...68
Firstfruits in the New Testament..69
How New Testament events align with Nisan's feasts 70
"Counting the omer" – *S'firat Ha-Omer*..............................72
The "promise of the Father" 73
Observance of Firstfruits 73
Observance of the omer count..74

Observance of the Feast of Firstfruits 77
Paper Plate Empty Tomb craft for children 78
Counting the Omer: *S'firat ha-Omer* 81
Omer Calendar...82

Weeks: The Descent of the Indwelling Holy Spirit ... 95
Why the term "Weeks"? ... 97
Why the term "Pentecost"? ... 97
The commandment to observe Shavuot ... 98
Shavuot is a special sabbath day ... 99
A feast of rejoicing... for *all* ... 99
One of three "pilgrimage feasts" ... 99
Another time that firstfruits is offered ... 100
A traditional explanation ... 100
The giving of Torah, God's instruction ... 101
Shavuot as a wedding celebration ... 101
Signs that accompanied the giving of Torah at Sinai ... 102
Signs that accompanied the giving of the indwelling Holy Spirit at Zion ... 103
A comparison graphic of the two Shavuot events ... 106
Why the number *seventy* at Shavuot? ... 107
Ten days after His last appearance ... 107
The book of Ruth and the Feast of Weeks ... 108
Traditions of Shavuot ... 109

Observance of the Feast of Weeks ... 111
Shehecheyanu: Who has granted us life ... 112
Aseret Ha Dibrot: The Ten Utterances ... 113
Tissue Paper Flower Garland craft for children ... 114
Blintzes Recipe ... 115

Trumpets: The Translation of Believers ... 117
The commandment to observe Yom Teruah ... 120
Other verses which include *teruah* ... 120
Themes repeated in the New Testament ... 121
The powerful symbolism of the shofar ... 122
Always returning, ever expanding ... 123
The "four calls" of the shofar – God's plan of the ages ... 124
Other titles and traditional concepts of Yom Teruah ... 125
What is a "civil" calendar year? ... 126
Traditional Jewish concepts of Yom Teruah ... 127
Other traditions of Yom Teruah ... 128

Shavuot (Pentecost), painting by Moritz Daniel Oppenheim, 1879.

In the Synagogue – Kol Nidre, painting by Wilhelm Wachtel, circa 1900.

Observance of the Day of Trumpets 131
Melech, Ozer: O King, O Helper 132
Adon Olam: Lord of the Universe (Eternal Lord) 133
Paper Crown craft for children 134
Party Horn Shofar craft for children 135
Recipe: Easy Apple Bundt Cake 136

Atonement: The Atonement of All Israel ... 139
The commandment to observe Yom Kippur 142
"Afflicting" and "denying" oneself 142
"The Fast" – Yom Kippur in the New Testament 142
The meaning of "atonement" 143
Atonement and the ark's "mercy seat": the *kapporet* 143
The symbols of the Day of Atonement 143
The procedures of the high priest on Yom Kippur (Leviticus 16)
and their symbolic meaning 144
Why "blood"? 146
Why have daily *and* yearly sin offerings? 146
Traditional Jewish understanding 148
The "pure soul" and "sealing" the book 149
Traditions of Yom Kippur 150
Kol Nidre – "All Vows" 151
Historical "Christian" antisemitism 151
Forced vows of renunciation 152
Say it... or die 153

Observance of the Day of Atonement 155
Avinu, Malkeinu: Our Father, Our King 156
Kol Nidre: All Vows 157
Al Chet: For the Sin 158

Tabernacles: The Millennial Kingdom ... 163
The commandment to observe the Feast of Booths ... 166
"Book-ended" by two special sabbaths ... 167
A joyful time of ingathering ... 167
A feast for eternity ... 167
One of the three pilgrimage feasts ... 167
For the foreigner and the homeless, too ... 167
The Messianic age of worldwide peace ... 168
The Feast of Ingathering ... 169
The four species ... 170
Waving the branches ... 171
The sukkah as a symbol of God's glory ... 172
The sukkah as a symbol of a dwelling ... 173
Water and light: Jesus in the Feast of Tabernacles ... 174
Yeshua – the water of Sukkot ... 174
Yeshua – the light of Sukkot ... 175
Hoshana Rabbah – The "Great Save Now" ... 176
Yeshua – fulfillment of Hoshana Rabbah ... 177
A Sukkot-like event – though not at Sukkot ... 178
Eighth Day of Assembly – Shemini Atzeret ... 179
Simchat Torah – Rejoicing in the Torah ... 180
A closing thought – the timing of Jesus' birth ... 181

Observance of the Feast of Tabernacles ... 183
To the sukkah: A song about the Feast of Tabernacles ... 184
Lulav waving ceremony ... 185
Sukkah building ideas ... 186
Children's crafts: Edible Sukkah, Kid's Craft Lulav ... 187

Appendix: Helpful Resources ... 189
Article: "Did Jesus die at the third or the sixth hour?" ... 190
Article: "Did Jesus spend 72 full hours in the grave?" ... 192
Article: "When was Jesus born?" ... 195
Glossary and Index ... 201
Indexes of Recipes; Children's Crafts and Activities;
Songs and Liturgy ... 209
Other Books By James T. and Lisa M. Cummins ... 211

Sukkot (Feast of Tabernacles), painting by Moritz Daniel Oppenheim, 1866.

When one of those who sat at the table with Him heard these things, he said to Him, "Blessed is he who will feast in the Kingdom of God!"

Jesus replied, "A certain man made a great feast, and he invited many people. He sent out his servant at supper time to tell those who were invited, 'Come, for everything is ready now.'"

Luke 14:15-17

Introduction

Welcome to Book 2 of the *Messiah's Calendar* series. If you have studied Book 1, you've already received the blessing of learning all about God's biblical calendar – how He defines a day, a week, a month and a year – as well as a brief overview of His *appointed times*, frequently called "the feasts of the LORD." If you have not yet had the chance to read Book 1, you will still be able to understand everything in Book 2, but we strongly advise that you go back and read Book 1 someday so that you can get a strong foundation in God's method of timekeeping. We can't stress enough how helpful and eye-opening a working knowledge of God's calendar will be in your personal Bible study.

Why people might read this book

People study the biblical feasts for many different reasons. Listed below are several possible reasons a person might study this book:

- **To honor and glorify Messiah Jesus,** by pondering the scriptures which speak about His holy days – spiritual "pictures" which God invented to point us toward the redemptive work of Jesus

- **To understand the timing of scriptural events** – God's feasts help us "pin down" the chronology of Old and New Testament events

- **To understand scriptural types, shadows and symbols** with respect to God's holy days – God's feasts reveal greater depth of meaning for events He has *already* fulfilled, while providing prophetic insight about future events *yet* to be fulfilled

- **To facilitate group worship between Jews and Gentiles** who believe in Jesus – God's holy days form a natural "bridge" of instant "common ground" between the two cultures

- **To express love for – and solidarity with – Israel** ("Israel" being the Jewish people in the Holy Land *and* those scattered throughout the world) by confirming as holy and precious the *same exact biblical dates* that *Israel* holds to be holy and precious

- **To receive the special anointing and sense of fulfillment** which comes from personally observing a feast of the LORD on the very date He ordered it to be done – even if quietly and privately in one's own home – a uniquely joyful, purposeful and memorable event

> *"Come to the feast, for everything is ready now."*
>
> The words of Jesus in the Parable of the Great Banquet, Luke 14:17

> *God's feasts are intended to be celebrations of His love for us and our love for Him.*

*Messianic congregations are mixed groups of Jews and Gentiles who believe Jesus is Messiah, Savior, Lord and God, and who worship Him together. They believe in being "born again," obtaining salvation through faith in Messiah's sacrificial death and resurrection, *purely* on the basis of the grace of God (*not* on the basis of human works, merit or effort). Messianic believers embrace both Old and New Testaments as "Torah" (that is, as God's divine and perfect "instruction") and celebrate the biblical calendar (which includes God's feast days). They also permit and encourage celebrations of other significant Jewish life cycle events which are aligned with scriptural principles (Jewish weddings, bar/bat mitzvah celebrations, yizchor/memorials, etc). All those who attend, be they Jew or Gentile, are invited to freely participate in any observances to whatever extent they feel comfortable, but are never compelled to do so.

How this book is arranged

Each chapter features a different feast. In it, we teach you the feast's position in God's yearly calendar, its place in Scripture, and its prophetic or symbolic significance, with careful attention to how it glorifies Jesus as Messiah.

We have spent decades teaching about God's appointed times (a.k.a., the "feasts") to churches, Messianic congregations* and home groups. Every time we teach this topic, we get the following statement from *someone* in the group:

> "I just loved learning about this feast day! But, now, I feel like I want to *do* this at home with my family! I mean, isn't there, like, stuff you can actually *do*, like songs and foods and what-not?"

The answer to this question is "Yes! There *is* stuff you can actually do." Best of all, the "stuff" we will show you will be either straight out of Scripture or aligned with Scripture. At the end of every chapter is a **special section on observance** with some Scripture verses to read aloud, songs to sing, foods to make, and children's crafts. Each special section on observance is printed on pages having a decorative black border, so that you can easily distinguish them from the "regular" pages in the book.

This brings us to a very important point. Please understand that **the sections on observance are provided only for those people who feel drawn by God to actively participate in *doing*, or *observing*, a particular feast.** Some of our readers may *never* experience that particular call of God, and they should feel neither guilty nor pressured to begin to observe *anything* that God has not personally confirmed to them in a spirit of peace. In fact, one reason we confined the observance materials to their own special sections was to make them easier to skip over, for the sake of those readers who are new to the feasts and not yet comfortable with the thought of observing them. We trust that the Holy Spirit will impress on each reader whatever ought to be his or her unique response to this book.

If you're feeling conflicted (i.e., "on the fence") about God's holy days in general, it might clarify things to take the perspective of the following parable. Let's say your best friend, whom you have trusted and loved your entire life, has a special anniversary coming up. He has invited you to the anniversary dinner. The *date* is crucial for him, because it reflects the date of a pivotal event which occurred in his life. The *gathering* is important to both of you, because you truly share his joy over this wonderful event that you are both commemorating. You are looking forward to this time of celebration, during which you can express your love for your friend. *That's* the attitude that should fill our hearts as we contemplate God's feasts.

Observing the feasts... is it mandatory?

Observing a feast day is one of those things that is *not* essential to salvation – *and never was!* If you think you will be able to "earn" salvation by observance of a feast (or by performance of *anything,* including any of God's commandments), you have a mistaken understanding of God's loving gift of *grace.* *Grace* is *unearned, unmerited, unconditionally loving favor.* It was the sacrifice of God's Son that did all the "earning" you will ever need. You *already* stand in a state of perfect acceptance by God, if you have asked Him to cleanse your sins in the shed blood of Jesus. That said, if you *do* begin to sense that God is calling you to participate in observing His feast days, by all means, enjoy! As a believer in Jesus, you are now a part of the family, and no one can refuse you the privilege of participating. Gentile or Jew, there's no difference in God's sight... *all* are invited!

Hebrew and Greek terms made easy

As we did in Book 1, we will give you simple definitions for all unfamiliar Hebrew or Greek terms along with their *transliterations* (pronunciations), so that you can learn how to say them.* Now, learning these terms isn't required for gaining a basic grasp of God's feasts, so don't become overly concerned about memorizing a bunch of foreign words. Just let yourself absorb whatever comes naturally as you read along at your own pace.

Also, be aware that we tend to use the names *Jesus* and *Yeshua* interchangeably in our writing. *Yeshua* is just Hebrew for *Jesus. Yeshua* (pronounced "yay-shoo-ah") is the actual name He was called by His earthly family and the disciples. *Yeshua* was translated into Greek in the New Testament as Ἰησοῦς (*Iesous,* pronounced "yay-ssooss") which eventually morphed through Latin then English into *Jesus.* But they're all really the *same name, just translated.* For example, a man might be called "Jack" in England, but, if he moved to France, he'd probably wind up being called "Jacques" by the French people there. An American named "Peter" might end up using the name "Pierre" in France.

Another reason we use the names *Yeshua* and *Jesus* interchangeably is that our readers come from both Jewish and Gentile backgrounds. In Hebrew, *Yeshua* connotes "salvation," so the use of this ancient Hebrew name can have a profound effect upon an observant Jew who may not yet know Him as Messiah. As we make use of the comfortable, familiar elements from people's cultures, we can help them connect more easily with challenging new concepts. We imitate the apostle Paul (Rav Sha'ul), who said, "I have become all things to all people" (1 Cor. 9:22). **Our heart's desire is to make everyone feel welcome and at ease,** especially those having to face a biblical truth they have never been taught in church or synagogue.

Ready to begin? We'll start with a nice overview in the next section.

Observing a feast day is one of those things that is not essential to salvation – and never was.

*Pronunciation note: Here's one helpful tip for pronunciation. Wherever you see the letters *ch* in our transliterations of Hebrew and Greek words, please pronounce the *ch* like in *Bach* or *Loch Ness.* It's a sort of rough "h" sound made by slightly closing the space between the back of the tongue and throat. (Now, if you can't make that noise, it's perfectly fine to just use a regular "h" sound. Lots of modern Israelis do this anyway!) This unique sound is often represented by a special character which looks an h with a dash going through it: ħ.

Important: You should never pronounce the Greek or Hebrew "ch" like the sound in *church,* because that sound does not exist in either the Hebrew or Greek languages. (We'll remind you about this as we go along; don't worry!)

"These are the appointed times of the Lord, even holy convocations, which you shall proclaim in their appointed season."

The words of God, Leviticus 23:4

PASSOVER · UNLEAVENED BREAD · FIRSTFRUITS · PENTECOST/WEEKS · DAY OF TRUMPETS · DAY OF ATONEMENT · TABERNACLES

For everything there is a season, and a time for every purpose under heaven... He has made everything beautiful in its time...

Ecclesiastes 3:1,11

Overview of the Biblical Year and God's Appointed Times

For those who have not had a chance to study Book 1 of our series, we'd like to present a brief overview of the biblical year, followed by an overview of the seven "feasts," or "appointed times," of the Lord.

Notes about the Biblical Year graphic

The graphic on the following two pages lists all the months of the biblical year. Unlike the months in our own calendar (which we call the *western* calendar or *Gregorian* calendar), the first day of every biblical month is determined by the occurrence of the phase of the *new moon*. Therefore, the biblical calendar is essentially a *lunar* calendar. Look at the bottom of the graphic, and you'll notice that the biblical months don't align at all with our western months; rather, they "straddle" part-way across our months.

Who invented this calendar in the first place? God did. At the time of the Exodus, God instructed Moses to tell the people Israel that the first month of their year was to be the month Abib, later called Nisan (Ex. 12:2). Up until that time, the Jewish people had always observed a different month as the start of their "new year." When it came to establishing God's calendar, the Jewish people themselves had absolutely *no* input. In fact, the Lord frequently had to *command* them to change their entire culture in order to bring them into alignment with His calendar. Jews even resisted observing God's calendar at certain times in their history. This is just one reason why it is more accurate to call this calendar a *biblical calendar* or a *Godly calendar,* rather than implying it to be merely a man-made, "Jewish" calendar. The only reason it came to be called "Jewish" is that Jewish people happened to be the first ones to observe it.

The names of the months came from two different cultures which influenced Israel. The oldest names, which are *pre-exilic* names, came from the Canaanite culture and language. After Israel was exiled to Babylon, a new set of names came into use: the *post-exilic* names, coming from the Babylonian culture and language. Many of these names may be found in Scripture (some are only found in extra-biblical writings), but the post-exilic names have remained in constant use by Jewish people from biblical times until today.

Please take a moment now to locate the **Biblical Holy Days** and **Biblical Events** which are listed toward the bottom of the graphic. Note that the biblical holy days are the ones that God Himself instituted in Leviticus chapter 23. They occur in the *first month*, the *third month* and the *seventh month*. These are the "feasts" which will be covered, each in its own chapter, in detail throughout this book. The other events (Chanukah and Purim), are mentioned in the Bible but were not specifically commanded by God, and so are considered "minor" feasts.

God Himself established the order of the months of the biblical year and invented the "feasts."

The Jewish people were merely the first group of people to observe them.

The Biblical Year

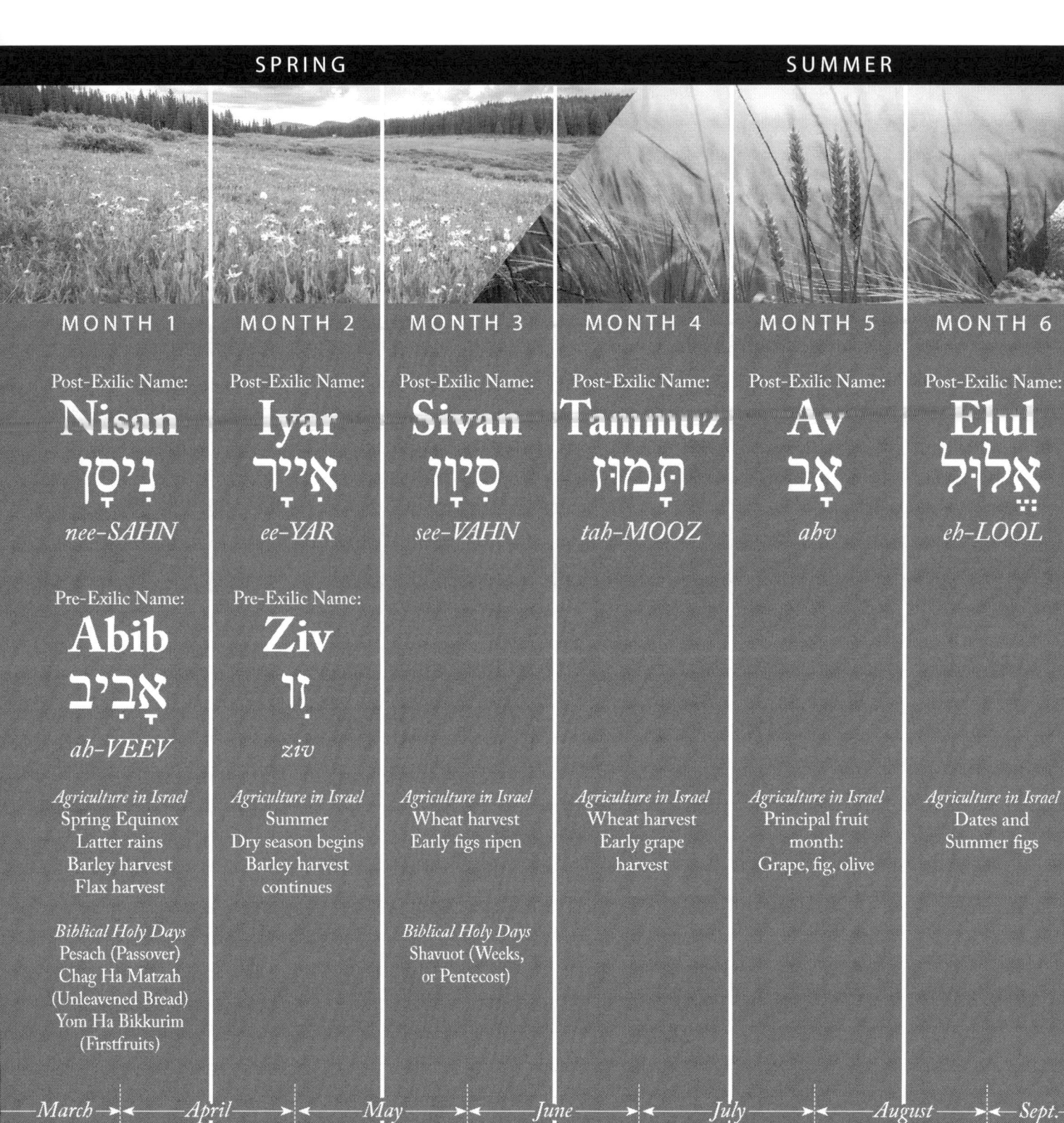

SPRING | **SUMMER**

MONTH 1
Post-Exilic Name:
Nisan
נִיסָן
nee-SAHN

Pre-Exilic Name:
Abib
אָבִיב
ah-VEEV

Agriculture in Israel
Spring Equinox
Latter rains
Barley harvest
Flax harvest

Biblical Holy Days
Pesach (Passover)
Chag Ha Matzah
(Unleavened Bread)
Yom Ha Bikkurim
(Firstfruits)

MONTH 2
Post-Exilic Name:
Iyar
אִיָּר
ee-YAR

Pre-Exilic Name:
Ziv
זִו
ziv

Agriculture in Israel
Summer
Dry season begins
Barley harvest
continues

MONTH 3
Post-Exilic Name:
Sivan
סִיוָן
see-VAHN

Agriculture in Israel
Wheat harvest
Early figs ripen

Biblical Holy Days
Shavuot (Weeks,
or Pentecost)

MONTH 4
Post-Exilic Name:
Tammuz
תַּמּוּז
tah-MOOZ

Agriculture in Israel
Wheat harvest
Early grape
harvest

MONTH 5
Post-Exilic Name:
Av
אָב
ahv

Agriculture in Israel
Principal fruit
month:
Grape, fig, olive

MONTH 6
Post-Exilic Name:
Elul
אֱלוּל
eh-LOOL

Agriculture in Israel
Dates and
Summer figs

March — *April* — *May* — *June* — *July* — *August* — *Sept.*

OVERVIEW OF THE BIBLICAL YEAR AND GOD'S APPOINTED TIMES | 21

Below is a graphic showing the order of the biblical months as they occur throughout the year.

The graphic spans both pages. Take a moment to read it over carefully, paying special attention to the Biblical Holy Days listed at the bottom of each column.

FALL | WINTER

MONTH 7

Post-Exilic Name:
Tishrei
תִּשְׁרֵי
tish-ray
or תִּשְׁרִי *tish-ree*

Pre-Exilic Name:
Etanim
אֵתָנִים
ay-tah-NEEM

Agriculture in Israel
Early rains
Seedtime
Plowing & sowing

Biblical Holy Days
Yom Teruah
(Day of Trumpets)
Yom Kippur
(Day of Atonement)
Sukkot (Tabernacles)

MONTH 8

Post-Exilic Name:
Cheshvan
חֶשְׁוָן
chesh-VAHN

Pre-Exilic Name:
Bul
בּוּל
bool

Agriculture in Israel
Wheat and
Barley sowing

MONTH 9

Post-Exilic Name:
Kislev
כִּסְלֵו
kiss-layv

Agriculture in Israel
Winter begins

Biblical Event
Chanukah
(Festival of the
Rededication of
the Temple)
(John 10:22)

MONTH 10

Post-Exilic Name:
Tevet
טֵבֵת
tay-VAYT

Agriculture in Israel
Rainy winter
months
Cultivation of
Jordan Valley
begins

MONTH 11

Post-Exilic Name:
Shevat
שְׁבָט
sh'-VAHT

Agriculture in Israel
Almond blossoms
Oranges ripening

MONTH 12

Post-Exilic Name:
Adar
אֲדָר
ah-DAR

אֲדָר שֵׁנִי
ah-DAR shay-NEE
(Second Adar),
a 13th month, is
sometimes added
to ensure Nisan 16
occurs after the
Spring Equinox.

Agriculture in Israel
Barley ripening
Citrus fruit
harvest

Biblical Event
Purim
(Memorial of
God's deliverance
of His people
in the book of
Esther)

Sept. → ← October → ← November → ← December → ← January → ← February → ← March

Seven major "appointed times" of the Lord

On the graphic on the preceding pages, we indicated the major "Biblical Holy Days." These special days, designated by God as "holy," are usually referred to in scripture by the Hebrew word **moadim** מוֹעֲדִים *(mo-ah-DEEM)*, **appointed times**, from the singular noun **moed** מוֹעֵד *(mo-AYD)*, meaning *appointed time, place or meeting*. These appointed times are often called "feasts," but not all of them involve feasting (one of them is actually a fast day).

The seven major appointed times are described in Leviticus 23, in which God describes His invention of these days of "holy assembly" and tells the people exactly what day of each month they are to be observed. God begins the chapter with the following key words:

> The Lord spoke to Moses, saying, "Speak to the children of Israel, and tell them, 'The appointed times of the Lord, which you shall proclaim to be holy convocations, even these are My appointed times'" (Lev. 23:1-2).

Notice the strong sense of personal ownership in verse 2. God calls them "My appointed times." It's important to remember that the people of Israel did *not* create or invent any of these observances. This fact is crucial because of the *prophetic significance* of God's appointed times.

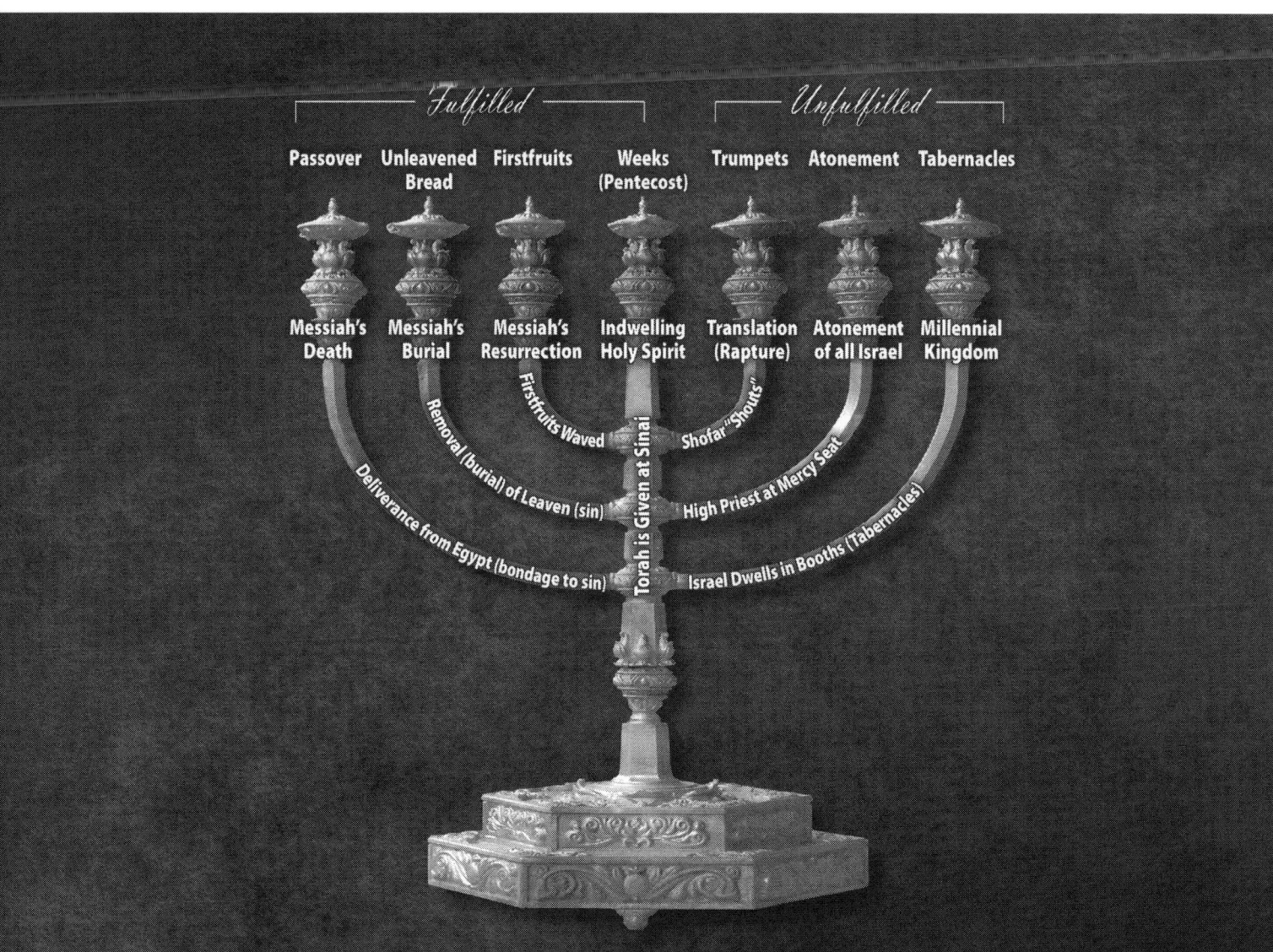

The prophetic significance of the seven major appointed times

The *moadim* have been set by God to occur in two time periods: **spring and fall.** These two time periods correspond to the first and second comings of Jesus the Messiah.

The SPRING *moadim* – fulfillment completed

Passover *(Pesach)* – Nisan 14, the date of Yeshua's crucifixion

Feast of Unleavened Bread *(Chag Ha Matzah)* – Nisan 15-21, a seven-day feast during which Yeshua was in the tomb

Feast of Firstfruits *(Yom Ha Bikkurim)* – Nisan 16, the date of Yeshua's resurrection

Feast of Weeks/Pentecost *(Shavuot)* – Sivan 6, the date that the believers in Acts chapter 2 were filled with the indwelling Holy Spirit

The FALL *moadim* – fulfillment in the future

Day of Trumpets *(Yom Teruah)* – Tishri 1, signifying the future translation of believers (aka *the Rapture*)

Day of Atonement *(Yom Kippur)* – Tishri 10, signifying the future atonement of all of the believing remnant of Israel

Tabernacles *(Sukkot)* – Tishri 15-21, a seven-day feast with an additional eighth day of assembly on Tishri 22, signifying the future millennial (thousand-year) reign of Yeshua on earth

Notes about the Appointed Times Graphic

The table on the following two pages provides a graphical overview of the **seven major appointed times of the Lord.** Please take some time now to carefully study it; take the time to read each Scripture reference in your own Bible, especially those taken from Leviticus 23. You will probably need to refer to this graphic frequently during your studies in this book, so we suggest you bookmark it or mark its place with a sticky note.

Following the graphic, we will begin our chapters which individually feature each feast of the Lord.

> *"The appointed times of the Lord... these are MY appointed times."*
>
> Leviticus 23:2, the words of God, emphasis ours

24 | OVERVIEW OF THE BIBLICAL YEAR AND GOD'S APPOINTED TIMES

 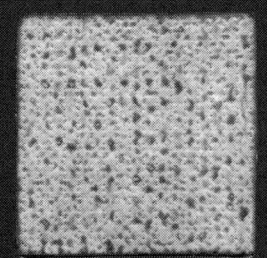  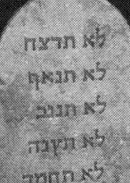

פֶּסַח	חַג הַמַּצּוֹת	יוֹם הַבִּכּוּרִים	חַג שָׁבֻעֹת
PEH-sach	chag hah-mah-TSŌT	yōhm hah-bih-koo-REEM	chag shah-voo-ŌT
Passover	**Unleavened Bread**	**Firstfruits**	**Weeks***
Nisan 14	Nisan 15-21	Nisan 16	Sivan 6
(in the FIRST month)	(in the FIRST month)	(in the FIRST month)	(in the THIRD month)
Leviticus 23:4-5	*Leviticus 23:6-8*	*Leviticus 23:9-14*	*Leviticus 23:15-22*
			Greek "Pentecost" = fifty

Spring Feasts – Already Fulfilled In Messiah

Messiah's Death	Messiah's Burial	Messiah's Resurrection	Indwelling Holy Spirit
(Deliverance from bondage in Egypt)	(Removal of all leaven / burial of sin)	(Firstfruits: first barley sheaves of the wave offering presented)	(Torah given at Sinai; first wheat sheaves presented)
...for indeed Christ, our Passover, has been sacrificed in our place. 1 Corinthians 5:7	*Purge out the old leaven, that you may be a new lump, even as you are unleavened...* 1 Corinthians 5:7	*But Christ has indeed been raised from the dead, the firstfruits of those who have fallen asleep. For since death came through a man, the resurrection of the dead comes also through a man. For as in Adam all die, so in Christ all will be made alive. But each in turn: Christ, the firstfruits; then, when He comes, those who belong to Him.* 1 Corinthians 15:20-23	*Now when the day of Pentecost had fully come, they were all with one accord in one place. Suddenly there came from the sky a sound like the rushing of a mighty wind, and it filled all the house where they were sitting. Tongues like fire appeared and were distributed to them, and one sat on each of them. They were all filled with the Holy Spirit...* Acts 2:1-4
The next day, [John] saw Jesus coming to him, and said, "Behold, the Lamb of God, who takes away the sin of the world!" John 1:29	*For Him who knew no sin He made to be sin on our behalf; so that in Him we might become the righteousness of God.* 2 Corinthians 5:21		
...you were redeemed... with precious blood, as of a faultless and pure lamb, the blood of Christ... 1 Peter 1:18-19			

OVERVIEW OF THE BIBLICAL YEAR AND GOD'S APPOINTED TIMES | 25

יוֹם תְּרוּעָה
yōhm t-ROO-ah

Day of Trumpets*

Tishri 1

(in the SEVENTH month)

Leviticus 23:23-25
*Literally, "Day of a shout"

יוֹם כִּפּוּר
yōhm kih-POOR

Day of Atonement

Tishri 10

(in the SEVENTH month)

Leviticus 23:26-32

סֻכּוֹת
soo-KŌT

Booths* (Tabernacles)

Tishri 15-21
plus Eighth Day of Assembly, Tishri 22

(in the SEVENTH month)

Leviticus 23:33-34
*Literally, "thicket shelters"

God's Appointed Times

Key:

← Hebrew name of the appointed time

← Transliteration (how it is pronounced)

← English name(s) of the appointed time

← Biblical date(s)

← Order of month

← Mentioned in Leviticus 23

Fall Feasts – Yet To Be Fulfilled

Translation of Believers

("Rapture")

For the LORD Himself will descend from heaven with a shout, with the voice of the archangel, and with God's trumpet. The dead in Christ will rise first, then we who are alive, who are left, will be caught up together with them in the clouds, to meet the LORD in the air... 1 Thessalonians 4:16-17

Behold, I tell you a mystery. We will not all sleep, but we will all be changed, in a moment, in the twinkling of an eye, at the last trumpet. For the trumpet will sound, and the dead will be raised incorruptible, and we will be changed. 1 Corinthians 15:51-52

Atonement of all Israel

(Israel recognizes Messiah Yeshua)

For I don't desire you to be ignorant, brothers, of this mystery, so that you won't be wise in your own conceits, that a partial hardening has happened to Israel, until the fullness of the Gentiles has come in, and so all Israel will be saved. Even as it is written, "There will come out of Zion the Deliverer, and he will turn away ungodliness from Jacob." Romans 11:25-26

Millennial Reign

(Yeshua's 1,000 year earthly reign)

It will happen that everyone who is left of all the nations that came against Jerusalem will go up from year to year to worship the King, the LORD of Armies, and to keep the feast of tabernacles. It will be, that whoever...doesn't go up to Jerusalem to worship the King, the LORD of Armies, on them there will be no rain. Zechariah 14:16-17

Now on the last and greatest day of the feast, Jesus stood and cried out, "If anyone is thirsty, let him come to Me and drink! He who believes in Me, as the Scripture has said, from within him will flow rivers of living water." John 7:37-38

← Past or future fulfillment

← New Testament event which this appointed time foreshadows

← Other significance of this appointed time

← Key verses describing this appointed time or its symbolic meaning, especially in the New Testament

Passover

Messiah's Death

"They shall take some of the blood [of the lamb], and put it on the two doorposts and on the lintel, on the houses..."
Exodus 12:7

"The Signs on the Door," painting by James Jacques Joseph Tissot, c. 1896–1902

"Lamb of God," painting by Francisco de Zurbarán, c. 1635–1640

"For indeed Christ, our Passover, has been sacrificed in our place."
1 Corinthians 5:7b

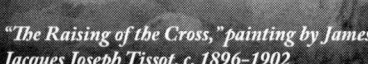

"The Raising of the Cross," painting by James Jacques Joseph Tissot, c. 1896–1902

"Behold, the Lamb of God, who takes away the sin of the world!"
John 1:29b

Passover

Passover is the first appointed time of the Lord which we will study, as it is the first to occur in God's biblical year, on the fourteenth day of the first month (Nisan). **Passover is a prophetic picture of the death of our Messiah, Jesus.**

From bondage to freedom

The Passover story originates in the Old Testament (Exodus 12), describing God's miraculous deliverance of the Jewish people from their **bondage to the Egyptians.** This feast is later completely fulfilled in the New Testament, in which God miraculously provided deliverance to the Jewish people (and all Gentiles who also choose to be "grafted in") from their **bondage to sin.** God purchased our freedom by offering Himself on the cross in payment of our own debt to sin (our death). He chose to accomplish all of this on the biblical date of **Passover, Nisan 14.**

Spiritual freedom in the Old Testament

The deliverance of Israel from Egypt was not just a deliverance from physical slavery, but from **spiritual slavery.** The Jewish people were to be set free from all the pagan influences that saturated the culture of Egypt, **in order to be free to serve (worship) God.** God reiterates this point in Scripture *seven times:*

> ...this is what the Lord, the God of Israel, says, "Let My people go, **that they may hold a feast to Me** in the wilderness" (Ex. 5:1).

> ...the Lord, the God of the Hebrews, has sent me to you, saying, "Let My people go, **that they may serve Me** in the wilderness..." (Ex. 7:16)

> ...this is what the Lord says, "Let My people go, **that they may serve Me**" (Ex. 8:1)

> ...this is what the Lord says, "Let My people go, **that they may serve Me**" (Ex 8:20).

> ...this is what the Lord, the God of the Hebrews, says: "Let My people go, **that they may serve Me**" (Ex. 9:1).

> ...this is what the Lord, the God of the Hebrews, says: "Let My people go, **that they may serve Me**" (Ex. 9:13).

> ...this is what the Lord, the God of the Hebrews, says: "How long will you refuse to humble yourself before Me? Let My people go, **that they may serve Me**" (Ex. 10:3).

"For, indeed, Messiah, our Passover lamb, has been sacrificed."

1 Corinthians 5:7b

On God's chosen date of Nisan 14, Yeshua hung in excruciating pain from the execution stake, choosing not to give up His spirit until the exact time that the Passover lamb was supposed to be slain in accordance with His Torah: "between the evenings."

Spiritual freedom in the New Testament

The purpose of Messiah's death was to provide all humans the opportunity to be **freed from our enslavement to sin.** Once freed from sin and death, we are intended to employ that freedom **in complete service of God.**

> For if we have become **united with Him in the likeness of His death,** we will also be part of His resurrection; knowing this, that **our old man was crucified with Him,** that the body of sin might be done away with, so that **we would no longer be in bondage to sin. For he who has died has been freed from sin...** But now, **being made free from sin, and having become servants of God,** you have your fruit of sanctification, and the result of eternal life. (Rom. 6:5-7, 22).

> "If anyone serves me, let him follow Me. Where I am, there will My servant also be. **If anyone serves Me, the Father will honor him**" (John 12:26, the words of Jesus).

The Passover lamb in the Old Testament

The Passover lamb was killed on Nisan 14, according to Exodus 12:6. God said,

> "...and you shall keep it until **the fourteenth day of the same month**; and the whole assembly of the congregation of Israel shall kill it between the evenings" (Ex. 12:6).

Many Bible translations of this verse speak of the lamb being killed "at twilight" or "in the evening." The more accurate translation of the original Hebrew is "between the two evenings," **ben ha arbayim** בֵּין הָעַרְבַּיִם *bayn ha-ar-BAH-yim*. According to the Talmud, the "first evening" is the time in the afternoon when the heat of the sun begins to decrease (about three o'clock), and the "second evening" begins with sunset. Josephus, the Jewish historian, relates that, at the time of Jesus, the Passover sacrifice (the slaying of the lamb) was offered from the "ninth hour" (3:00 pm) to the "eleventh hour" (5:00 pm).*

The Passover lamb in the New Testament

Jesus, our Passover Lamb, **died on Nisan 14.** Not only that, but **He waited to give up His life specifically during the period "between the evenings."**

> Now from the sixth hour [noon] there was darkness over all the land until the ninth hour [3:00 pm]. **About the ninth hour,** Jesus cried with a loud voice, saying, "Eli, Eli, lama sabachthani?" That is, "My God, my God, why have you forsaken me?" (Mat. 27:45,46)

---

* Titus Flavius Josephus, *The Wars of the Jews* 6.9.3.

Applying the blood in the Old Testament

The Israelites were instructed to **apply the blood of the slain Passover lamb to the doorposts** of their homes so that the Lord's Angel of Death would "pass over" the house and not slay their firstborn children (Ex. 12:7). In fact, this is where the word "Passover" comes from. In Hebrew, the word for Passover is **Pesach*** פֶּסַח *(PEH-saḥ)*, which is the noun form of the Hebrew verb **pasach** פ.ס.ח *(pah-saḥ)*, meaning *to leap or hop (over), to spring over without touching, to skip,* thereby *to pass or spare*. In Greek, the word *passover* is **pascha*** πάσχα *(PAHS-ḥah)*, from which we get our English adjective "paschal" as in the terms *paschal lamb* or *paschal season*. You can actually hear the Hebrew origins of these Greek and English words if you listen closely to their consonant sounds.

Applying the blood in the New Testament

God applies the blood of Jesus to our lives in a miraculous manner at the moment we are born again. His blood cleanses us from all sin, gives us triumph over the Enemy (Satan) and provides access into God's Most Holy Place:

> ...and the **blood** of Jesus, His Son, cleanses us from all sin (1 John 1:7). Therefore Jesus also, that He might sanctify the people through His own **blood**, suffered outside the gate (Heb. 13:12).

> ...they overcame him because of the Lamb's **blood**, and because of the word of their testimony... (Rev. 12:11)

> Having therefore, brothers, boldness to enter into the holy place by the **blood** of Jesus, by the way which He dedicated for us, a new and living way, through the veil, that is to say, His flesh... (Heb. 10:19-20)

Jesus is the door of salvation

In the last scripture above we see that Yeshua's slain body and blood became the doorway for our entry into the Holy Place. That "door" was pictured in *the blood on the doorpost* in Exodus. In Deuteronomy 6:9 and 11:20, God told His people to write His words "on their doorposts and on their gates," a practice which continues to this day. Observant Jewish people affix a *mezuzah case* containing small scrolls of these scriptures on the doorposts of their houses. The mezuzah is affixed with nails at the top and the bottom, just as our Savior's body was affixed with nails through hands and feet. The *blood on the doorpost*, the *scriptures on the doorpost* (the "Word made flesh"), and the *door itself* all represent Jesus.

> Jesus therefore said to them again, "Most certainly, I tell you, I am the sheep's **door**... **I am the Door. If anyone enters in by Me, he will be saved...** (John 10:7,9)

"They shall take some of the blood, and put it on the two doorposts and on the lintel, on the houses in which they shall eat [the lamb]."

Exodus 12:7

*Pronunciation note: Recall that the Hebrew *ch* sounds like the *ch* in *Bach* or *Loch Ness*. The word *Pesach* sort of rhymes with "bedrock." Similarly, the Greek *ch* sound in *Pascha* is pronounced *ch* as in *Bach*.

"...let us keep the feast...with the unleavened bread of sincerity and truth."

1 Corinthians 5:8

A Feast Without Leaven (Old Testament)

The Passover was to be celebrated **without leaven.** In fact, Passover is the day that "kicks off" the entire seven-day Feast of Unleavened Bread. Throughout both the Old and New Testaments, *leaven* is a spiritual symbol of *sin*. The Hebrew word for *unleavened bread* is **matzah** מַצָּה *(mah-TSAH).* This word is spelled a variety of ways in English: *matsah, matza, matsa,* etc. The first place in the Bible where God issues a commandment to eat matzah is in Exodus 12:8, in which He instructs the people to eat it along with the roasted Passover lamb.

> They shall eat the flesh in that night, roasted with fire, and **unleavened bread**... (Ex. 12:8)

Not only does God command the eating of unleavened bread, but He insists that *all leaven itself* be removed from the houses of all the people, in verses 14 through 20 of the same chapter. We will discuss this topic in greater detail in the next chapter of this book, titled "Unleavened Bread."

A Feast Without Leaven (New Testament)

The Feast of Passover was celebrated in the New Testament by both Jewish and Gentile believers in Jesus, not only in continued obedience to God's several Old Testament commandments to do so "forever," but also because of its wonderful additional significance of now being a *memorial* of the sacrificial death of Messiah. Naturally, these believers celebrated the feast using unleavened bread as they always had before, but Paul needed to remind them that this "leaven" was actually a symbol of *sin* in the believer's life. As God-honoring as it was to painstakingly remove the tiniest crumbs of leaven from their homes, it was even more important to the LORD that their *sin* be removed (repented of) before they participated in God's Passover. Paul cautioned them repeatedly that, if they permitted even the smallest amount of such sin to persist by their approval, it would quickly spread and grow, contaminating the entire life of the individual, eventually spreading through the entire local body of believers.

> A little leaven grows through the whole lump (Gal. 5:9).

> Your boasting [about sin in the local body of believers] is not good. Don't you know that a little leaven leavens the whole lump? Purge out the old leaven, that you may be a new lump, even as you are unleavened. For indeed Christ, our Passover, has been sacrificed in our place. Therefore let us keep the feast, not with old leaven, neither with the leaven of malice and wickedness, but with the unleavened bread of sincerity and truth (1 Cor. 5:6-8).

Passover/Unleavened Bread as a unit

God views Passover (a single-day event, Nisan 14) and the Feast of Unleavened Bread (a seven-day event, Nisan 15-21) **together as a unit.** Occasionally in Scripture, He refers to the *entire time period* by either or both names. One reason for this is because Passover is also a day that is celebrated *without leaven.*

> In the first month, in the fourteenth day of the month, you shall have the Passover, a feast of seven days; unleavened bread shall be eaten (Ezek. 45:21).

Even though the verse above has "merged" both feasts together under the shorthand title of "Passover," God really instituted Passover as a one-day celebration on Nisan 14 and Unleavened Bread as a seven-day celebration commencing on Nisan 15. This practice of referring to the *entire* period of Nisan 14-21 as *either* Passover *or* Unleavened Bread continued throughout New Testament times (and persists among Jewish people to this day). Two examples in Mark 14 demonstrate how these terms became "intermingled."

> It was now two days before the Passover and the Unleavened Bread... (Mark 14:1)

> On the first day of Unleavened Bread, when they sacrificed the Passover lamb, [Jesus'] disciples asked him, "Where do you want us to go and prepare that you may eat the Passover?" (Mark 14:12)

We already know from Scripture (as well as from Josephus and from other historical sources) that the Passover lamb was sacrificed on Nisan 14 ("Passover," technically). In Mark 14:12, though, Mark used both terms *interchangeably*, assuming his readers would know, of course, that the Passover lamb was sacrificed on the 14th, while "Unleavened Bread" technically began on the 15th.

We use many such "language shorthands" ourselves. Americans will say "Washington," but it doesn't usually refer to the physical city; it refers to "those who hold power at the federal level." The "Oval Office" is not about some round room in a white building; it is a synonym for "the presidency." Christian college students will say they are "going home for Christmas." Everyone in western culture knows that this refers not just to a single day – December 25 – but to all the weeks of winter break between the semesters. Imagine you are a historian living two thousand years in the future and attempting to translate our documents. Even assuming you still spoke the same English that we do today, you would also need to understand the tiniest details of our culture in order to accurately translate our writings. How much more necessary it is, then, to have at least a *basic* working knowledge of God's calendar while we navigate the writings of the Bible – speaking to us across massive distances of foreign cultures and thousands of years. Thank God for His Spirit, who teaches us His Word!

Scripture has a habit of referring to the Feasts of Passover and Unleavened Bread as if they were a single unit.

The habit persists to this day throughout the land of Israel and among Jewish communities worldwide.

The Hebrew word "olam" – "forever" – is used in the Bible to describe the eternal nature of God's Word, His kingdom, His love and mercy, and all of His eternal covenants. This word is also translated "universe" or "eternity" – i.e., all of space or all of time.

A memorial forever

God repeatedly commanded that Passover be kept by His people as a memorial *forever*. In passages describing Passover, you will see the Hebrew word **olam** עוֹלָם *(o-LAHM)* translated as *forever, everlasting, for eternity, [a] lasting [ordinance], [a] permanent [ordinance], never-ending,* or *without end,* depending on your Bible translation. This same Hebrew word is used to describe God's covenants with Noah, Abraham, Isaac, Jacob, David and others. It is used to describe God's personal Holy covenant Name, which He says would never be changed. The Psalms use this very word, *olam*, to say that God's love endures *forever*, that He will reign *forever*, and that He shall be praised *forever*. The references throughout the Old Testament to Messiah's seed and kingdom lasting *forever* all have this Hebrew word. Psalm 119:89 uses *olam* to speak of the very Word of God: "Your word, O Lord, is *eternal*."

A separate phrase also found in several of these Bible verses is the phrase *throughout your generations*. As if to bind the two ideas together like two strands of a single cord, God doubles the strength of His statement about the eternal nature of Passover: "throughout your generations, as an everlasting ordinance."

Each of the following verses speaks of the *permanent* nature of God's memorial Feast of Passover. Notice, too, God's *personal ownership* of this feast.

> This day shall be to you for a **memorial**, and you shall keep it a feast to the Lord: **throughout your generations** you shall keep it a feast by an ordinance **forever** (Ex. 12:14).

> You shall observe [Passover] for an ordinance to you **and to your sons forever** (Ex. 12:24).

> It is a night to be much observed to the Lord for bringing them out from the land of Egypt. This is that night of the Lord, to be much observed of all the children of Israel **throughout their generations** (Ex. 12:42).

> **You shall tell your son in that day**, saying, "I do this because of that which the Lord did for me when I came forth out of Egypt." It shall be for a sign to you on your hand, and for a **memorial** between your eyes, that the law of the Lord may be in your mouth; for with a strong hand the Lord has brought you out of Egypt. You shall therefore keep this ordinance in its season **from year to year.** (Ex. 13:8-10).

Passover isn't just for Jews

Although the commandments on the preceding page were given at the time to the sons of Israel, the ultimate fulfillment of Passover (freedom from sin's bondage through Messiah's sacrifice) was to be a gift for the entire world, not just for Israel. God had always intended that Israel be "a light to the nations," so that the nations would be drawn to her holy way of living and her relationship with a loving God, then willingly join with her in joyful participation of God's wonderful memorial feasts. Long before the time of Christ, all foreigners living in the land of Israel were invited to participate, according to God's words:

> If a foreigner lives among you, and desires to keep the Passover to the LORD; according to the statute of the Passover, and according to its ordinance, so shall he do. You shall have one statute, both for the foreigner, and for him who is born in the land (Num. 9:14).

A memorial forever - the New Testament

Keeping the feasts was *never* intended as a means of "earning" salvation. In the Old Testament, God was only pleased by *faith*, and people back then still needed to receive His *grace* as His free *gift*. God's salvation has never changed over all the centuries: hearts must *first* be saved, and *then* the keeping of His commandments will follow, but only as the *outward expression* or *fruit* of an already cleansed, born-again heart. The New Testament explains that Moses did *not* keep Passover as a means of justification by his own works or merit.

> **By faith, [Moses] kept the Passover,** and the sprinkling of the blood, that the destroyer of the firstborn should not touch them (Heb. 11:28).

The New Testament is filled with examples of people keeping the Passover *by faith through grace*. Jesus kept Passover throughout His lifetime on earth (the Gospels mention Jesus keeping *three* Passovers during His ministry years alone). His family and disciples kept it, too. Gentiles in Corinth also celebrated Passover and Unleavened Bread *several decades after* Messiah's resurrection.

> [Jesus'] parents went every year to Jerusalem at the feast of the Passover. When He was twelve years old, they went up to Jerusalem according to the custom of the feast (Luke 2:41-42).

> The Passover of the Jews was at hand, and Jesus went up to Jerusalem (John 2:13, the Passover of the first year of Yeshua's ministry).

> [Jesus] said to them, "I have earnestly desired to eat this Passover with you before I suffer..." (Luke 22:15, the Passover of Yeshua's death)

> Therefore let us keep the feast...with the unleavened bread of sincerity and truth (1 Cor. 5:8, the words of Paul to the Corinthians).

> *"By faith, Moses kept the Passover, and the sprinkling of the blood, that the destroyer of the firstborn should not touch them."*
>
> Hebrews 11:28

The seder, or "order" of the feast of Passover, is packed from beginning to end with symbols that illustrate the unique, specific ministry of Yeshua. It was a portion of this very seder that Yeshua instructed to be "done in remembrance" of Him.

Do "this" in remembrance of Me

At that final Passover feast which Jesus shared with His disciples, He led them in a traditional Passover **seder** *(SAY-der)*. A *seder* is just an *order* or *procedure*, coming from the Hebrew word which means "order; orderly arrangement." So, the "Passover seder" is the order in which the prayers are said, songs are sung, food is eaten, story is told, and symbols are explained at the Passover feast. Nowadays, the seder is printed in a convenient little booklet called a *haggadah*. The word *haggadah* is a Hebrew word meaning "telling," because God commands that we *tell* the story of Passover to our children and to one another as we keep this feast.

Yeshua instructed the twelve to "do this" – that is, **keep the Passover** – in memory of Him.

> ...the Lord Jesus on the night in which He was betrayed took bread. When He had given thanks, He broke it, and said, "Take, eat. This is My body, which is broken for you. **Do this in memory of Me.**" In the same way He also took the cup, after supper, saying, "This cup is the new covenant in My blood. Do this, as often as you drink, in memory of Me." **For as often as you eat this bread and drink this cup,** you proclaim the Lord's death until He comes (1 Cor. 11:23-26).

"Eat this bread and drink this cup" is a very specific reference to the *unleavened bread* and the *cup after the meal* of the Passover seder.

The "cup after the meal"

Certain phrases in the book of Luke reveal that elements of the traditional seder were purposely employed by Yeshua and given another layer of significance as His sacrificial death drew near. If you are a Jewish person who has participated in Passover seders all your life, certain familiar words describing the seder elements will practically jump out of the New Testament at you; you can't miss them!

One such phrase is "the cup after the meal."

> Likewise, He took **the cup after the supper**, saying, "This cup is the new covenant in my blood, which is poured out for you" (Luke 22:20, cf. 1 Cor. 11:25).

There are four cups of wine/grape juice during the traditional seder. Each holds a different significance. The third cup, the cup *after* the meal, has always had the distinction of being called "the cup of redemption," since even before the time of Christ. It was *this* cup to which Messiah assigned new, deeper meaning, by stating it would be the new covenant in His blood, which would *redeem* us.

"The Last Supper," painting by James Jacques Joseph Tissot, c. 1896–1902

Other powerful seder symbols

There are several other elements of the traditional seder which appear in the gospels. Two are the **breaking of the bread** after **having given thanks,** which we just read from the verses of Scripture on the preceding page. Note that the Greek of the New Testament is careful not to say "blessed *it;*" for no observant Jew ever blesses an *object*, like bread or wine. They always bless *God*, and they do so by saying a *traditional blessing*. This is termed "making the **b'rachah**" ("making the blessing"). Jewish traditional blessings begin with, "Blessed are You, Lord our God, King of the Universe." The traditional blessings over "bread" and "fruit of the vine" are still used today in everyday Jewish life, and they are all the more recited at holy feasts like the Passover seder. The words of the blessings are the same today as they were hundreds of years before Christ, as extra-biblical writings demonstrate. You can actually *know* the blessings Yeshua would have used during the seder as He blessed His Father before breaking the bread. You can read them in the excerpts of the seder on the following pages.

During a seder, there are certain times in which the blessing over bread is said, after which the matzah is broken and shared. At one point in the seder, three special squares of matzah are stored in a cloth pouch having three compartments, called a "**unity**." The center piece of matzah is drawn out, the blessing is said, and the bread is ceremoniously **broken** in half by the leader. Half of it is wrapped in a white linen cloth and "buried" (hidden) for a time, then "found" later in the evening, broken, and eaten by all present. Jesus' words after making the b'rachah and breaking the matzah were, "Take, eat. This is My body, which is **broken** for you." After the cross, His own broken body was wrapped in linen and buried for a time, then resurrected. We believers are partakers of His body and thus His resurrection. The "unity" of the three pieces of matzah is a symbol of the triunity of our God.

There are many glorious symbols of our Messiah in the seder. On the following pages, we have included only the briefest possible excerpts from a typical "Haggadah" – the booklet of the seder order – a term which comes from a Hebrew word meaning "telling." God has always been adamant that the historical story of Passover be "told," especially to one's children; see Exodus 12:25-27, 13:8.

The traditional seder order has been handed down from generation to generation. Most elements of the seder have been in place since before the time of Christ, so He and His disciples would have performed them many times in their lives as they observed Passover each year. Within the traditional elements of the Passover seder, the symbolism of Yeshua the Messiah and His sacrificial death is unmistakable – for those who have eyes to see and ears to hear.

If you feel the call to partake in a Passover seder after reading these excerpts, we definitely urge you to experience it in "real life." Check your neighborhood notice boards, social media, or local ads during the weeks before Passover for invitations to public seders. Christian churches will often hold abbreviated seder "demonstrations" which provide glimpses into some of the symbolism. Messianic congregations tend to hold the entire traditional sit-down seder meal, while explaining all the symbolic significance as it relates to Messiah Jesus. You can also just dive right in and hold your own seder at home with your family. There are several fine Messianic "Haggadot" (plural for "Haggadah") available on the internet, both in the form of free pdf downloads and inexpensive printed booklets for purchase. The foods of the seder are not difficult to obtain or prepare, and the booklets make observance easy, even if it's your first time.

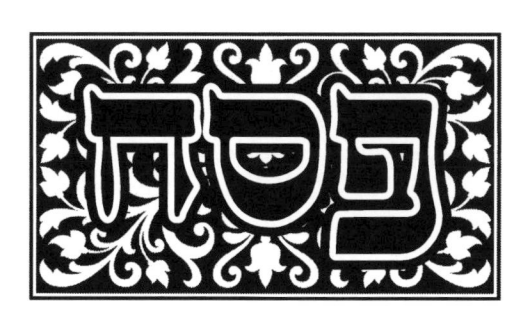

Passover

Excerpts from the Haggadah
Passover Recipes

Order of the Excerpts from the Passover Seder

The excerpts on the following pages do not necessarily follow the order of the seder. Only a few excerpts have been included to provide a brief glimpse into some of the wonderful symbolism of the Passover seder.

Messianic Version

The following excerpts are typical of a Messianic haggadah. A Messianic haggadah differs from a traditional haggadah in that it expands upon the words and elements of the traditional seder by including commentary that clearly proclaims Jesus to be Passover's fulfillment.

Pronunciation Key

a is pronounced *ah* as in *father*
ai is pronounced *eye* as in *Adonai* or *jai alai*
ch is pronounced ℏ as in *Bach* or *Loch Ness*
ei is pronounced *ay* as in *reign*
i is pronounced *ee* as in *marine*
u is pronounced *oo* as in *soon*

The Seder Plate

Leader: On the table is a seder plate, holding the ceremonial items of Passover: bitter herbs, a roasted egg, a sweet apple mixture, parsley, and a bone. They all tell the story of Passover, a story that has been retold for thousands of years. Each food is symbolic of a different element of the story, which tells how we were freed from a life of physical bondage in Egypt and spiritual bondage to sin.

beitzah *bay-tsah*
roasted egg
Symbolism: A reminder of mourning over the temple and over the sin and rebellion which necessitated its loss. (The egg was often eaten in houses of mourning.)

בֵּיצָה

זְרוֹעַ

zeroa *z'-RO-ah*
lamb shankbone
literally, arm, foreleg, shoulder, *figuratively*, strength. In Scripture, zeroa appears in the phrase "My outstretched *arm*" to express God's mighty, saving power. Symbolism: A reminder of the sacrificial lamb that was offered in the temple in Jerusalem and eaten at Passover. A symbol of Messiah, the Passover lamb, who saves us with His own outstretched arm.

כַּרְפַּס

karpas *kar-pas*
parsley
Symbolism: Life, created and sustained by God. Dipped in salt water, it is a reminder of the tears and life of suffering experienced by Israel in Egypt.

חֲזֶרֶת

chazeret *ḥah-ZEH-ret*
horseradish root
Symbolism: One of the two bitter herbs. This one is usually eaten together with the matzah, the bread of affliction, to induce "tears of compassion" for the sorrow of Israel during her bondage in Egypt.

maror *mah-ror*
bitter herb
Symbolism: One of the two bitter herbs eaten to remind us of the bitter slavery of the children of Israel and the bitter consequences of our own former enslavement to sin.

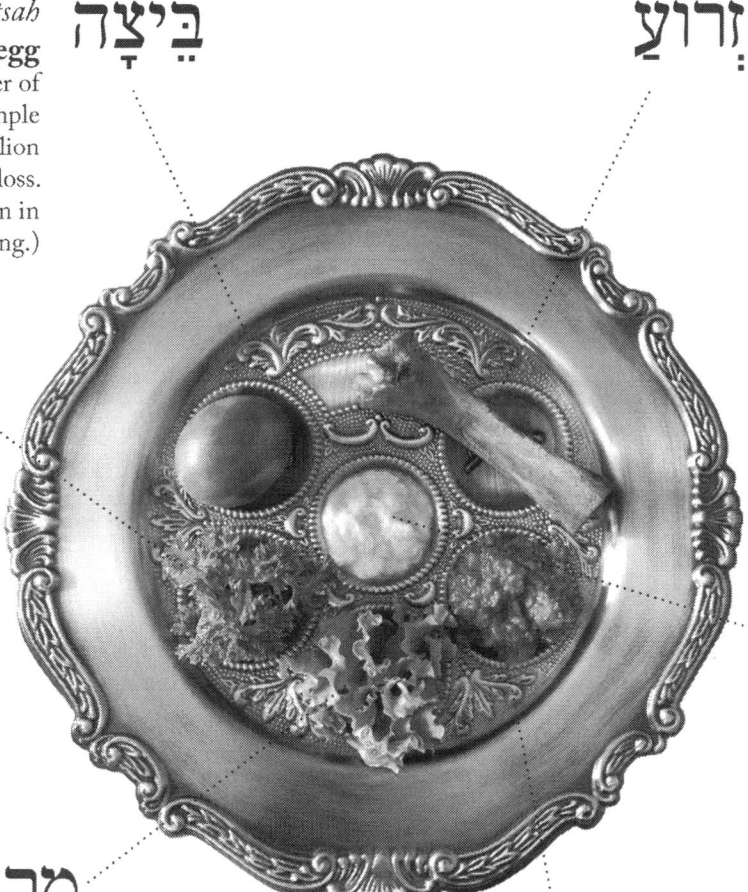

מָרוֹר

charoset *ḥah-ro-set*
chopped apples & nuts

חֲרֹסֶת

Symbolism: From a Hebrew root *cheres*, meaning "clay," charoset's texture and color remind us of the mortar that the Israelite slaves used to make bricks for the Egyptians. Its sweetness reminds us of God's intervention during even the most bitter circumstance.

The Four Cups

Leader: Tonight we will celebrate the redemption of our mighty God by drinking from our cups four times. With each cup, we remember the miracles that God has done for us, and continues to do for us every day.

The first cup:	*The second cup:*	*The third cup:*	*The fourth cup:*
The Cup of Sanctification	**The Cup of Plagues**	**The Cup of Redemption**	**The Cup of Praise**
We will drink from this cup to inaugurate the seder. This cup reminds us of the holiness of this event which God commanded to be kept forever.	We will drink from this cup partway through the seder and before the meal. Before drinking, we will first dip a little finger into the cup ten times, letting one drop of liquid fall for each of the ten plagues God brought on Egypt.	*"The Cup After The Meal"* We will drink from this cup after the meal. This is the cup which symbolizes the blood of the Passover lamb. Jesus calls this cup His "blood of the covenant."	Just as Jesus and the disciples did, we will drink from this cup to close out the seder while singing a hymn of praise from the *Hallel* (*Hallel* means "praise," Psalm 136).

Before drinking each cup, we bless the LORD, saying or singing the traditional blessing (b'rachah):

בָּרוּךְ אַתָּה יהוה אֱלֹהֵינוּ מֶלֶךְ הָעוֹלָם בּוֹרֵא פְּרִי הַגָּפֶן

Ba-ruch ah-tah, Adonai, Elohaynu, Meh-lech hah-Olam, bo-ray p'ree hah-gah-fen.

"Blessed are you, LORD, our God, King of the Universe, who creates the fruit of the vine."

All: Yeshua the Messiah took up the cup after the meal, saying, "This cup is the new covenant in my blood, which is poured out for you" (Luke 22:20). As the blood of the lamb brought us physical redemption in Egypt, the Messiah's death brings us spiritual redemption today.

The Bread of Affliction

Leader: *(Lifting a piece of matzah)* This is matzah, the Bread of Affliction. It symbolizes the bread of the lowly and poor, of our fathers in Egypt, but more so, it symbolizes the Bread of Life, Yeshua, who was afflicted because of our sins. See how it is pierced? Our Messiah was pierced. See how it is striped? Our Messiah was flogged. See how it is unleavened? Our Messiah was completely free from the leaven of sin. The Sinless One died to remove our sins.

All: "But He was wounded for our transgressions, He was bruised for our iniquities: the chastisement of our peace was upon Him; and with His stripes we are healed" (Isaiah 53:5).

Leader: *(Lifting the matzah-tash – the cloth bag with three compartments containing three pieces of matzah)* Three matzot are wrapped together for Passover in a Unity. This is a symbol of the unity of Father, Son and Holy Spirit. *(Removing the centermost piece of matzah and breaking it in half)* Just as the middle piece of the Bread of Affliction is broken, so Messiah was afflicted and broken. *(Wrapping one half in a white cloth and hiding it while the children cover their eyes)* The hidden half is called the afikomen. It has been wrapped in white, just as Messiah's body was wrapped for burial. At the end of our seder, it will be found and returned to the table, just as Messiah was hidden in the grave for a short time before he rose again and reappeared. *(Breaking off a piece from the remaining half and distributing the remainder among the people)* Let us recite the traditional b'rachah (blessing) and eat the unleavened bread of Passover.

All:

בָּרוּךְ אַתָּה יהוה אֱלֹהֵינוּ מֶלֶךְ הָעוֹלָם
הַמּוֹצִיא לֶחֶם מִן הָאָרֶץ

Ba-ruch ah-tah, Adonai, Elohaynu, Meh-lech hah-Olam, hah-mo-tsee leh-chem min hah-ah-retz.

"Blessed are you, LORD, our God, King of the Universe, who brings forth bread from the earth."

OBSERVANCE OF PASSOVER

The Four Questions

Leader: In Exodus 12:26-27 God commanded, "When your children ask you, 'What does this ceremony mean to you?' Then tell them...'" Throughout tonight's seder, our children's questions are answered as we tell the Passover story.

A Child: *(Rising to sing the song of the four questions)*

Ma Nishtanah מַה נִּשְׁתַּנָּה

Mah nish-ta-nah hah lai-lah ha-zeh mih-kol hah-lay-lot! mih-kol hah-lay-lot! She-b'chol ha-lay-lot a-nu o-chlin cha-maytz u-mah-tzah cha-maytz u-mah-tzah. Hah-lai-lah ha-zeh, hah-lai-ah ha-zeh, ku-lo mah-tzah?

How different this night is from all other nights!

On all other nights we eat leavened and unleavened bread. On this night why do we eat only unleavened bread?

On all other nights we eat all kinds of vegetables. On this night why do we eat bitter herbs?

On all other nights we don't dip our vegetables even once. On this night why do we dip them twice?

On all other nights we eat our meals sitting or reclining. On this night why do we eat only reclining?

מַה נִּשְׁתַּנָּה הַלַּיְלָה הַזֶּה מִכָּל הַלֵּילוֹת!

Ma nish-tah-nah hah-lai-lah hah-zeh mih-kol hah-lay-lot!

שֶׁבְּכָל הַלֵּילוֹת אָנוּ אוֹכְלִין חָמֵץ וּמַצָּה. הַלַּיְלָה הַזֶּה כֻּלּוֹ מַצָּה?

Sheb-chol hah-lay-lot anu o-chleen chamaytz oo-matzah. Hah-lai-lah hah-zeh koo-lo matzah?

שֶׁבְּכָל הַלֵּילוֹת אָנוּ אוֹכְלִין שְׁאָר יְרָקוֹת. הַלַּיְלָה הַזֶּה מָרוֹר?

Sheb-chol hah-lay-lot anu o-chleen sh'-ar y'-rah-kot. Hah-lai-lah hah-zeh mah-ror?

שֶׁבְּכָל הַלֵּילוֹת אֵין אָנוּ מַטְבִּילִין אֲפִילוּ פַּעַם אֶחָת. הַלַּיְלָה הַזֶּה שְׁתֵּי פְעָמִים?

Sheb-chol hah-lay-lot ayn anu mat-bee-leen ah-fee-loo pa'am eh-chat. Hah-lai-lah hah-zeh sh'-tay f'-ah-meem?

שֶׁבְּכָל הַלֵּילוֹת אָנוּ אוֹכְלִין בֵּין יוֹשְׁבִין וּבֵין מְסֻבִּין. הַלַּיְלָה הַזֶּה כֻּלָּנוּ מְסֻבִּין?

Sheb-chol hah-lay-lot anu o-chleen bayn yosh-veen oo-vayn m'-soo-been. Hah-lai-lah hah-zeh koo-lah-noo m'-soo-been?

Favorite Passover Recipes

Charoset

Apple and nut mixture for the seder plate

4 to 6 medium chopped or grated apples, not peeled
1 cup finely chopped nuts (pecans, walnuts or almonds)
1 tbsp honey
1 tsp sugar
2 tsp cinnamon
4 tbsp sweet red wine or grape juice

Mix all ingredients; keep chilled in the refrigerator. May be served immediately, but flavors blend and intensify after chilling all day or overnight. Serves at least 3 tables of 8 people each (providing about 1 cup per communal seder plate).

Matzah Chocolate Layer Cake

Super-easy, no-bake recipe that's always a big hit

21 ounces of Hershey's milk chocolate bars (plain, no almonds)
5 to 7 matzah squares
grape juice (a moderate amount; you won't need the whole bottle)

Melt chocolate, either in a double boiler or in the microwave. (If melting in microwave, run it no longer than 1 or 2 minutes at a time, removing chocolate and stirring it frequently to prevent it from burning.) Pour grape juice into a square pan, just enough to immerse a square of matzah in it. Let the matzah soak 45 to 60 seconds (not too long, or it will disintegrate). Gently lift the soaked matzah square from the grape juice and place it on a clean dinner plate. Spread a layer of melted chocolate over the matzah square with the back of a fork or spoon, enough to cover it fairly well. Repeat; lay another soaked matzah on top, then more chocolate, and so on. Top off the last matzah with a final layer of melted chocolate. Chill in refrigerator for at least an hour. After cake is set, use sharp knife to cut into squares and serve. Once set, cake may be stored at room temperature.

Unleavened Bread

Messiah's Burial

"We have been buried therefore with Him by baptism into death..."

Romans 6:4

"For Him who knew no sin He made to be sin on our behalf; so that in Him we might become the righteousness of God."

2 Corinthians 5:21

Jesus in the Sepulchre (Jésus dans le sépulcre), James Tissot, 1886–1894.

Unleavened Bread

The **Feast of Unleavened Bread** (**Chag ha Matzot*** חַג הַמַּצּוֹת *ḣahg hah-mah-TSŌT*) is a symbol of two things: **Messiah's burial** in the grave and the **purging of sin** from the believer's life. As we will learn in this chapter, the two are intertwined. To understand this important feast, we'll need to study two things: God's own description of this feast, and the meaning of **leaven** as His Word explains it.

What is leaven?

Before we embark on a study of the Feast of Unleavened Bread, it would be helpful to have a solid working definition of leaven itself. In English dictionaries, two definitions are provided: **Leaven** is any **substance** (typically yeast) that may be added to dough to cause it to **ferment and rise**. Figuratively, any **pervasive influence** that modifies or transforms something else may be also termed "leaven." Common synonyms in the English language for leaven's activity are *make rise, puff up, expand* or *permeate, infuse, pervade*. From these English definitions of leaven, we can already see why leaven is a symbol of the effects of sin. Once sin is allowed to persist in a believer's life or a community's culture, it will *infuse and transform every aspect* and – if left unaddressed – will eventually cause a *puffing up* of arrogant, willful rebellion.

Scriptural terms for leaven

Here are the **Hebrew** terms used in the **Old Testament** for *leaven:*

חָמֵץ	**chametz** *(ḣah-MAYTZ)*	leavened; i.e., "that which is leavened" (from a verb meaning "to leaven")
שְׂאֹר	**s'or** *(s'-OR)*	leaven (a noun; the actual agent used to leaven the dough)

In the **Greek** of the **New Testament**, here is the term for *leaven:*

ζύμη	**zumē** *(ZOO-may)*	leaven; *figuratively*, corruption

"Purge out the old leaven, that you may be a new lump, even as you are unleavened..."

1 Corinthians 5:7

***Pronunciation note:** Recall that the Hebrew "ch" is always pronounced "ch" as in "Bach," something like a rough, back-of-the-throat "h" sound. The term *chag*, meaning "feast" sounds a bit like our word "hog." The term *matzot* has a long ō sound in the last syllable; it rhymes with "boat."

This feast also goes by the slightly different name *Chag ha Matzah*. The Hebrew word for unleavened bread in singular form is *matzah*; the plural form is *matzot*.

Just as Israel was commanded to put away leaven during and after the Exodus, we too have been commanded to put away our sinful ways, now that we have been set free from sin by the saving power of Messiah's death and resurrection.

Scriptural terms for "unleavened"

Here are the **Hebrew** terms used in the **Old Testament** for *unleavened bread*:

מַצָּה   **matzah** *(mah-TSAH)*   unleavened bread (or cake), singular

מַצּוֹת   **matzot*** *(mah-TSŌT*)*   unleavened breads (or cakes), plural

In the **Greek** of the **New Testament**, here is the term for *unleavened*:

ἄζυμος   **azumos** *(AH-zoo-mahss)*   an adjective meaning "unleavened;" *figuratively*, "uncorrupted, sincere"

The remainder of this chapter provides our own summary of the truths that are revealed in both the Old and New Testaments wherever the above six Hebrew and Greek terms appear in Scripture.

God's Feast of Unleavened Bread

God instituted the Feast of Unleavened Bread just prior to the great exodus from Egypt. In Exodus 12:14-20, He said,

> [14]This day shall be to you for a memorial, and you shall keep it a feast to the Lord: throughout your generations you shall keep it a feast by an ordinance forever. [15]**Seven days you shall eat unleavened bread**; even the first day you shall **put away leaven out of your houses,** for whoever eats leavened bread from the first day until the seventh day, that soul shall be cut off from Israel. [16]In the first day there shall be to you a holy convocation, and in the seventh day a holy convocation; no kind of work shall be done in them, except that which every man must eat, that only may be done by you. [17]You shall observe the **feast of unleavened bread**; for in this same day have I brought your armies out of the land of Egypt: therefore you shall observe this day throughout your generations by an ordinance forever. [18]**In the first month, on the fourteenth day of the month at evening, you shall eat unleavened bread, until the twenty first day of the month at evening.** [19]**Seven days shall there be no leaven found in your houses**, for whoever eats that which is leavened, that soul shall be cut off from the congregation of Israel, whether he be a foreigner, or one who is born in the land. [20]**You shall eat nothing leavened. In all your habitations you shall eat unleavened bread.**

*Pronunciation note: The last syllable of *matzot* is pronounced with a long ō sound, so that it rhymes with "boat."

You probably noticed that this passage provides an excellent example of the way that God views **Passover and Unleavened Bread as a unit**. Why is it viewed as a unit? Passover is a single day (the 14th of Nisan, see verse 18) that, upon its conclusion, then kicks off the seven-day-long Feast of Unleavened Bread (Nisan 15-21; see its concluding date, also stated in verse 18). Throughout the *entire period* from Passover (Nisan 14) through Unleavened Bread (Nisan 15-21), no leaven may be eaten or found in the homes of the people. This is why, in both modern conversation and ancient Scripture, the term "Feast of Unleavened Bread" can imply the inclusion of Passover as well. You will always need to study the full context of a passage to understand whether God might be referring to both feasts together as a unit, or if He is speaking of only the seven-day feast itself.

For the sake of illustration, let us put this in purely Gentile terms. Everyone understands that when a college student says she is "going home for Christmas," she is really saying she will be staying there right on through New Year's day. In that particular usage of the term "Christmas," New Year's day is *understood* to be included in the time period. But, if that same student says, "We always open our presents together on Christmas morning," she is speaking only about the day of Christmas itself, December 25th. She is not including New Year's day in that particular usage. We must use the context to understand her meaning. Bible scholars do the same thing when studying Scripture.

There are other important things to notice about the passage on the previous page, such as God's commandment about the **leaven itself.** Not only did God command that no unleavened *bread* be eaten for seven days, but He went a step further in verse 19, commanding that no actual leavening *agent* (yeast, etc.) be found in their houses. This additional layer of commandment is very important because of leaven's symbolism of sin's pervasive quality. Observant Jews (and all those Gentiles who choose to enjoy partaking in the feasts) will remove all leavened foods as well as leaven itself from their houses the day before Nisan 14. They will keep their homes "leaven free" until the conclusion of the seven-day Feast of Unleavened Bread on Nisan 21.

Another item of note is the **holiness** of the event. Notice that God has "book-ended" the seven-day period with two special sabbaths (verse 16). Such special sabbaths don't necessarily fall on the seventh day of the week. Depending on the moon's cycle that year, they can and often do occur mid-week. The two special sabbaths of Unleavened Bread always occur on the 15th and 21st of Nisan, no matter what day of the week those dates fall on. They *can*, of course coincide with the weekly seventh-day sabbath, but they don't *have* to. You may think of your own birthday as an example. It always occurs on the same *date* every year, but not on the same *day of the week* every year. Knowing about these "special sabbaths" will be very helpful to you later, when we discuss Firstfruits and the Feast of Weeks.

> *Unleavened Bread is a seven-day-long feast, affixed to and continuing forth from the day of Passover. It is a holy event unto itself, book-ended by two special sabbaths.*

"You shall eat unleavened bread... seven days, even the bread of affliction, for you came forth out of the land of Egypt in haste..."

Deuteronomy 16:3

Repetitions of the commandment

As if to underscore the great importance God places on the Feast of Unleavened Bread, God repeated His commandment *three more times* in Scripture. We have included those three passages below. We put some of the key facts in **boldface type**.

⁴These are the **set feasts of the LORD**, even **holy convocations**, which you shall proclaim in their appointed season. ⁵In the first month, on the fourteenth day of the month in the evening, is the LORD's Passover. ⁶**On the fifteenth day of the same month is the LORD's feast of unleavened bread. Seven days you shall eat unleavened bread.** ⁷In the **first day** you shall have a **holy convocation**. You shall do no regular work. ⁸But you shall offer an offering made by fire to the LORD seven days. In the **seventh day** is a **holy convocation**: you shall do no regular work (Lev. 23:4-8).

¹⁶In the first month, on the fourteenth day of the month, is the LORD's Passover. ¹⁷On the **fifteenth day of this month shall be a feast: seven days shall unleavened bread be eaten.** ¹⁸In the **first day** shall be a **holy convocation:** you shall do no servile work... ²⁵On the **seventh day** you shall have a **holy convocation:** you shall do no servile work (Num. 28:16-18, 25).

¹Observe the month of Abib,* and keep the Passover to the LORD your God; for in the month of Abib the LORD your God brought you forth out of Egypt by night. ²You shall sacrifice the Passover to the LORD your God, of the flock and the herd, in the place which the LORD shall choose, to cause His name to dwell there. ³You shall eat **no leavened bread** with it. **You shall eat unleavened bread with it seven days**, even **the bread of affliction**; for you came forth out of the land of Egypt in haste: that you may remember the day when you came forth out of the land of Egypt all the days of your life. ⁴**No leaven shall be seen with you in all your borders seven days**... ⁸Six days you shall eat **unleavened bread**; and on the **seventh day** shall be a **solemn assembly to the LORD your God**; you shall do no work [therein] (Deut. 16:1-4, 8).

We once knew a pastor who had a favorite saying: "When God says something, it's important. When God *repeats* it, it's really, really important." The Feast of Unleavened Bread, then, is very important indeed, and it's certainly not just about eating yeast-free bread for seven days.

*****Abib** is the pre-exilic name for the first month of the biblical year, a month which later came to be called Nisan. Refer to pages 20-21 for a review of pre- and post-exilic month names.

Unleavened Bread's prophetic significance

We know from New Testament Scripture that Yeshua was placed in the grave during the Feast of Unleavened Bread. It is significant that He was "put away" during this time, for Scripture states that Messiah literally "became sin" for our sakes, so that "in Him, we might become the righteousness of God."

> [15]**He died for all, that those who live should no longer live to themselves, but to Him who for their sakes died** and rose again... [18]But all things are of God, who reconciled us to Himself through Jesus Christ, and gave to us the ministry of reconciliation; [19]namely, that God was in Christ reconciling the world to Himself, not reckoning to them their trespasses, and having committed to us the word of reconciliation... [21]**For Him who knew no sin He made to be sin on our behalf;** so that **in Him we might become the righteousness of God** (2 Cor. 5:15-19,21).

Notice a few important things here. First, the context of this passage is a chapter in which Paul is describing the process of the death of a believer's body. He speaks of us groaning in our present form, weighed down by the burden of sinful corruption in our mortality. He speaks of the day that we will be transformed, clothed with immortality. When Messiah died and was buried during the Feast of Unleavened Bread, he actually "became sin on our behalf," and God put that leaven away, into the grave. What was the entire purpose of this? That the leaven of sin would be removed from our lives so that we "no longer live to ourselves, but to Him who for our sakes died and rose again."

Now that we are born again, it is incumbent on us to continually allow the Holy Spirit to put the leaven of sin out of our lives. We must let Him conform us, minute by minute, to the righteousness of God Himself. God has *already* put us in a position in which He views us as righteous, all because of His righteous Son's death. In return, our act of loving worship should be to prayerfully make every effort to put away sin's polluting force from our lives, every single day. As beings of free will, we have the choice to cooperate on a daily basis with the powerful grace of God. It's His grace that creates the desire within us to remove sin from our lives in the first place. It's that same powerful grace that empowers us to put away sin's pervasive corruption from our daily lives. *That* is the enduring message of the Feast of Unleavened Bread.

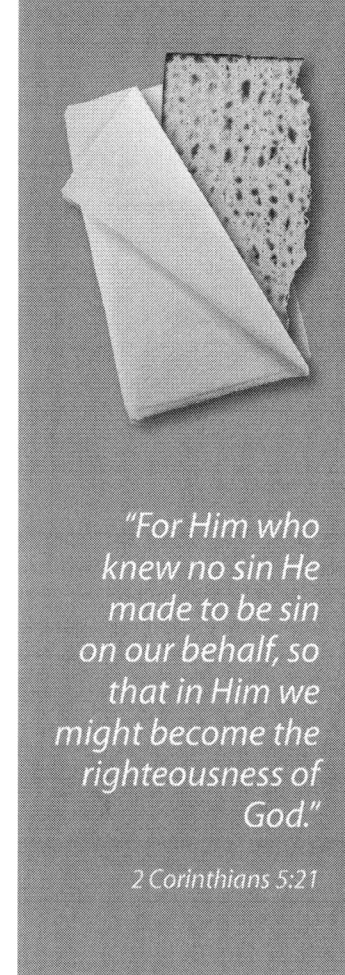

> "For Him who knew no sin He made to be sin on our behalf, so that in Him we might become the righteousness of God."
>
> 2 Corinthians 5:21

Scripture speaks of leaven as a symbol of hypocrisy, malice and wickedness. The Bible teaches that the effect of such leaven is a boastful arrogance – a "puffing up" – which will infect all aspects of individual and communal life.

Leaven in the New Testament

It is important for all believers to understand how the New Testament actually describes leaven. Let's read some of the words of Jesus and the apostle Paul.

"Beware of the **leaven** of the Pharisees, which is **hypocrisy**" (the words of Jesus, Luke 12:1).

"Take heed: beware of the **leaven** of the Pharisees and the **leaven** of Herod" (the words of Jesus, Mark 8:15).

⁷You were running well! Who interfered with you that you should not obey the truth? ⁸This persuasion is not from Him who calls you. ⁹A little **leaven** grows through the whole lump. ¹⁰I have confidence toward you in the Lord that you will think no other way. But he who troubles you will bear his judgment, whoever he is (the words of Paul in his letter to the Galatians, chapter 5, warning of the dangerous infection of false teaching).

¹It is actually reported that there is sexual immorality among you, and such sexual immorality as is not even named among the Gentiles, that one has his father's wife. ²You are **puffed up**, and didn't rather mourn, that he who had done this deed might be removed from among you... ⁶Your **boasting** is not good. Don't you know that a little **leaven** leavens the whole lump? ⁷Purge out the old **leaven**, that you may be a new lump, even as you are unleavened. For indeed Christ, our Passover, has been sacrificed in our place. ⁸Therefore let us **keep the feast**, not with old **leaven**, neither with the **leaven** of malice and wickedness, but with the unleavened bread of sincerity and truth (the words of Paul admonishing the believers who lived in Corinth, 1 Cor. 5)

To summarize, then, Scripture makes leaven a symbol of **pervasive hypocrisy, malice,** and **wickedness**. Leaven is symbolized as that agent which **puffs up in arrogant boasting**. When it symbolizes sin that is left unaddressed, it is described as **spreading through the whole body** of believers, just as it **infects every aspect** of an individual believer's life.*

---

*In all of Scripture, there is only one usage of the term *leaven* which (some think) may hold a neutral symbolism rather than its standard symbolism of evil. This is when Yeshua describes the silently pervasive quality of the Kingdom of Heaven as "leaven-like" (Mt. 13:33, Lk. 13:21). There is sharp division of opinion on this topic, however. Some scholars see this usage of leaven as *positive* (the expansive growth of the Kingdom with its positive influence); some see it as *negative* (an abnormally large, unwieldy growth as implied by the preceding "parable of the mustard seed" in which "the birds of the air come and lodge in its branches.") Scholars from the latter group note that the "birds of the air" are biblical symbols of evil spirits, who infiltrate the body of believers to do harm.

Unleavened Bread in the New Testament

It will be well worth your time to carefully re-read the passage from 1 Corinthians 5 on the previous page. Perhaps read the entire chapter in your own Bible. We urge you to do so now, before proceeding to read any of our commentary below.

Scholars date Paul's first letter to the Corinthians as having been written sometime between 53 and 57 CE.* Notice that these born-again, blood-bought believers who lived in Gentile-dominated Corinth **continued to observe the Feast of Unleavened Bread as late as twenty years after the resurrection of Jesus.**

We can learn even more about the culture of first-century believers from the very way in which Paul spoke in 1 Corinthians 5. We get the strong impression that Paul *assumed* that the Corinthian believers were observing the Feast of Unleavened Bread. Paul didn't even bother to command them to keep the feast, for he knew it was *already* their usual practice. Rather, Paul was writing to remind the believers to observe the feast *properly* – with purity and humility, putting away sin. Paul merely used the occasion of the Feast of Unleavened Bread to remind these believers of its true meaning: to avoid spiritual contamination by putting willful sin completely out of their communal life. This, indeed, is the whole point of this feast.

In our own ministry over the years, we have met many wonderful non-Jewish brothers and sisters who joyfully embarked on observing the feasts of the LORD, only to be immediately opposed by a well-meaning friend or relative who feared that it was somehow *wrong* to observe Unleavened Bread. The opposer usually gave the reason that Jesus, by His resurrection, had "done away with" such things as the feasts. Our confused brother or sister would often return to us and ask, "How is it *wrong* to be observing a feast that God invented as a memorial to Himself for all eternity? I am literally *doing* His word, and *pondering* His word, for seven straight days, and He has shown me the areas of sin that I needed to confess and get cleaned up. I'm overjoyed, I feel released, and I am drawing closer to Jesus than ever before. God's peace and direction have never been more evident in my entire life! So, how is this supposed to be *bad* for me?"

In answer to this, we made it our habit to point our brother or sister to this very passage in 1 Corinthians. Paul himself endorsed the observance of the Feast of Unleavened Bread some *twenty years after the resurrection of Jesus*. Not only that, but he went a step further: he insisted that, *whenever* and *wherever* it was observed, it had to be observed *in the right spirit*. Unleavened Bread must be observed in a manner that invites the Holy Spirit to use the feast as the powerful object lesson in the believer's life that it was always intended to be.

If you are fully submitted to the Holy Spirit while you observe a feast of the LORD, and if you are observing the feast for the *right* reasons (i.e., to humbly experience His grace through faith) and not for the *wrong* reasons (i.e., to boast as though you've earned some kind of special status by doing so), then you will please God greatly. So, if you are hearing the call of God to do so, then, by all means, *allow yourself the freedom to enjoy His feasts*. All His children are invited.

Those who choose to observe God's Feast of Unleavened Bread must do so in a manner that allows the Holy Spirit to speak to their hearts about the hidden leaven (sin) in their lives. They must fully cooperate with the grace of God, confessing sin and allowing Him to cleanse their lives by His power.

*The abbreviation CE just means "common era." It is the standard academic and scientific synonym for the abbreviation AD (which stands for *Anno Domini*, Latin, "in the year of the Lord.") Similarly, BCE simply means "before common era." Scientific and academic publications use the CE and BCE terminology in order to maintain a neutral position with regard to religious beliefs. The terminology has also been adopted by many Jewish publications.

Bedikat Chametz – the traditional search for leaven – and its Messianic symbolism

As we have seen from Scripture, God places a high priority on removing the leaven from one's house during the Feast of Unleavened Bread because of its symbolism of the removal of sin from one's life. Therefore, the search for leaven in the home has evolved in Jewish culture into a beautiful family tradition known as **Bedikat Chametz*** בְּדִיקַת חָמֵץ *(b'-dee-KAHT ħah-MAYTS)*, literally, the "examination for that which is leavened," better known as "the search for leaven."

During the day preceding Passover, the head of the house examines (with the light of a candle) all the cupboards, corners and remote places of the house in order to find any stray crumbs of leavened food (chametz). Any chametz that is found is swept with a feather onto a wooden spoon and disposed of into a paper or cloth bag. Usually, the entire bag is disposed of by burning it the following morning. For centuries, the tradition was that the man of the house led his children in the ceremonial search, but the woman of the house participated as an equally important partner, for she knew best where all the leaven was stored in the home.

To hold the interest of the youngest children, the practice has emerged of "seeding" the home with several well-hidden pieces of chametz for them to find (usually ten pieces). Some traditions also include the father carrying a small bell, which he rings each time a child finds chametz in the house.

The symbols of this ceremony are powerful representations of the ministries of Father, Son and Holy Spirit.

> The **candle**: This represents the Light of the World, Yeshua the Messiah. It His light that illuminates the darkest corners of our lives, revealing our sin to us.
>
> The **feather**: A symbol of the Holy Spirit. It is only by His activity that sin may be swept out of our lives.
>
> The **wood**: The wooden spoon, upon which the leaven is collected, will later be discarded or destroyed by fire because of its contamination with leaven. The wood represents the despised cross upon which Messiah was affixed as He "became sin for us."
>
> The **fire**: This represents the lake of eternal fire into which God the Father will one day cast death and hell itself (Rev. 20:14). Our sins are as far removed from us as east is from west (Psalm 103:12).

The traditional Jewish ceremony of Bedikat Chametz is rich with beautiful symbols of the work of grace carried out by Father, Son and Holy Spirit in the life of the believer.

*Pronunciation note: the word *chametz* begins with a rough "h" sound like the "ch" in "Bach."

The father of the house leads the children in "Bedikat Chametz," the search for leaven. The mother has hidden bits of leavened bread for her family to find. Note the candle and feather being used by the father and son at lower right.

THE SEARCH for the LEAVEN &c.
The Mistress of the family puts Leavened Bread in various places, to the end that her Husband in his search may find it.

The Search for the Leaven, etching by Bernard Picart, circa 1733.

Although hiding exactly *ten* pieces of chametz is not necessarily a worldwide practice among all Jews, there is a certain biblical symbolism in that number. The number ten is viewed as a complete and perfect number, symbolizing a *thorough* search. In Scripture, the number ten signifies testimony, law, responsibility and the completeness of order. God created the world with *ten* statements (His order). God initiated His Torah with *ten* commandments/utterances (His law). A tithe is a *tenth* of our earnings (our responsibility and response in faith). The Passover lamb was chosen on the *tenth* day of Nisan (Exodus 12:3). The Day of Atonement occurs on the *tenth* day of the seventh month.

The Bedikat Chametz ceremony is a powerful object lesson that tends to leave a marked impression on young children. We have seen God use this ceremony as a strong reminder in the lives of teenagers and young adults. The Holy Spirit is able to bring to mind the childhood memories of this ceremony and its symbols when it comes time for a young person to make his first responsible effort to seek out and remove sinful behavior on his own.

We hasten to remind you that the ceremony of Bedikat Chametz is not described anywhere in the Bible. It is purely optional. It is just a God-honoring cultural tradition, no different from the myriad of God-honoring Gentile traditions which cannot be found in the Bible, yet are enjoyed by the Church today. Bedikat Chametz is one way to let your entire family participate in a Jesus-honoring, annual event which is fully aligned with God's Word. We think it's a fantastic way to spiritually prepare hearts young and old for the Feast of Unleavened Bread.

The simple, traditional blessing for Bedikat Chametz, the Search for Leaven, is provided in the following pages, so that you can lead your own family in this beautiful tradition if you desire. In this version, along with the traditional liturgy, we have added our own Messianic liturgy which is intended to glorify Jesus as Messiah. Please feel free to modify it or write your own Scripture-based liturgy if you feel so led! The emphasis shouldn't be on pronouncing Hebrew blessings correctly or saying certain words. Instead, it should be on spending family time together in worship, remembering Yeshua's sacrificial death and burial, exposing and removing the leaven of sin from our lives – the true, <u>spiritual</u> purposes of His Feast of Unleavened Bread.

Also included are a few matzah-based recipes (recipes using unleavened bread) which we hope you will enjoy. Seven days without leaven can make it challenging to prepare meals that hold your family's interest, so the more good, leaven-free recipes you can acquire, the better!

Unleavened Bread

Bedikat Chametz Ceremony and Matzah-based recipes

Bedikat Chametz
The Search for Leaven   בְּדִיקַת חָמֵץ

Carry out the search on the night before Passover. You will need a candle, a feather, a wooden spoon and a paper bag. (For small children, it is best to let each child use his or her own flashlight for the search, rather than a candle.) An adult should hide small pieces of bread (ten pieces is a traditional number) throughout the house. Before the search begins, light the candle and say the traditional blessing:

Family

The head of the household leads the entire family in the blessing...

Blessed are You, LORD our God, King of the Universe, Who instilled within us the holiness of His commandments and Who commanded us to remove all leaven.

בָּרוּךְ אַתָּה, יהוה, אֱלֹהֵינוּ מֶלֶךְ הָעוֹלָם, אֲשֶׁר קִדְּשָׁנוּ בְּמִצְוֹתָיו וְצִוָּנוּ עַל בִּעוּר חָמֵץ.

Bah-ruch ah-tah Adonai, Eh-lo-hay-nu Meh-lech hah-o-lahm ah-shayr kid-shah-nu b'-mitz-vo-tahv v'-tsih-vah-nu ahl b'-oor chah-maytz.

Head of household

Thank You, Father for inscribing Your Law, and all Your commandments therein, on our hearts (Jer. 31:33, Heb. 8:10). Thank You, Holy Spirit, for choosing to dwell within us, applying the Word so that we may be sanctified daily (2 Tim. 1:14, 1 Cor. 6:19). Thank You, Yeshua, for Your work on the execution stake, becoming sin for us, being buried away during the feast of Unleavened Bread, then rising again, in order that we may stand pure and blameless before God (2 Cor. 5:21).

(Lifting up the candle to show the children) This candle represents Yeshua – Jesus – the Light of the World. He lets us see the darkest corners of our hearts to find any sin that may be hiding there.

(Picking up the feather) This feather represents Ruach ha Kodesh – the Holy Spirit. He is the only one powerful enough to sweep sin out of our lives. We cannot do it on our own. We ask Him to help us.

(Lifting up the wooden spoon) This wooden spoon represents the execution stake – the cross that everyone despised. Yeshua died on that cross when He took away our sin. All of our sins were forgiven, once and for all, because Jesus died for us on the wooden cross.

One of the adults leads the youngest children in the search for the ten pieces of chametz. Use the feather to sweep the crumbs onto the wooden spoon, then dump the contents from the spoon into the paper bag. In the morning, when the bag of chametz and wooden spoon are burned, it is traditional to recite:

All chametz in my possession which I have inadvertently not seen or removed is hereby nullified and ownerless as the dust of the earth.

This is symbolic of confessing and disavowing all sin in our lives, even sin of which we are unaware.

Matzah Balls (for soup)

Prep time 20 minutes. Cook time 25 minutes. Ready in 1 hour 15 minutes.

- 4 eggs
- 6 tablespoons olive oil
- ⅓ cup club soda plus 2 tbsp club soda
- ½ tsp salt
- 1 ½ cups matzah meal (or more)
- 4 quarts water

In a bowl, whisk eggs and olive oil together until well blended. Stir in both amounts of the club soda, and the salt, into the egg mixture. Mix the 1 ½ cups matzah meal into the egg mixture, adding up to another ¼ cup if needed to arrive at a doughy consistency. Cover; refrigerate for 30 minutes. Bring water to a boil in a large pot. With wet hands, form balls from the dough, about 1-inch diameter. Gently lower the matzah balls into the boiling water, then reduce heat to low, cover the pot and simmer until matzah balls are tender, 25 to 30 minutes. Remove them from the water and store them separately (in the fridge, if storing long term) until you are ready to add them to your soup, or they will fall apart. You can heat them together with the soup just before serving.

Apple Matzah Cake

A moist, tasty, apple and cinnamon cake

2 tbps vegetable shortening, room temp.

Cake Batter:
- 4 eggs, separated into yolks & whites
- ¾ cup vegetable oil
- ½ cup orange juice
- 1 ½ cups white sugar
- 1 ½ cups matzah cake meal*
- ¾ tsp salt
- 1 ½ tsp vanilla

Apple Layer:
- ¾ cup white sugar
- ½ tsp ground cinnamon
- 3 Granny Smith apples, peeled and thinly sliced

*If matzah cake meal is unavailable, you may substitute regular matzah meal which you have first ground in a blender until it is very fine.

Preheat oven to 350° F. Grease an 8" square baking dish with shortening. In glass, metal or ceramic bowl, beat egg whites with electric mixer until stiff peaks form and hold their shapes when lifting beater straight up from the mixture. Set aside. In a mixing bowl, beat egg yolks, oil, orange juice and vanilla until thick (about 5 minutes). Stir in 1 ½ cups sugar; mix well. Lightly stir in matzah cake meal and salt. Use rubber spatula or whisk to gently fold about a third of the beaten egg whites into the batter until incorporated throughout. Then add the remaining egg whites, repeating the process. That's your batter. Now, mix ¾ cup sugar with the cinnamon in a bowl. Spread half the batter into the greased pan. Sprinkle about a third of the sugar-cinnamon mixture on the batter. Layer the apple slices evenly over that. Over the apple layer, sprinkle half of the remaining sugar-cinnamon mixture. Spread remaining batter over this. Sprinkle remaining sugar and cinnamon over the top of the cake. Bake until golden brown, about 45 minutes.

Firstfruits

Messiah's Resurrection

But Christ has indeed been raised from the dead, the firstfruits of those who have fallen asleep. For since death came through a man, the resurrection of the dead comes also through a man. For as in Adam all die, so in Christ all will be made alive. But each in turn: Christ, the firstfruits; then, when He comes, those who belong to Him.

1 Corinthians 15:20-23

Firstfruits

The **Day of Firstfruits, Yom Ha Bikkurim*** יוֹם הַבִּכּוּרִים *(yōhm hah-bih-koo-REEM)* is a symbol of **Messiah's resurrection** and the fact that He is the **firstfruits of all who are resurrected**. This glorious feast falls every year on Nisan 16, the third day after Passover and smack dab in the middle of the seven-day-long Feast of Unleavened Bread. Our Messiah, the Passover Lamb, was slain "between the evenings" at the beginning of Nisan 14, was in the grave over a time period spanning three different biblical days, and was raised from the dead during the third day, Nisan 16, the Feast of Firstfruits.

The commandment of the feast

In order to understand all the beautiful symbols of Firstfruits, it will be helpful to read God's exact words about the feast He invented. The passage below may seem lengthy at first, but its entire context is necessary because Firstfruits is intricately linked to the feasts which occur before, during and after it. These relationships are vital to the feast's true meaning. As you read God's words below, notice that He set the wave offering of the firstfruits to be done *after* Passover and *during* Unleavened Bread; specifically, on the day after "the sabbath" (i.e., the first special sabbath of Unleavened Bread). From this date of the firstfruits offering, exactly *fifty days* are to be counted to arrive at the next holy event, which is called the Feast of Weeks, also known as Pentecost. (We'll clarify these details for you on the next pages, but just take a moment now to carefully read the entire passage, taken from Leviticus 23.)

> [4]These are the set feasts of the LORD, even holy convocations, which you shall proclaim in their appointed season. [5]In the first month, on the fourteenth day of the month in the evening, is the LORD's Passover. [6]On the fifteenth day of the same month is the feast of Unleavened Bread to the LORD. Seven days you shall eat unleavened bread. [7]In the first day you shall have a holy convocation. You shall do no regular work... [8]...In the seventh day is a holy convocation: you shall do no regular work. [10]...When you have come into the land which I give to you, and shall reap its harvest, then you shall bring the **sheaf of the first fruits of your harvest** to the priest: [11]and he shall wave the sheaf before the LORD, to be accepted for you. **On the next day after the sabbath the priest shall wave it**.... [14]...This is a statute forever throughout your generations in all your dwellings. [15]**You shall count from the next day after the sabbath, from the day that you brought the sheaf of the wave offering**; seven weeks shall be completed: [16]even to the next day after the seventh week you shall number fifty days...

The presentation of the sheaf of Firstfruits is a statute forever throughout Israel's generations in all her dwellings.

Leviticus 23:14

***Pronunciation note:** The Hebrew word *yom*, meaning "day" or "day of," has a long *ō*, so it rhymes with *dome* or *roam*. Try to avoid pronouncing it so it rhymes with *mom*, because that makes it sound exactly like a completely different Hebrew word, the word for *sea*.

God's timing of the Feast of Firstfruits

We realize that the passage on the preceding page might seem confusing to those who have never observed God's biblical feasts. So we took excerpts from the passage and set them underneath a graphic to help you visualize the time periods God was describing. Recall that the biblical day begins at sunset, so the dates on our graphic follow biblical timekeeping, rather than the modern-day western concept of starting the day at midnight.

The graphic spans two pages.

←─────────────── **Passover** ───────────────→ ←─ **Special Sabbath; 1st Day of Unleavened Bread** ─

This special sabbath may fall on any day of the week; it is not restricted to just Saturdays

**Evening –
Nisan 14
begins**

**Evening –
Nisan 15
begins**

"In the first month, on the fourteenth day of the month in the evening, is the Lord's **Passover**" (Lev. 23:5).

"On the fifteenth day of the same month is the feast of **Unleavened Bread** to the Lord. Seven days you shall eat unleavened bread. In the **first day you shall have a holy convocation**. You shall do no regular work..." (Lev. 23:6-7a)

THE FEAST OF FIRSTFRUITS | 67

← Feast of Firstfruits; Also Day 1 of the 50-day countdown → | **← Day 2 of the 50-day countdown →**
Day 2 of the 7-day Feast of Unleavened Bread | *Day 3 of the 7-day Feast of Unleavened Bread*

**Evening –
Nisan 16
begins**

**Evening –
Nisan 17
begins**

" ...then you shall bring the **sheaf of the first fruits of your harvest** to the priest: and he shall wave the sheaf before the Lord, to be accepted for you. **On the day after the sabbath the priest shall wave it...** " (Lev. 23:10b-11a)

"**You shall count from the day after the sabbath, from the day that you brought the sheaf of the wave offering**; seven weeks* shall be completed: even to the day after the seventh week **you shall number fifty days**..." (Lev. 23:15-16a)

---

*Some of our readers who like to read along in their own Bibles might see a different phrase used here – "seven sabbaths." That's because many older translations opted to translate the countdown period in this verse very literally, as "seven sabbaths" rather than "seven weeks." They arrived at this translation from the verse's Hebrew word *shabbatot*, "sabbaths," which can literally mean "holy days of rest," but can *also* be used to imply generic "periods of seven days." The "seven days" usage arose because there is always one holy sabbath within any seven day period. To count the number of *weeks* in a given time period, one could just as easily count the number of *sabbaths* that had gone by, so in general conversation, the two ideas became interchangeable. Jewish people would often substitute the term "sabbath" for the word "week," as in the sentence, "It's been at least five sabbaths since I last saw him." From this context, a translator would understand the intended meaning of "five weeks." In fact, this "double usage" carried over into the Greek of the New Testament, where "sabbaths" in Greek may be understood to refer to either literal "holy days of rest" or just plain old, regular "weeks." To clarify His meaning in the Leviticus passage above, God repeated the commandment for the fifty-day countdown in a parallel passage, Deuteronomy 16:9. There, He made Himself crystal clear by saying, *literally*, "seven weeks." The Hebrew word He used in Deuteronomy 16:9 was *shavuot* instead of *shabbatot*. *Shavuot* literally means "weeks" or "periods of seven." It was from this very word, *shavuot*, that the "Feast of Weeks" got its Hebrew name.

> *Jesus is the "firstfruits of the resurrection."*
>
> *Believers are firstfruits of redemption, not only spiritually, but – one day – physically. Our resurrected bodies will be firstfruits of the restoration of all creation which is yet to come.*
>
> *As firstfruits, we are living sacrifices, "separated" (set apart) to a holy God and to a life of loving service.*

Scriptural terms for *firstfruits*

God uses two **Hebrew** terms to refer to *firstfruits* in the **Old Testament**.

רֵאשִׁית   **reshith** *(ray-SHEET)*   beginning, first in place, time, order or rank. First phase, step or element in a course of events. Earliest of produce, i.e., "first fruits." (*By extension*, finest, foremost, chief, choicest)

בִּכּוּרִים   **bikkurim** *(bih-koo-REEM)*   first fruits. (from a root *bakar* ב.כ.ר. meaning *to bear new fruit* or *to constitute as first born*)

In the **Greek** of the **New Testament**, here is the term for *firsfruits*:

ἀπαρχή   **aparchē*** *(ah-par-HAY)*   firstfruits (*literally*, "a separation of the first;" i.e., a beginning of sacrifice, or a setting apart of the "first" of a harvest to the LORD)

The Feast of Firstfruits occurs during the month Nisan, the time of year when the barley is harvested. Taking the definitions of the three words above all together, we get an excellent picture of the symbolism. **Firstfruits are:**

first in time   In the land of Israel, barley is the *first* grain crop harvested in the *first* month of God's biblical year. It acts as a pledge (earnest) of what is to come. As such, it represents a promise, a *forerunner*, of a bountiful harvest. As a forerunner, firstfruits can also symbolize Godly *leadership* – those who forge ahead in righteousness and shepherd the people toward a harvest of spiritual prosperity. The same symbolism of pledge and leadership extends to the first born child of a human family.

first in place   God commanded that, once they had established themselves in the land, the people present their firstfruits at His holy city, Jerusalem – the city where He would place His Name – the *chief* place in all the world.

first in rank   The barley sheaves of firstfruits were to be of the *choicest* and *best* barley, not the discards. This symbolizes Godly leadership of the highest moral character.

first sacrifice   The beginning of the barley harvest was an opportunity to present the *first sacrifice* of the biblical year, transforming an otherwise mundane agricultural task into a beautiful outward act of worship. By presenting the first produce of the year in faith, the worshipper publicly declared his gratitude and remembered his utter reliance on God.

***Pronunciation note:**
The last syllable of **aparchē** *(ah-par-HAY)* is pronounced with a rough "h" sound. It does not have the sound *ch* as in *church*. The Greek language has no such sound.

Firstfruits in the New Testament

These meanings of firstfruits have been applied throughout the New Testament.

Messiah Yeshua is the **firstfruits of the resurrection:**

> [20]But now Christ has been **raised from the dead. He became the firstfruits of those who are asleep.** [21]For since death came by man, the resurrection of the dead also came by man. [22]For as in Adam all die, so also in Christ all will be made alive. [23]But each in his own order: **Christ the firstfruits**, then those who are Christ's, at His coming (1 Cor. 15:20-23).

Believers have the **firstfruits of the Spirit,** an **earnest** of promised **redemption**:

> [18]For I consider that the sufferings of this present time are not worthy to be compared with the glory which will be revealed toward us. [19]For the creation waits with eager expectation for the children of God to be revealed... [22]For we know that the whole creation groans and travails in pain together until now. [23]Not only so, but ourselves also, who have the **firstfruits of the Spirit**, even we ourselves groan within ourselves, waiting for adoption, the **redemption** of our body (Rom. 8:18-19,22-23).

The holy root of Israel is a **firstfruit of holiness:**

> [12]Now if [Israel's] fall is the riches of the world, and their loss the riches of the Gentiles; how much more their fullness? ... [15]For if the rejection of them is the reconciling of the world, what would their acceptance be, but **life from the dead**? [16]If the **firstfruit is holy**, so is the lump. If the root is holy, so are the branches (Rom. 11:12,15-16)

Believers are **firstfruits** of the restoration of all creation:

> [18]Of His own will He brought us forth by the word of truth, that we should be a kind of **firstfruits of His creatures** (James 1:18).

The 144,000 redeemed ones are set apart as **firstfruits to God and the Lamb**:

> [4]...These were redeemed by Jesus from among men, the **firstfruits to God and to the Lamb** (Rev. 14:4b).

Paul speaks of the household of Stephanas as Achaia's **firstfruits**:

> [15]Now I beg you, brothers (you know the house of Stephanas, that it is the **firstfruits** of Achaia, and that they have set themselves to serve the saints)... (1 Cor. 16:15)

> *"But now Christ has been raised from the dead. He became the firstfruits of those who are asleep."*
>
> *1 Corinthians 15:20*

How New Testament events align with Nisan's feasts

Now that you understand what Firstfruits is all about, you are fully equipped to see how the order of the feasts of the month Nisan – Passover, Unleavened Bread and the Feast of Firstfruits – aligns with the death, burial and resurrection of Messiah.[1] (This graphic is a duplicate of the one on the pages 66-67, except this one contains references to New Testament events.)

Jesus held the Passover seder "when evening came" (Mt 26:20, Mk 14:17), at the start of Nisan 14. **He prophesied that Peter would deny him three times** "this day, even in this night" before the cock crowed (Mk 14:30). After the conclusion of the seder and through the night hours, these events occurred: **Jesus wept in Gethsemane. Judas betrayed Jesus. Jesus was taken to the high priest's house. Peter denied Jesus.**

Jesus was taken before the council of elders "as soon as it was day" (Lk 22:66), at which time Jesus avowed His Messiahship and Godhead. He was condemned for blasphemy and then mocked.

Jesus was taken before Pilate for sentencing "early in the morning" (Mt 27:1, Mk 15:1, Jn 18:28). While still very early in the morning, Pilate sent Him to Herod and Herod returned Him to Pilate.

Judeans demanded Barabbas' release. Pilate had Jesus scourged at "about the sixth hour" (Jn 19:14). John was using *Roman* timekeeping,[2] so this equated to roughly 6 or 7 a.m. It was the "preparation of the Passover" (Jn 19:14).

Jesus was affixed to the cross. "It was the third hour, and they crucified him" (Mk 15:25. In *Jewish* timekeeping,[2] this equated to about 9 a.m.)

Darkness covered the land "from the sixth hour until the ninth hour" (Mt 27:45, Mk 15:33, Lk 23:44, i.e., from about noon until 3 p.m.)

Jesus gave up His spirit "at the ninth hour" (Mt 27:46, Mk 15:34; about 3 p.m., "between the evenings" when the Passover lamb must be slain, Ex. 12:6)

"When evening had come" (Mt 27:57, Mk 15:42) **Joseph of Arimathaea wrapped Jesus' body in linen and quickly laid it in the tomb** "for it was the day of preparation, and the sabbath was drawing near" (Lk 23:54). The women with him noted how the body was laid, then went home to prepare spices and ointments.

Jesus in the grave. On the sabbath, the women "rested, according to the commandment" (Lk 23:56).

Evening – Nisan 14 begins

Evening – Nisan 15 begins

⟵——— **Passover** ———⟶ ⟵ **Special Sabbath; 1st Day of Unleavened Bread**

Also termed "preparation day" or "the preparation of the passover" in anticipation of the special sabbath (high day or high sabbath) on the following day

This special (high) sabbath may fall on any day of the week; it is not restricted to just Saturdays

[1] We hasten to add that this graphic represents just *one* of several possible alignments of events that fit the scriptural accounts. For example, some believe that Jesus may have held His seder sometime during the hours of Nisan 13, and so they adjust all the events that follow by a certain number of hours accordingly. The graphic below happens to represent our own favorite theory, and we're not clinging to it as though it's gospel truth. There are several good alternative theories to this one. We certainly respect the excellent scholarship and logical rationale which support other reasonable theories, too.

[2] For more information about Roman vs. Jewish timekeeping in the gospels, see the article in the appendix entitled, "Did Jesus die at the third or the sixth hour?"

[3] Jesus spent time in the grave during the biblical dates of Nisan 14, 15 and 16, then was raised on the 16th, the *third day*. For more information on how any portion of a biblical day may be reckoned as "a day," see the article in the appendix entitled, "Did Jesus spend 72 full hours in the grave?"

The women and some others came to the tomb at early dawn, bringing the prepared spices "when the sabbath was past, very early in the morning the first day of the week at the rising of the sun" (Mk 16:1), "when it was still dark" (Lk 24:1). (Nisan 16, the Feast of Firstfruits, fell on the first day of the week that particular year.) **Mary of Magdala ran to Simon Peter to say the body had been taken. The other women remaining at the tomb saw two men in dazzling clothing who announced Messiah's resurrection.**[3] **Upon Mary's later return to the tomb, Jesus appeared to her** (Jn 20:10-18).

Jesus appeared to certain of the women on their return to the city (Mt 28:8-10, Mk 16:8, Lk 24:9-11).

Peter and John ran to the tomb and found it empty (Lk 24:12, Jn. 20:3-10). At some point shortly after, **Jesus was seen by Peter** (cf Lk 24:34, 1 Cor 15:5).

Jesus walked and talked with two disciples on the road to Emmaus "that very day" (Lk 24:13).

Not recognizing Him, the two urged Him to stay, "for it is almost evening, and the day is almost over" (Lk 24:29). **As they ate supper together, He vanished.** "They rose up that very hour and returned to Jerusalem" (Lk 24:33).

As eleven of the disciples were hiding in a locked room "the same day at evening, being the first day of the week" (Jn 20:19), **Jesus suddenly appeared in their midst.**

Evening – Nisan 16 begins

Evening – Nisan 17 begins

⇐ **Feast of Firstfruits; Also Day 1 of the 50-day countdown** ⇒ ⇐ **Day 2 of the 50-day countdown** ⇒

Day 2 of the 7-day Feast of Unleavened Bread   *Day 3 of the 7-day Feast of Unleavened Bread*

> *"Counting the omer" is nothing more than the obedient practice of counting off fifty days, beginning on the Feast of Firstfruits and concluding on the Feast of Weeks, also known as Pentecost.*

"Counting the omer" – *S'firat Ha-Omer*

God uses a particular Hebrew phrase in Scripture when He refers to a **sheaf** of firstfruits. In the Hebrew, this phrase is written as follows:

עֹמֶר רֵאשִׁית   **omer reshith** *(OH-mehr ray-SHEET)* – sheaf of the firstfruits

The term **omer** עֹמֶר *(OH-mehr)*, "sheaf," is still used in conversation today by observant Jews (and by those Gentiles who choose to observe God's feasts), so it is a good term for you to learn. Notice the references to this Hebrew word in the text of Leviticus 23 concerning the Feast of Firstfruits and its fifty-day countdown to the Feast of Weeks (Pentecost):

> ⁹The Lord spoke to Moses, saying, ¹⁰"Speak to the children of Israel, and tell them, 'When you have come into the land which I give to you, and shall reap its harvest, then you shall bring the **sheaf** *[omer]* of the firstfruits of your harvest to the priest: ¹¹and he shall wave the **sheaf** *[omer]* before the Lord, to be accepted for you. On the next day after the sabbath *[the special sabbath of the first day of Unleavened Bread]* the priest shall wave it...'" ¹⁵**"You shall count** from the next day after the sabbath, **from the day that you brought the sheaf** *[omer]* **of the wave offering; seven sabbaths shall be completed:** ¹⁶**even to the next day after the seventh sabbath you shall number fifty days**; then you shall offer a new meal offering to the Lord" (Lev. 23: 9-11, 15-16).

The repeated mention of the "sheaf" in the above passage has given rise to the phrase *s'firat ha-omer*, **"counting the omer,"** a shorthand expression for the counting of the fifty days from Firstfruits to the Feast of Weeks (Pentecost). Our next chapter will be devoted entirely to the Feast of Weeks, so we won't discuss its meaning in great depth here, except to say that on that date occurred both the giving of Torah at Mount Sinai (Exodus 19 and 20) and the giving of the indwelling Holy Spirit (Acts 2). God established His fifty-day countdown to forever memorialize these two earth-shaking, mind-blowing events.

Leviticus 23 is interspersed repeatedly with the statement, "This is a statute forever throughout all your generations and all your dwellings." In fact, this statement occurs within the context of the passage above. "Counting the omer" was observed dutifully by Jewish people for generations. In ancient times, they counted off the fifty days with a hopeful expectation of the restorative power of God's righteous Torah (instruction) in their lives. Believing Jews clung by faith to God's promise that He was able to save them by grace, "writing His Torah on their hearts" (Jer. 31:33). In New Testament times, the Jewish followers of Jesus continued to obediently "count the omer," holding to the same hope and expectation of their ancestors. However, along with this hope, they had been given an *additional* expectation: the "promise of the Father."

The "promise of the father"

In the last, evening hours of that wonderful Feast of Firstfruits on which Yeshua was resurrected, Yeshua appeared to the disciples as they were gathered together behind locked doors for fear of the Judeans. "*Shalom aleichem,*" He said to them, meaning "Peace be to you." He calmed their fear and invited them to touch Him, for they thought at first that they were seeing a ghost. He ate a piece of fish and some honeycomb, further proving His bodily resurrection. He spoke to them about how the events of the preceding days were all fulfillments of Scripture. He opened their minds so they could understand how the Law, the Prophets and the Writings (*Torah, N'viim* and *Ch'tuvim* – the *TaNaCH*, or Old Testament) all spoke about Him. Then He said:

> "And, look! I am sending **the promise of My Father** upon you, but wait in the city of Jerusalem until you are **endued with power from on high**" (Luke 24:49).

The disciples waited obediently in Jerusalem for the promise of the Father. Today, we know *exactly* how long that wait was, for they observed the commandment to count the omer for *fifty days* while they waited. On the very day of the Feast of Weeks – exactly fifty days after Firstfruits – the promise of the Father was fulfilled with the descent of His indwelling Holy Spirit.

Observance of Firstfruits

How do Messianic believers* today – both Jewish and Gentile – actually *observe* the Feast of Firstfruits?

There is little in Scripture teaching us how to observe Firstfruits, but the Talmud records some of its ancient traditions, which included carrying the first produce of the land (including sheaves of barley) in large baskets up to Jerusalem, accompanied by much dancing and singing of psalms. Today, Messianic believers gather with their families on Nisan 16, the day of Firstfruits, to read aloud the Gospel accounts of Yeshua's resurrection. Some families set out a basket of barley stalks on the dining table during Firstfruits, as an object lesson for the kids. Other families let their children make a cave out of playdough or paper mache to fashion a tomb, along with the disk-shaped stone to roll across the entrance. They also make angels from clay, felt, wood or paper. On resurrection day, the day of Firstfruits, the children position the angels at the tomb and roll away the stone, demonstrating that the tomb is now empty. You can find many "instructables" for easy children's crafts of angels and caves on the internet. We include one on the following pages.

> "And, look! I am sending the promise of My Father upon you, but wait in the city of Jerusalem until you are endued with power from on high."
>
> *The words of Jesus, Luke 24:49*

*Messianic Jews are born-again Jews who believe Jesus is Messiah, Savior and Lord. After being born again, they continue to observe a biblically Jewish lifestyle (observing *b'rit milah, bar mitzvah* and *yizchor*, for example). The Messianic Jewish lifestyle naturally includes observing all the holy days God established in the Bible. Many born-again Gentiles answer God's call to join Messianic congregations; hence the more inclusive term **"Messianic believers."** This term encompasses both Messianic Jews *and* those Gentiles who opt to worship in unity with their Jewish brothers and sisters in a Messianic congregational setting. In addition to celebrating God's feasts, Messianic congregations may offer other unique benefits like Hebrew classes, reading from a real Torah scroll or performing traditional Jewish songs, worship dances and liturgy.

When a child learns to count the fifty days while waiting for Pentecost to arrive, he learns a powerful object lesson about taking time to prepare the heart while prayerfully asking, seeking and knocking.

Observance of the omer count

If you would enjoy participating in the fifty-day "counting of the omer," there are many wonderful ways to do it. The traditional way is to pronounce a blessing at the biblical start of every day (just after sunset) followed by a simple statement of which day of the fifty days has arrived. Orthodox Jews recite this in Hebrew, but you can just say it in English – for example, "Today is the fifteenth day of the omer count." Most people also like to write the number of each day on a regular calendar. If you want to go the "traditional" route, we've included the traditional blessing in the following special section on observance.

Many Messianic families like to augment this tradition by reading a different verse of Scripture each day of the omer count, together as a family. It's a great opportunity to discuss the application of God's Word in real life situations together. This kind of "family worship time" brings the counting of the omer in line with God's original intent for the fifty-day period: a devotional time to prepare the heart, to expectantly look for and receive a better understanding of His Word, and to walk in a way more yielded to His Spirit.

We, the authors of this book, were inspired (like many others) to create an omer "advent calendar" to aid in celebrating the omer count. The concept will be familiar to those of our readers who have used advent calendars to count the twenty-five days leading up to Christmas. An omer calendar is exactly the same idea, except it has fifty days on it rather than twenty-five. The internet is filled with ideas for making inexpensive, DIY advent calendars, which may be repurposed into your own personalized omer calendar. Many DIY calendars incorporate envelopes tacked to a bulletin board, or paper bags clothes-pinned to a clothesline, or rows of empty matchboxes hot-glued to each other, in which parents can hide candies, stickers or small party favors. If you design your calendar with such containers, we would encourage that you also include in each day's container a small slip of paper (folded or rolled up like a tiny scroll) on which you've written a Bible verse for the child to read aloud to the family. You might choose verses which fit the dual themes of the upcoming holy day of the Feast of Weeks – the goodness of God's Torah (instruction/law) and the fruits of His Spirit. The goal is to whet the appetite of the children, to fill them with expectation of the mighty power associated with the day of Pentecost. Patiently opening a calendar every day for fifty days while looking forward to Pentecost is a powerful object lesson about persistence in prayerful asking, seeking and knocking (Mt. 7:7).

In the following special section on the observance of Firstfruits, you'll find a series of tear-out pages for a ready-made omer calendar you can use immediately with your family. It can be used "as is," but we encourage you to use your imagination to modify it to fit your family's unique personality.

This hand-painted omer calendar (ink and gouache on parchment) was made in the Netherlands in the 18th century. It was a gift of Dr. Harry G. Friedman to the Jewish Museum. The number of each day is surrounded by hand-painted colorful birds and flowers. Under each day is the proclamation which the head of the house would read aloud in Hebrew, for example, "Today is twenty-two days of the omer."

This piece of paper-cut art had two functions: It served as both an omer calendar and as a memorial of the honored deceased members of the congregation, whose names are inscribed along the sides and bottom. Positioned around the large circle are the proclamations for the days of the omer count. The traditional blessing for counting the omer is inscribed along the top of the circle. The artist, Baruch Zvi Ring, created the art using ink, paint, pencil, watercolor, and layers of intricately hand-cut paper (1904, Rochester, New York). The calendar was a gift of Temple Beth Hamedresh-Beth Israel of Rochester to the Jewish Museum.

Simple children's craft ideas for Resurrection Morning – Nisan 16, The Day of Firstfruits – are included in this section. We also include the traditional blessing for the Counting of the Omer, the fifty-day countdown beginning on Firstfruits and ending on the Feast of Weeks (Pentecost). We hope you enjoy using the ready-to-use omer calendar in the tear-out pages. Feel free to repurpose it to use with your own unique omer calendar ideas.

Firstfruits

Children's Crafts for the Day of Firstfruits
S'firat Omer – **the Counting of the Omer**
Omer Calendar Tear-Out Pages

Paper Plate Empty Tomb
Craft for Children

For the empty tomb, you will need:

- Two or three large, sturdy paper plates having a "lip" (deep plates like Chinet work very well)
- Brown paper bags or brown kraft paper, crumpled and wrinkled then spread flat again
- Scissors
- Scotch tape or a stapler (or a hot glue gun if you have one)
- Elmer's white all-purpose glue (inexpensive "school" glue is fine)
- Optional: Acrylic paints in "stone-like" colors: beiges, tans, grays, and browns

For the angels, you will need:

- White paper (can be construction paper or just regular copier paper)
- Scissors
- Optional: Diamond dust glitter and white school glue or spray adhesive for applying the glitter

Tomb Instructions

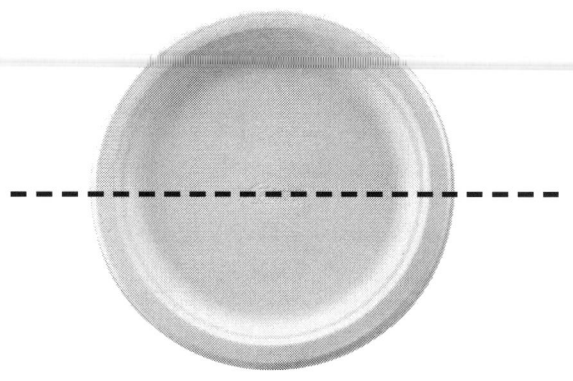

1. Cut one of the paper plates in half (on dotted line as shown).

2. Set one half aside. In the other half, cut out the tomb's opening in a rough arch, as shown. (It can be a bit jagged or crooked; it doesn't have to be perfect.)

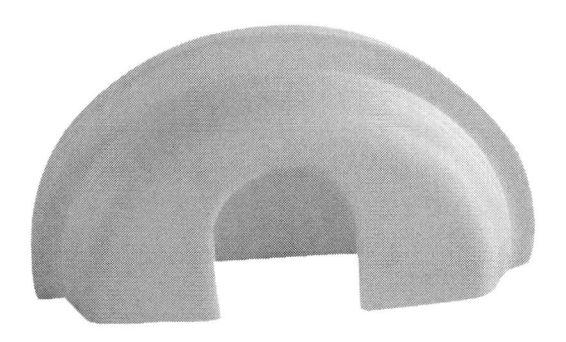

3. Put the two halves of the plate together like this to make a cave. Secure the lips of the plate halves together using tape, staples or hot glue.

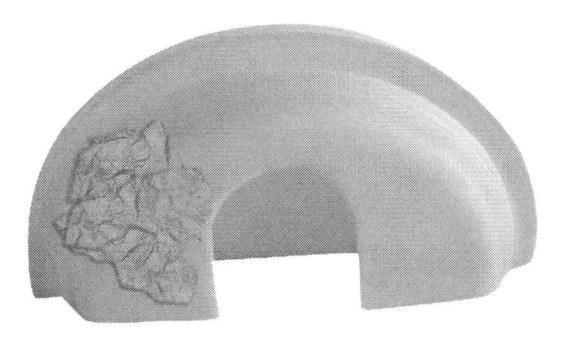

4. Glue torn pieces of the crumpled brown paper to the tomb with the Elmer's glue. Cover the front of the tomb completely. You can paint the paper, too.

Tomb Instructions, continued

5. From another paper plate (or two plates, if needed), cut two rough circles of about the same size. Be sure to make them large enough to be able to fully cover the tomb's opening. Tape or glue them together, one on top of the other. This will make a thick, strong, two-ply disc that will be the "stone" that rolls in front of the tomb's entrance.

6. Glue pieces of torn, crumpled brown paper to the disc. If you want, you can also dab gray, beige and brown paint all over it to make it look even more like stone.

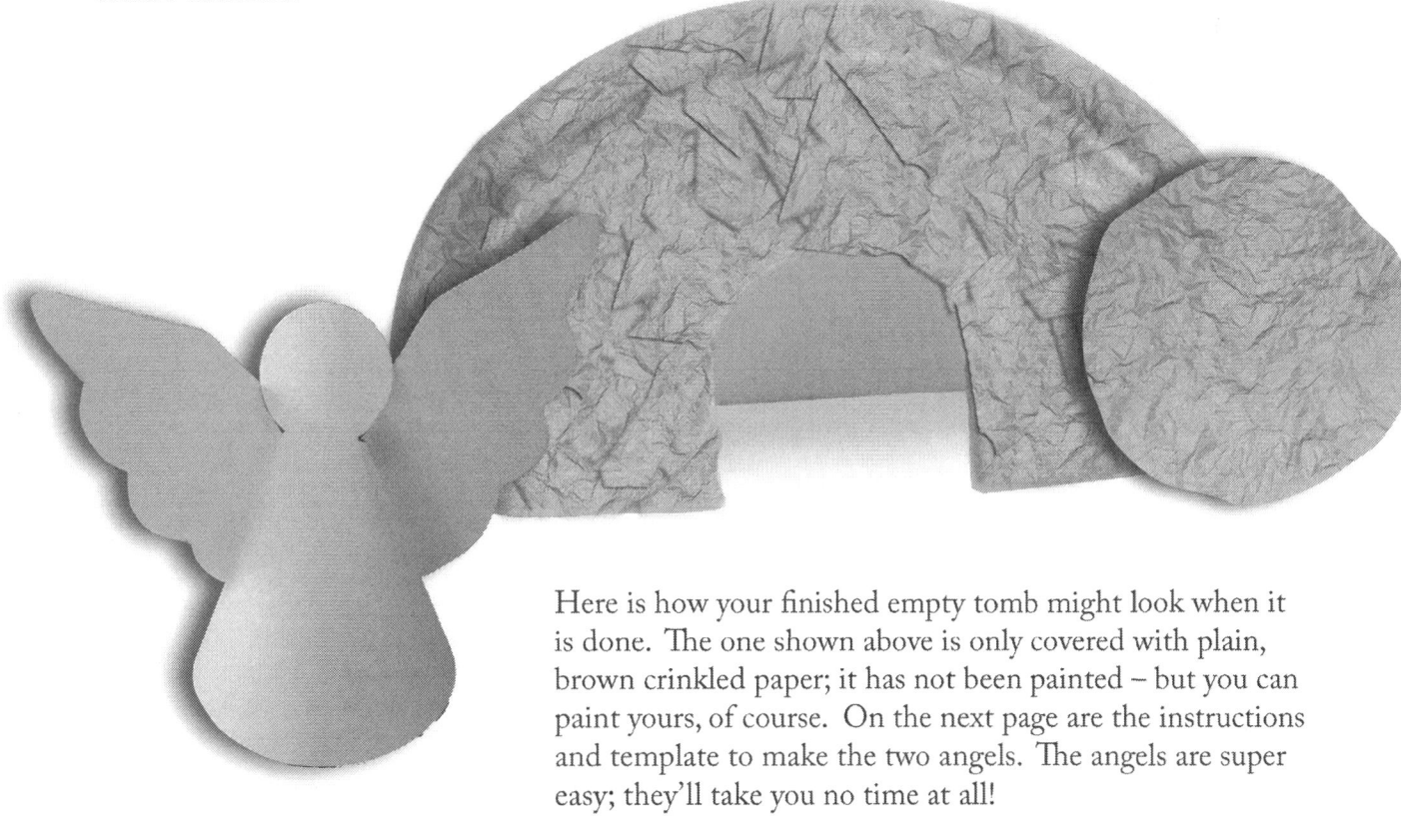

Here is how your finished empty tomb might look when it is done. The one shown above is only covered with plain, brown crinkled paper; it has not been painted – but you can paint yours, of course. On the next page are the instructions and template to make the two angels. The angels are super easy; they'll take you no time at all!

While you work on this craft project with the kids, you can talk with them about the resurrection story or read short excerpts from the Gospels about it.

Angel Instructions

1. Cut out this template (or you can just trace over it if you like). Trace around the template to duplicate its shape onto a sheet of white paper. Then cut out the shape that you traced on your white paper. Be sure to also cut along the straight line "slots" that are shown.

Optionally, you might also apply glitter to your paper angel before assembly. You could also attempt this craft using any flat material that holds its shape and can stand upright. It just needs to be flexible enough to curl.

2. Gently curl the paper angel backward until you are able to interlock the two slots together, as in the photo at left which shows the back of the angel. If needed to hold the angel more securely together, apply a couple pieces of Scotch tape just under the point where the wings interlock toward the bottom.

Back of angel

Finished angel shown at right.

Front of angel

Counting the Omer
S'firat Ha-Omer סְפִירַת הָעוֹמֶר

Family — *The head of the household leads the entire family in the traditional blessing...*

Blessed are You, LORD our God, King of the Universe, Who has instilled within us the holiness of His commandments and Who has commanded us regarding the counting of the Omer.

בָּרוּךְ אַתָּה, יהוה, אֱלֹהֵינוּ מֶלֶךְ הָעוֹלָם,
אֲשֶׁר קִדְּשָׁנוּ בְּמִצְוֹתָיו וְצִוָּנוּ עַל סְפִירַת הָעוֹמֶר.

Bah-ruch ah-tah Adonai, Eh-lo-hay-nu Meh-lech hah-o-lahm ah-shayr kid-shah-nu b'-mitz-vo-tahv v'-tsih-vah-nu ahl s'fee-raht hah-o-mehr.

Head of household

Thank You, Father for inscribing Your Law, and all Your commandments therein, on our hearts (Jer. 31:33, Heb. 8:10). Thank You, Holy Spirit, for choosing to dwell within us, applying the Word so that we may be sanctified daily (2 Tim. 1:14, 1 Cor. 6:19). Thank You, Yeshua, for Your death on the execution stake at Passover, Your burial during the Feast of Unleavened Bread, and Your resurrection on the Feast of Firstfruits, in order that we may stand pure and blameless before God (2 Cor. 5:21). We all look forward now to Your beautiful Feast of Weeks! We are thankful that You apply Your Word mightily in our hearts by the power of the Holy Spirit.

In obedience to Your commandment of Leviticus 23:15-16, we now joyfully count the omer.

Today is the _____ day of the omer count *(insert the day of the count, for example, "twentieth")*.

(If an omer calendar is available, have one of the children open that day's door, bag, box, or envelope. If he or she is able to read, the child should read the enclosed Bible verse to the rest of the family. If not, an adult may read. Discuss the meaning of the verse and pray over it as a family.)

Omer Calendar

The calendar on the following pages consists of fifty double-sided cards which will form the picture shown below once they are assembled in the correct order in a 5x10 grid. Arrange as shown in the simple diagram below. A nice activity for the children might be to have them color the picture pages with crayons or colored pencils <u>before</u> you cut the cards apart, immediately after you tear out the pages from the book.

There are two ways to use the calendar. One way is to pin all the cards (in the order of the grid shown) to a wall, with the picture side hidden against the wall so that the number side is facing outward. Each day of the omer count, the child selects the correct card, takes it down, reads the verse and then replaces the card in its original position, but flipping the card over so that the picture side is now showing. As the days pass, more and more of the "big picture" is revealed. We have found it helpful to have an adult align the "flipped" cards, butting one against the next, and then Scotch tape each one to the next as the picture is formed. This will keep the picture looking neat.

Another way to use this calendar is to store each card in its own numbered envelope, and keep all the envelopes in a wicker basket (perhaps along with a small sheaf of some stalks of barley – a symbol of the baskets of sheaves that were separated out to the Lord during Firstfruits). Each day, the child opens the appropriately numbered envelope and pulls out the card. He or she reads the verse and then flips the card over, attaching it to a wall as above. An alternative to displaying the cards on a wall is to lay them out on a large table designated for the purpose. After flipping each card, align it by its borders to its neighboring card and Scotch tape it (to prevent the picture from getting all mixed up by a sudden breeze!). After the Feast of Weeks has come and gone, cut the tape with scissors to free the cards; they may be reused the next year.

Lay out the numbered cards like this.

1	2	3	4	5	6	7	8	9	10
11	12	13	14	15	16	17	18	19	20
21	22	23	24	25	26	27	28	29	30
31	32	33	34	35	36	37	38	39	40
41	42	43	44	45	46	47	48	49	50

When you flip a card over, set it back in its original position. The picture will look this like after you flip all the cards over:

OBSERVANCE OF THE FEAST OF FIRSTFRUITS | 83

1 — But now Christ has been raised from the dead. He became the firstfruits of those who are asleep.
1 Corinthians 15:20

2 — I have hidden Your word in my heart, that I might not sin against You.
Psalm 119:11

11 — Now the Lord is the Spirit and where the Spirit of the Lord is, there is liberty.
2 Corinthians 3:17

12 — I will walk in liberty, for I have sought Your precepts.
Psalm 119:45

21 — There is one body, and one Spirit, even as you also were called in one hope of your calling.
Ephesians 4:4

22 — Let my tongue sing of Your word, for all Your commandments are righteousness.
Psalm 119:172

31 — ...for the Kingdom of God is not eating and drinking, but righteousness, peace, and joy in the Holy Spirit.
Romans 14:17

32 — But we know that the law is good, if a man uses it lawfully.
1 Timothy 1:8

41 — ...in [Messiah] you also are built together for a dwelling of God in the Spirit.
Ephesians 2:22

42 — But it is easier for heaven and earth to pass away, than for one tiny stroke of a pen in the law to fall.
The words of Jesus, Luke 16:17

OBSERVANCE OF THE FEAST OF FIRSTFRUITS

Unleavened Bread
Nisan 15-21

Firstfruits
Nisan 16

1 2 3 4 5 6 7 8 9 10 11 12 13 14 15 16 17 18 19 20 21 22

OBSERVANCE OF THE FEAST OF FIRSTFRUITS | 85

4 Open my eyes, that I may see wondrous things out of Your law.

Psalm 119:18

3 But we received, not the spirit of the world, but the Spirit which is from God, that we might know the things that were freely given to us by God.

1 Corinthians 2:12

14 I will delight myself in Your commandments, because I love them.

Psalm 119:47

13 For God didn't give us a spirit of fear, but of power, love, and self-control.

2 Timothy 1:7

24 The Lord's law is perfect, restoring the soul.

Psalm 19:7a

23 It is through Messiah that Jews and Gentiles alike have access through one Spirit to the Father.

Ephesians 2:18

34 For I delight in God's law in my innermost self.

Romans 7:22

33 Now may the God of hope fill you with all joy and peace in believing, that you may abound in hope, in the power of the Holy Spirit.

Romans 15:13

44 "Heaven and earth will pass away, but My words will by no means pass away."

The words of Jesus, Luke 21:33

43 God also testifying with them, both by signs and wonders, by various works of power, and by gifts of the Holy Spirit...

Hebrews 2:4

86 | OBSERVANCE OF THE FEAST OF FIRSTFRUITS

OBSERVANCE OF THE FEAST OF FIRSTFRUITS | 87

6
I run in the path of Your commandments, for You have set my heart free.

Psalm 119:32

5
For you didn't receive the spirit of bondage again to fear, but you received the Spirit of adoption, by whom we cry, "Abba! Father!"

Romans 8:15

16
Your word is a lamp to my feet, and a light for my path.

Psalm 119:105

15
But you, beloved, keep building up yourselves on your most holy faith, praying in the Holy Spirit.

Jude 1:20

26
Do we then nullify the law through faith? May it never be! No, we establish the law.

Romans 3:31

25
For in one Spirit we were all baptized into one body, whether Jews or Greeks, whether bond or free; and were all given to drink into one Spirit.

1 Corinthians 12:13

36
For this is the covenant that I will make with the house of Israel. After those days... I will put my laws into their mind, I will also write them on their heart.

Hebrews 8:10a

35
My speech and my preaching were not in persuasive words of human wisdom, but in demonstration of the Spirit and of power.

1 Corinthians 2:4

46
In the beginning was the Word, and the Word was with God, and the Word was God.

John 1:1

45
...who preached the Good News to you by the Holy Spirit sent out from heaven; things which angels desire to look into.

1 Peter 1:12b

88 | OBSERVANCE OF THE FEAST OF FIRSTFRUITS

OBSERVANCE OF THE FEAST OF FIRSTFRUITS | 89

8 Direct me in the path of Your commandments, for I delight in them.
Psalm 119:35

7 The Spirit himself bears witness with our spirit that we are children of God.
Romans 8:16

18 The law of Your mouth is better to me than thousands of pieces of gold and silver.
Psalm 119:72

17 I will pour on the house of David, and on the inhabitants of Jerusalem, the spirit of grace and of supplication.
Zechariah 12:10a

28 But he who looks into the perfect law of freedom, and continues, not being a hearer who forgets, but a doer of the work, this man will be blessed in what he does.
James 1:25

27 It will happen afterward, that I will pour out my Spirit on all flesh; and your sons and your daughters will prophesy. Your old men will dream dreams. Your young men will see visions.
Joel 2:28

38 "Don't think that I came to destroy the law or the prophets. I didn't come to destroy, but to fulfill."
The words of Jesus, Matthew 5:17

37 ...our Good News came to you not in word only, but also in power, and in the Holy Spirit, and with much conviction.
1 Thessalonians 1:5a

48 *(Continued from previous card)*
"For John indeed baptized in water, but you will be baptized in the Holy Spirit not many days from now."
The words of Jesus, Acts 1:5

47 Being assembled together with [the disciples], Yeshua commanded them, "Don't depart from Jerusalem, but wait for the promise of the Father, which you heard from me."
Acts 1:4

90 | OBSERVANCE OF THE FEAST OF FIRSTFRUITS

OBSERVANCE OF THE FEAST OF FIRSTFRUITS | 91

10 — Turn my heart toward Your statutes, not toward selfish gain.
Psalm 119:36

9 — ...we who have the firstfruits of the Spirit groan within ourselves, waiting for the adoption... the redemption of our body.
Romans 8:23

20 — Those who love Your law have great peace. Nothing causes them to stumble.
Psalm 119:165

19 — There are different kinds of spiritual gifts, but the same Spirit is the source of them all.
1 Corinthians 12:4

30 — Therefore the law indeed is holy, and the commandment holy, and righteous, and good.
Romans 7:12

29 — But the fruit of the Spirit is love, joy, peace, patience, kindness, goodness, faith, gentleness, and self-control...
Galatians 5:22-23a

40 — "For most certainly, I tell you, until heaven and earth pass away, not even one smallest letter or one tiny pen stroke shall in any way pass away from the law, until all things are accomplished."
The words of Jesus, Mt. 5:18

39 — Don't you know that you are a temple of God, and that God's Spirit lives in you?
1 Corinthians 3:16

50 — Now when the day of Pentecost had fully arrived, they were all with one accord in one place... They were all filled with the Holy Spirit...
Acts 2:1,4

49 — *(Continued from previous card)* "But you will receive power when the Holy Spirit has come upon you. You will be witnesses to Me in Jerusalem, in all Judea and Samaria, and to the uttermost parts of the earth."
Acts 1:8

92 | OBSERVANCE OF THE FEAST OF FIRSTFRUITS

Happy Firstfruits!

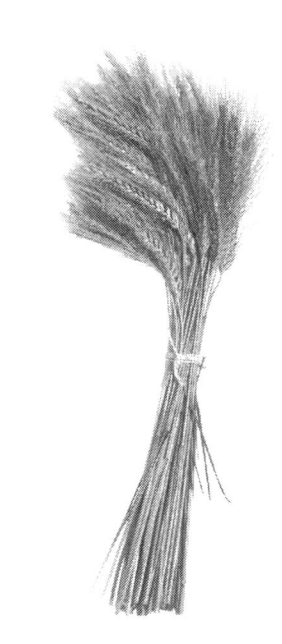

שבועות

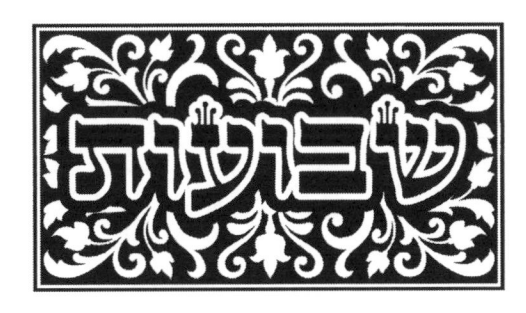

Weeks

The Descent of the Indwelling Holy Spirit

...there were thunders and lightnings, and a thick cloud on the mountain, and the sound of an exceedingly loud trumpet...
All Mount Sinai smoked, because the Lord descended on it in fire; and its smoke ascended like the smoke of a furnace, and the whole mountain quaked greatly...
Exodus 19:16,18

Now when the day of Pentecost had fully come, they were all with one accord in one place. Suddenly there came from the sky a sound like the rushing of a mighty wind, and it filled all the house where they were sitting. Tongues like fire appeared and were distributed to them, and one sat on each of them.

Weeks (Pentecost)

By the time the biblical month Sivan arrives, observant Jews and Messianic believers throughout the world will have completed nearly all fifty days of the omer count. Beginning on the Feast of Firstfruits (Nisan 16), they start the daily count. They continue to count through the end of the month Nisan, then all the way through the second month (Iyar), and then on into the first days of the third month (Sivan). Finally, finally, finally... on the date of Sivan 6, the "fullness" of the fifty day count arrives – the **Feast of Weeks**, also known by the name **Pentecost**.

In Hebrew Scripture, the term **Feast of Weeks** is written **Chag Shavuot*** חַג שָׁבֻעֹת *(ḥag shah-voo-ŌHT).* In casual conversation today, people often drop the word *chag*, "feast of," and simply refer to this special day as *Shavuot*, "Weeks."

Why the term "Weeks"?

The biblical Hebrew word for *week* means "seven of something," somewhat like the English word *dozen* means "twelve of something." The Bible speaks of a "week of days" (seven days), but also a "week of years" (seven years). God employed powerful symbolism when He decided to call this feast by the term "Weeks." The day of Shavuot comes at the conclusion of "seven sevens" of days – literally, a "week" of weeks. So, **Shavuot represents completion and perfection to the highest degree.** It is the very symbol of the perfection and wholeness of both God's Law and God's Spirit. How fitting that two related, pivotal events – the **giving of Torah** to Moses and the people of Israel at Mount Sinai (Exodus 19) and the **giving of the indwelling Holy Spirit** to the believers at Mount Zion (Acts 2) – both occurred on this very date!

Why the term "Pentecost"?

The term *Pentecost* came about as Jewish people began to speak Greek once it became a worldwide common language. A Greek translation of the Hebrew Bible was eventually written. Recall that God commanded in Scripture that His people count to the "fiftieth" day to arrive at the date of the Feast of Weeks. The word "fiftieth" in Greek is **pentēkostos** πεντηκοστός *(pen-tay-koss-toss).* Its feminine noun form is **pentēkostē** πεντηκοστή *(pen-tay-koss-tay).* Jewish people who spoke Greek used the word *pentēkostē* to refer to the "fiftieth" day, or the day of Shavuot. It is from this Greek word, *pentēkostē,* "fiftieth," that we get our English term "Pentecost."

"It will be in the last days," says God, "that I will pour out my Spirit on all flesh... I will show wonders in the sky above, and signs on the earth beneath; blood, and fire, and billows of smoke..."

Peter's quote of the prophet Joel during his famous speech at Pentecost, on the date of Sivan 6 (Acts 2:17,19)

***Pronunciation note:** The first sound in the word *chag*, meaning "feast of," is pronounced with a rough "h" sound, like the "ch" in "Bach" or "Loch Ness." The word *shavuot*, meaning "weeks," has a long ō sound in the last syllable, and that syllable is emphasized, so the whole word rhymes roughly with "power boat:" *shah-voo-ŌHT.*

> *"You shall keep the feast of weeks to the LORD your God... and you shall rejoice before the LORD your God..."*
>
> *Deuteronomy 16:10a, 11a*

The commandments to observe Shavuot

It will be helpful to read some of the places in the Bible where God initiated this most wonderful feast day. To help you discern its place among the other feasts described in the passages, we have inserted helpful *italicized* descriptions. We have also **bolded** some of the more important features of these commandments. We'll explain their meanings on the following pages.

> ⁹The LORD spoke to Moses, saying, ¹⁰"Speak to the children of Israel, and tell them, 'When you have come into the land which I give to you, and shall reap its harvest, then you shall bring the sheaf *[omer]* of the firstfruits of your harvest to the priest: ¹¹and he shall wave the sheaf before the LORD, to be accepted for you. On the next day after the sabbath *[the special sabbath of the first day of Unleavened Bread]* the priest shall wave it...'" ¹⁵**"You shall count** from the next day after the sabbath, from the day that you brought the sheaf of the wave offering *[the Feast of Firstfruits]*; **seven sabbaths shall be completed:** ¹⁶**even to the next day after the seventh sabbath you shall number fifty days**; then you shall offer a new meal offering to the LORD... ²¹You shall make proclamation on the same day: it shall be **a holy convocation** to you *[another special sabbath – the Feast of Weeks]*; **you shall do no regular work. This is a statute forever in all your dwellings throughout your generations**" (Lev. 23: 9-11, 15-16, 21).

> ⁹You shall **count for yourselves seven weeks**: from the time you begin to put the sickle to the standing grain *[Firstfruits]* **you shall begin to number seven weeks**. ¹⁰You shall keep the **feast of weeks** to the LORD your God with a tribute of a freewill offering of your hand, which you shall give, according as the LORD your God blesses you: ¹¹and **you shall rejoice** before the LORD your God, **you, and your son, and your daughter, and your male servant, and your female servant, and the Levite who is within your gates, and the foreigner, and the fatherless, and the widow, who are in the midst of you, in the place which the LORD your God shall choose, to cause His name to dwell there** (Deut. 16:9-11).

These passages are rich with information. We'll discuss some of the details on the following pages.

Shavuot is a special sabbath day

In the passages on the preceding page, God commands the day of Shavuot (Weeks/Pentecost) to be a *holy convocation* and *a special sabbath* on which no regular work is to be done. This commandment is a "statute forever... throughout all your generations" (Lev. 23:21). Why *holy*? Why *forever*? Because Shavuot is the very date on which our holy God "descended" in two earth-shaking events. His purpose was simple: to dwell among us in love and holiness. Centuries before Yeshua's incarnation, on the first Shavuot, He gave His holy Word (His "instruction," the root meaning of the Hebrew word *Torah*). Centuries later, again on Shavuot, He gave His indwelling Holy Spirit. The Word and the Spirit are One – as He Himself is One Lord and One God, the never-changing, Great "I AM."

Recall that a special sabbath doesn't always fall on the regular weekly "seventh day" sabbath. A special sabbath may occur on *any* day of the week. The biblical date of Shavuot – Sivan 6 – is derived by counting fifty days from Nisan 16 (the biblical date of Firstfruits). Just like your birthday, Sivan 6 can occur on *any* day of the week.

A feast of *rejoicing*... for *all*

Notice God's emphasis on *rejoicing* in the passage from Deuteronomy on the previous page. In verse 10, God not only says, "You shall keep the feast of weeks," but He specifically states, "You shall keep the feast of weeks *to the Lord your God.*" The whole purpose of the feast is a *celebration* of *love*, in a *personal relationship*. To use a modern example, if close friends and family members are invited to attend a wedding, the true spiritual purpose in their attending is to *show their love* for the couple and to *rejoice over the union*. In His great love, God extends His inclusive invitation to *everyone*, not just the Israelites or the well-to-do land-owners. God commands that servants, Levites, foreigners, orphans and widows – rich or poor, Jew or Gentile, bond or free – *all* be invited to His feast (vs. 11).

One of three "pilgrimage feasts"

There were three specific feasts that God commanded to be held in Jerusalem, i.e., "the place the Lord your God shall choose to cause His name to dwell there." These three "pilgrimage" feasts were **Passover/Unleavened Bread, Weeks** and **Tabernacles**. Because people traveled on foot to Jerusalem to celebrate these days, they came to be called in Hebrew the **shalosh regalim** שָׁלוֹשׁ רְגָלִים *(shah-lōhsh r'-gah-leem)*, literally, "the three feet" or "the three steps." The New Testament speaks of "God-fearing Jews from every nation" and "many going up from the countryside to Jerusalem" during these three feasts. Those who could afford to do so would arrive in time for Passover and just stay right there in Jerusalem, all fifty-plus days, until the day of Shavuot had fully come.

"...you, and your son, and your daughter, and your male servant, and your female servant, and the Levite who is within your gates, and the foreigner, and the fatherless, and the widow, who are in the midst of you..."

God's invitation to celebrate the Feast of Weeks, Deuteronomy 16:11

Another time that firstfruits is offered

There is one slightly confusing reference to Weeks/Shavuot that you need to be aware of in case you come across it in Scripture. In Numbers 28, Shavuot is actually referred to as a sort of "day of firstfruits."

> ²⁶Also in the day of the first fruits, when you offer a new meal offering to the Lord in your **feast of weeks**, you shall have a holy convocation; you shall do no servile work... (Num. 28:26)

The context of the surrounding verses is clear; God is truly speaking of the Feast of *Weeks*. Yet, He calls it "the day of the first fruits." Why? Isn't the Feast of Firstfruits on Nisan 16, which occurs fifty days earlier?

A brief overview of Israel's agricultural cycle will clear things up easily. In first biblical month, Nisan, at the very beginning of the *barley* harvest, the first harvested sheaves of barley were presented as firstfruits on Nisan 16 (which is indeed the "Feast of Firstfruits"). As the Omer count progressed through the month of Iyar, people continued to gather in the full harvest of the barley; this was an ongoing process. But all the while, the *wheat* was growing into maturity, too. By early Sivan, the wheat had *just* ripened, so it was finally time to start harvesting the *wheat*. On Sivan 6, people brought a firstfruit offering of the wheat, and probably that of several other crops as well. The "firstfruits" that God is speaking about in Numbers 28:26 is the first produce of the *wheat*. Therefore, this cannot refer to the Feast of Firstfruits which always occurs during Unleavened Bread in Nisan, but, rather, it must refer to a "firstfruit offering" of the *wheat* harvest which occurs in Sivan.

A different, more traditional explanation

In a large collection of Jewish traditional writings called the *Mishnah*, the rules about how to gather and present all seven types of firstfruits were recorded in a chapter called *Bikkurim* ("firstfruits"). Here's a paragraph from Bikkurim 1:3.

> One does not bring bikkurim before *Atseret* [the day of "refraining" from work, i.e., Shavuot]. People from *Har Tsevo'im* [Mount Zeboim] brought their bikkurim and they [the priests] did not accept [the fruits] because of the verse in the Torah, "And the harvest festival, the firsfruits of your labor that you plant in the field" (Ex. 23:16).

So, Jewish tradition says that everyone would *set aside* the firstfruits of the barley harvest on Nisan 16, and *wait* fifty days until Shavuot (Sivan 6) to present them in Jerusalem (along with the firstfruits of the wheat and other crops). This is one possible reason that the Feast of Weeks is called a "day of firstfruits."

Israelis have held annual Shavuot parades in Jerusalem since their return to the land, as shown in this photo from the mid 1900s. Men, women and children all participate in the parades, dancing, singing, wearing flower garlands and carrying baskets of firstfruits.

The giving of Torah, God's instruction

Scripture describes in Exodus 19 and 20 how God gave His Torah to His people through His servant, Moses. While this passage doesn't explicitly state the exact date of Shavuot (Sivan 6), it is clear from the context that Sivan 6 was within the exact time frame that Moses was on the mountain receiving God's Torah.

> [1]On **the first day of the third month** [Sivan] after the Israelites left Egypt—on that very day—they came to the Desert of Sinai. [2]... Israel camped there in the wilderness in front of the mountain (Ex. 19:1, 2b).

Shavuot as a wedding celebration

Traditional Judaism views the Feast of Weeks as a kind of wedding day between God and His people. The written commandments which God gave to Moses on the tablets was their *ketubah*, or set of written wedding vows. The groom (God) professed His gracious promises to His people throughout the commandments. In turn, Israel (the bride) vowed that they would be faithful to these commandments, out of great love and gratitude. God officially stated that Israel would be His own people, and they officially stated Him to be their God. He expressed a very personal desire to "set His tent among them" to dwell intimately with them, the "tent" being a symbol of both the husbandly coverage of the *tallit* (prayer shawl) and the *chuppah* (the wedding canopy). He repeatedly reminded Israel of this special "marriage" relationship in Scripture, usually framing His reminders to keep His commandments in the context of a "renewal of vows." The only way to please God, even back then, was through *faith*. The commandments could only be obeyed in the right spirit through the *grace of God*.

> [3]If you walk in my statutes, and keep my commandments, and do them... [11]I will set my tent among you... [12]I will walk among you, and will be your God, and you will be My people (Lev. 26:3a, 11a, 12a).

> [27]My tent also shall be with them; and I will be their God, and they shall be my people (Ezek. 37:27).

This same marriage relationship of faith has been extended even to non-Jews, indeed to *anyone* who by faith has accepted God's gracious offer of love and forgiveness through the atoning work of Messiah. Yeshua frequently referred to Himself as the bridegroom of Israel, yet He never failed to extend the same relationship to any Gentile who would receive Him in love. What a great wedding celebration awaits *all* of us who love Him!

> Let us rejoice and be exceedingly glad, and let us give the glory to Him. For the marriage of the Lamb has come, and his wife has made herself ready... Blessed are those who are invited to the marriage supper of the Lamb... (Rev. 19:7, 9)

God's commandments fill the role of His wedding vows to Israel, His bride. Israel's acceptance of the commandments at Sinai officially declared the union. Through many generations, Jews who accepted salvation by faith and grace continued to abide faithfully in this union as they awaited their Messiah. "The bride" expanded to include Gentiles who attached themselves to the God of Israel, having been born again in the Jewish Messiah, Yeshua. He is the Bridegroom of Israel, and He is "the living Torah."

Signs that accompanied the giving of Torah at Sinai

Amazing details from the giving of Torah on Sinai find many parallels in the giving of the indwelling Holy Spirit on Zion. Take a moment to read the Scripture passages below which describe God's gift of His commandments to His people Israel. We bolded the key details that you will find fascinating once you compare them to the details of the descent of the indwelling Holy Spirit in Acts 2.

As Israel encamped before Mt. Sinai, God presented His official "marriage" vows with Israel, and the people responded in agreement.

⁴You have seen what I did to the Egyptians, and how I bore you on eagles' wings, and brought you to Myself. ⁵Now therefore, if you will indeed obey My voice, and **keep My covenant**, then **you shall be My own possession from among all peoples**; for all the earth is Mine; ⁶and **you shall be to Me a kingdom of priests, and a holy nation**... ⁸All the people answered together, and said, "**All that the LORD has spoken we will do**" (Ex. 19:4-6,8).

There was thunder, lightning, a thick cloud and the sound of an exceedingly loud shofar (ram's horn wind instrument). The shofar is symbolic of the "wind of God" or "breath of God."

¹⁶It happened on the third day, when it was morning, that there were **thunders and lightnings**, and a **thick cloud** on the **mountain**, and the sound of an exceedingly **loud shofar**; and all the people who were in the camp **trembled**. ¹⁷Moses led the people out of the camp to meet God; and they stood at the lower part of the mountain (Ex. 19:16-17).

The Lord descended on the mountain in fire; it smoked and quaked.

¹⁸Mount Sinai, all of it, **smoked**, because **the LORD descended on it in fire**; and its smoke ascended like the smoke of a furnace, and the whole mountain **quaked** greatly (Ex. 19:18).

After God gave His "book of the covenant" to Moses and Moses read it to the people, God invited seventy elders and Aaron, Nadab and Abihu to see Him.

⁹Then Moses, Aaron, Nadab, Abihu, and **seventy of the elders** of Israel went up. ¹⁰**They saw the God of Israel**. Under His feet was like a paved work of sapphire stone, like the skies for clearness (Ex. 24:9-10).

God then called Moses to ascend to Him on the mountain, to receive the stone tablets which He Himself had written with "His finger" (Ex. 31:18).

¹²The LORD said to Moses, "**Come up** to Me on the **mountain**, and **stay** here, and I will give you the **tablets of stone with the law and the commands that I have written**, that you may teach them"... ¹⁷The appearance of the glory of the LORD was like **devouring fire** on the top of the mountain in the eyes of the children of Israel (Ex. 24:12,17).

Moses descended from the mountain to find that the people were worshipping a golden calf idol. He threw down God's tablets and broke them. God ordered the camp cleansed of all who rejected His Word and proclaimed themselves His enemies – about three thousand men.

²⁵When Moses saw that the people had broken loose (for Aaron had let them loose for a derision among their enemies), ²⁶then Moses stood in the gate of the camp, and said, "Whoever is on the LORD's side, come to me!" All the sons of Levi gathered themselves together to him. ²⁷He said to them, "Thus says the LORD, the God of Israel, 'Every man put his sword on his thigh, and go back and forth from gate to gate throughout the camp, and every man kill his brother, and every man his companion, and every man his neighbor.'" ²⁸The sons of Levi did according to the word of Moses: and there fell of the people that day about **three thousand men** (Ex. 32:25-28).

Signs that accompanied the giving of the indwelling Holy Spirit at Zion

Compare the details above with those of the descent of the indwelling Holy Spirit, described in the following passages. You'll see some striking parallels.

After seeing Messiah ascend into heaven near the Mount of Olives, the disciples gathered and went up (ascended) to Jerusalem (Mount Zion), obediently awaiting both Shavuot and the promise of the Father which Yeshua had told them to await.

¹²Then they returned to **Jerusalem** from the mountain called Olivet, which is near Jerusalem, a Sabbath day's journey away. ¹³When they had come in, **they went up** into the upper room, where they were **staying**; that is Peter, John, James, Andrew, Philip, Thomas, Bartholomew, Matthew, James the son of Alphaeus, Simon the Zealot, and Judas the son of James. ¹⁴All these with one accord continued steadfastly in prayer and supplication, along with the women, and Mary the mother of Jesus, and with His brothers (Acts 1:12-14).

> **When the day of Shavuot had "fully" come on the fiftieth day, the entire group (about 120, see Acts 1:15) of faithful disciples gathered themselves in one place to celebrate the feast. The Holy Spirit descended. (The Hebrew and Greeks words for "spirit" also mean "breath" or "wind.")**

¹Now when the day of Pentecost had fully come, they were all with one accord in one place. ²Suddenly there came from the sky a **sound** like the **rushing of a mighty wind**, and it filled all the house where they were sitting. ³**Tongues like fire** appeared and were distributed to them, and one sat on each of them. ⁴They were all filled with the Holy Spirit, and began to speak with other languages, as the Spirit gave them the ability to speak. (Acts 2:1-4)

> **Jewish people had assembled in Jerusalem for Shavuot; they had come from "every nation under heaven." (The biblical "number of nations" is seventy, derived from the nations who sprang from the seventy grandsons of Noah listed in Genesis 10, cf.)**

⁵Now there were dwelling in Jerusalem Jews, devout men, **from every nation under the sky**. ⁶When this sound was heard, the multitude came together, and were bewildered, because everyone heard them speaking in his own language. ⁷They were all amazed and marveled, saying to one another, "Behold, aren't all these who speak Galileans? ⁸How do we hear, everyone in our own native language? ⁹Parthians, Medes, Elamites, and people from Mesopotamia, Judea, Cappadocia, Pontus, Asia, ¹⁰Phrygia, Pamphylia, Egypt, the parts of Libya around Cyrene, visitors from Rome, both Jews and proselytes, ¹¹Cretans and Arabians: we hear them speaking in our languages the mighty works of God!" ¹²They were all amazed, and were perplexed, saying one to another, "What does this mean?" ¹³Others, mocking, said, "They are filled with new wine" (Acts 2:5-13).

> **Peter stood up and addressed the Jewish representatives of all the nations, mentioning certain signs of God's miraculous power – fire and billows of smoke.**

¹⁴But Peter, standing up with the eleven, lifted up his voice, and spoke out to them, "You men of Judea, and all you who dwell at Jerusalem, let this be known to you, and listen to my words. ¹⁵For these aren't drunken, as you suppose, seeing it is only the third hour of the day. ¹⁶But this is what has been spoken through the prophet Joel: ¹⁷ 'It will be in the last days, says God, that I will pour out my Spirit on all flesh. Your sons and your daughters will prophesy. Your young men will see visions. Your old men will dream dreams. ¹⁸Yes, and on my servants and on my handmaidens in those days, I will pour out my Spirit, and they will prophesy. ¹⁹I will show wonders in the sky above, and signs on the earth beneath; blood, and **fire, and billows of smoke** (Acts 2:14-19).

Peter explained to the men that Jesus was their Messiah and their salvation.

²² "Men of Israel, hear these words! Jesus of Nazareth, a man approved by God to you by mighty works and wonders and signs which God did by Him in the midst of you, even as you yourselves know, ²³Him, being delivered up by the determined counsel and foreknowledge of God, you have taken by the hand of lawless men, crucified and killed; ²⁴whom God raised up, having freed him from the agony of death, because it was not possible that He should be held by it... ³²This Jesus God raised up, to which we all are witnesses. ³³Being therefore exalted by the right hand of God, and **having received from the Father the promise of the Holy Spirit, He has poured out this, which you now see and hear**" (Acts 2:22-24, 32-33).

Three thousand of them received the Word, believed and were saved.

³⁷Now when they heard this, they were cut to the heart, and said to Peter and the rest of the apostles, "Brothers, what shall we do?" ³⁸Peter said to them, "Repent, and be baptized, every one of you, in the name of Jesus Christ for the forgiveness of sins, and you will receive the gift of the Holy Spirit. ³⁹**For the promise is to you, and to your children, and to all who are far off, even as many as the Lord our God will call to Himself.**" ⁴⁰With many other words he testified, and exhorted them, saying, "Save yourselves from this crooked generation!" ⁴¹Then those who gladly **received his word** were baptized. There were added that day about **three thousand souls** (Acts 2:37-41).

A comparison graphic of the two Shavuot events

Sinai		Acts
God told Moses to come up (**ascend**) to Him (Ex. 24:12).	**ascent**	Yeshua told the disciples to go up (**ascend**) to Jerusalem and wait for the promised Holy Spirit (Acts 1:12). They **ascended** to an upper room.
God **descended** to give the people His Torah (Ex. 19:18).	**descent**	The Holy Spirit **descended** to indwell believers.
The Father chose to give His Torah to Israel through Moses who waited on **Mount Sinai.**	**mountain**	The Father chose to send the indwelling Holy Spirit to believers who waited on **Mount Zion.**
God descended in **fire** (Ex. 19:18).	**fire**	The Holy Spirit descended with tongues like **fire** (Acts 2:3).
God descended with the sound of a loud **shofar** (Ex. 19:16). The shofar is a symbol of the "breath of God."	**wind**	The Holy Spirit descended with a sound from the sky like a mighty rushing **wind** (Acts 2:2).
Smoke ascended from Mount Sinai "like the smoke of a furnace (Ex.19:18).	**smoke**	Peter preached to those assembled in Jerusalem about mighty signs of the Spirit, including fire and "billows of **smoke**" (Acts 2:19).
God wrote His covenant with His finger on **tablets** of stone (Ex.31:18).	**tablets**	The Holy Spirit writes God's covenant on the **tablets** of men's hearts (Prov. 7:3, 2 Cor. 3:3, cf. Jer. 31:33).
God invited **seventy** elders, representatives of all the tribes of Israel, to meet Him and see His personal appearance (Ex. 24:9-10).	**seventy**	Through the miraculous speaking in tongues, God invited listeners representing all **seventy** nations to know Him personally (Acts 2:5).
God cleansed Israel of **three thousand** people who rejected His Word and declared enmity against Him (Ex. 32:28).	**three thousand**	God forgave, cleansed and saved **three thousand** people who embraced His Word in faith (Acts 2:41).

Why the number *seventy* at Shavuot?

God invited **seventy** of the elders of Israel to meet Him – to actually *see* Him and eat and drink – at the time that He gave His Torah (Ex. 24:9-11). These were representatives of *all the tribes of Israel* encamped before the mountain. Centuries later, as the Holy Spirit descended and the disciples spoke in the languages of "all the nations," men from all **seventy** nations of the world were there to see it (Acts 2). These were representatives of the *entire world*. We see this same extension of grace "to all nations" set forth in the words of the Great Commission: "Go, and **make disciples of all nations**, baptizing them in the name of the Father and of the Son and of the Holy Spirit" (Matthew 28:19).

The number seventy is preeminent in Scripture. Seventy descendants of Noah repopulated the world – ancestors of the nations. Seventy children of Jacob went down to Egypt. Seventy elders were appointed by Moses in the book of Numbers. The Israelites were exiled in Babylon seventy years. Jesus commanded us to forgive "seventy times seven." Seventy disciples were sent out by Yeshua to preach the gospel. At least seventy parables of Jesus have been recorded in the New Testament. Seventy weeks are set forth in the end-time prophecy of the book of Daniel.

Why *seventy*? The number is the product of two other special numbers: seven and ten. Seven is a symbol of *perfection* and *completion*. Ten, too, represents *completion*, but it also is the spiritual symbol of God's law, best exemplified by His "ten commandments." During the first Feast of Weeks, God's "perfect law" was given to the *seventy elders of Israel* at Mount Sinai. Centuries later, God wrote His perfect law on the hearts of men from all *seventy nations* (Acts chapter 2).

Ten days after His last appearance

Yeshua told His disciples to wait in Jerusalem for the "promise of the Father" – the indwelling Holy Spirit. Jesus made His first post-resurrection appearance to the disciples on Firstfruits. In Acts 1:3-5, we learn that Jesus continued appearing to them "over a period of forty days."

> ³To these He also showed himself alive after He suffered, by many proofs, appearing to them **over a period of forty days**, and speaking about God's kingdom. ⁴Being assembled together with them, He commanded them, "Don't depart from Jerusalem, but wait for the promise of the Father, which you heard from Me. ⁵For John indeed baptized in water, but you will be baptized in the Holy Spirit not many days from now."

There are fifty days between Firstfruits and Weeks, so the disciples waited **ten days** between Yeshua's last appearance and the descent of the Holy Spirit. *Ten* days – the numerical symbol of God's law, which was written on their hearts by His Spirit.

The numbers ten and seventy feature prominently in the Feast of Weeks... and they have special meaning.

The Pilgrims of Emmaus on the Road (Les pèlerins d'Emmaüs en chemin), opaque watercolor over graphite, James Tissot, c. 1886-1894.

Jesus appeared for a period of forty days following His resurrection. The disciples waited ten more days for Shavuot to arrive.

When Boaz left the gleanings of his harvest for the poor and the foreigner, he was obeying one of God's commandments which is strongly connected to the Feast of Weeks. God used this commandment to introduce Ruth to her kinsman redeemer and bring her into the family of God.

Ruth Gleaning, James Tissot, c. 1886-1894.

The book of Ruth and the Feast of Weeks

The book of Ruth is traditionally read on the day of Shavuot. The setting of the book is during the time period leading up to Shavuot (between the barley harvest and the firstfruits of the wheat harvest), and it is filled with concepts related to the Feast of Weeks. Here are just a few important symbols:

The **threshing floor** – represents the spiritual sifting and refining process which all believers undergo, especially important during the fifty-day countdown from Firstfruits to Weeks.

The **kinsman redeemer** – Boaz, the kinsman redeemer, typifies Messiah Yeshua, who redeemed us from our helpless spiritual condition when we were far away from His family, and without hope (Mt. 20:28, Gal. 4:5, Eph. 2:12-13, Rev. 5:9)

The **marriage** – the marriage of Boaz and Ruth is a symbol of the marriage between God and man in both the giving of Torah and the giving of the indwelling Holy Spirit. Just as Ruth, the foreigner (a Moabitess) was redeemed and declared "one" with both Israel and with God, so too believing Gentiles have been included in the same covenant. "Grafted in" Gentile believers echo Ruth's declaration of faith: "Your people shall be my people, and your God my God" (Ruth 1:16, Rom. 11).

The **barley and the wheat** – one popular Shavuot day tradition involves the presentation of one loaf of barley bread and one loaf of wheat. The two different loaves represent the first harvest (symbolic of mostly Jews) and the second harvest (symbolic of mostly Gentiles). Ruth the Gentile was redeemed, married to a Jew, and became the great grandmother of King David and an ancestor of Yeshua Himself. In Messiah, Gentile and Jew have become "one new people" (Eph. 2:11-14).

The **gleaning for the foreigner and poor** – God says in Leviticus 23:22, "When you reap the harvest of your land, you shall not wholly reap into the corners of your field, neither shall you gather the gleanings of your harvest: you shall leave them for the poor, and for the foreigner. I am the LORD your God." This verse stands out like a sore thumb in the middle of an entire chapter of commandments describing when and how to observe God's feasts. Interestingly, **the gleaning commandment follows directly after God's commandment to observe the Feast of Weeks.** (Read it in context now.) Because Boaz obeyed this very gleaning commandment, the needy foreigner Ruth was able to meet her kinsman-redeemer when she went out to glean in his field. Their Godly union brought great blessing to herself, to Boaz, to her mother-in-law, to the local community, and to the earthly lineage of Messiah Yeshua Himself.

Traditions of Shavuot

Jewish people (along with those Gentiles who join with them in observing the feasts) have many wonderful traditions for celebrating the Feast of Weeks.

The **Ten Commandments** – When the congregation gathers for the special sabbath day of Shavuot, the portion that is read from the Torah always includes the verses containing the "ten commandments" (titled the "ten utterances" in Judaism).

Bible study – In many congregations, a considerable part of the day of Shavuot may be devoted to reading the Bible together as a group. Remembering God's commandment to "rejoice" on this day, people make it a festive gathering, with special foods and music. Messianic believers include New Testament verses that complement and illuminate any readings from the Old Testament.

Shavuot (Pentecost) (Das Wochen- oder Pfingst-Fest), painting by Moritz Daniel Oppenheim, 1879. Note the rose garlands decorating the synagogue and the flower petals on the floor.

Barley and wheat loaves – As described on the previous page, a loaf of barley and a loaf of wheat may be presented and shared by everyone.

Dairy foods – Many Bible verses link faithful obedience to God's commandments to the reward of a good, promised land – a land "flowing with **milk** and honey." Therefore it is a tradition to prepare special dairy-based foods for the day of Shavuot. Two crowd favorites served at Shavuot celebrations are cheesecakes and cheese blintzes, drizzled with sweet fruit toppings.

Roses – Synagogues often decorate the Torah scroll, the ark (the scroll's special cabinet), and the sanctuary with roses for the Feast of Weeks. Israelis wear garlands of flowers at Shavuot parades. Judaism claims several reasons for this ancient tradition, some of them scriptural, as in Song of Songs 2:2 which extols the "beloved" as "a flower among thorns." There may be some truth to an ancient Jewish legend that, on Shavuot, Mount Sinai was miraculously covered with greenery and flowers (though it was a desert region), for the Bible states that God commanded the people "not to let the flocks or herds graze in front of the mountain" (Ex. 34:3). The

Children wearing wreaths of flowers in a Shavuot parade, photograph circa 1940-1950. Note the bowls and baskets of firstfruits.

tradition of decorating with flowers on Shavuot dates back to before the Babylonian exile, according to some sources. At least as far back as the 1300s CE, it was a tradition to spread fragrant flowers on the floor of the synagogue, in honor of "the joy of the holiday of Shavuot," as Rabbi Yaakov Moelin wrote at the time.

This section includes some of the traditional songs, blessings and recipes of the Feast of Weeks. Of course, the day of Shavuot is rich with centuries of traditional liturgy; entire books (called "Machzorim") have been devoted to keeping track of the many centuries' worth of Hebrew prayers, songs, scriptures and poems associated with this high pilgrimage sabbath. We have included just the briefest examples here, to give you a taste of the traditions of Shavuot. However, if you would like to experience "the whole megillah," you might try to locate an "observant" Messianic congregation — one which treasures and practices the ancient, biblically-based traditions of the holiday.

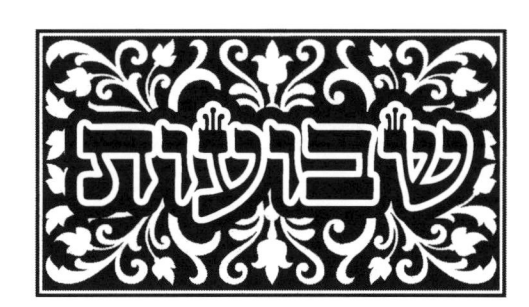

Weeks

Songs, Readings, Liturgy, Crafts and Recipes

Shehecheyanu

Who has granted us life   שֶׁהֶחֱיָנוּ

This ancient blessing is sung to celebrate special occasions which bring joy, pleasure or benefit, or to express gratitude to God for new, pleasant experiences. Therefore, it is usually sung at the start of each of God's annual feasts. The words of this blessing may be found in the Talmud, where it is indicated that it has been recited for centuries, perhaps as far back as two thousand years.

Leader — *Leading everyone in the traditional melody so they can sing along:*

Ba-ruch a-tah A-do-nai El-o-hay-nu meh-lech ha o-lam Sheh-heh-che-ya-nu v' kee-y' ma-nu v' hig-ee-a-nu laz-man ha-zeh

Leader — *Rather than singing, the leader may just lead the others in pronouncing the blessing without the melody:*

Blessed are You, LORD our God, King of the Universe, Who has granted us life and sustained us and enabled us to reach this season.

בָּרוּךְ אַתָּה, יהוה, אֱלֹהֵינוּ מֶלֶךְ הָעוֹלָם,
שֶׁהֶחֱיָנוּ וְקִיְּמָנוּ וְהִגִּיעָנוּ לַזְּמַן הַזֶּה.

Ba-ruch a-tah Adonai, El-o-hay-nu Meh-lech ha-O-lam Sheh-heh-cheh-ya-nu, v'-kee-y'-ma-nu, v'-hig-ee-a-nu, laz-man ha-zeh.

The leader may add the following as a corporate prayer:

LORD, our God, on this holy day of Shavuot we thank You in the Name of our Messiah Yeshua. Thank You for the privilege of Your Holy Torah, which was made flesh and dwelled among us in the person of Yeshua. Thank You for abiding within us, Holy Spirit, and for imprinting Your Torah on our hearts.

OBSERVANCE OF THE FEAST OF WEEKS | 113

Aseret Ha Dibrot

The "Ten Utterances" or "Ten Statements" עֲשֶׂרֶת הַדִּבְּרוֹת

*We're all familiar with the famous phrase "The Ten Commandments." However, the Hebrew scriptures of the Old Testament contain not merely 10, but 613 commandments. The New Testament repeats many of these commandments and even builds upon them, adding further nuance or clarification. All of God's commandments in both Testaments fall under **ten basic categories, or principles**, which God issued as **ten statements** in Exodus 20:1-17. Each statement provides "example" commandments which encompass the many nuances of the entire category it represents. The man-made term "the ten commandments" is somewhat misleading; it engenders the misunderstanding that the ten basic principles are <u>all</u> the commandments that God ever gave.*

Leader — *The Leader chooses ten people to read the following ten Scripture passages aloud. He or she should announce each category before each reader reads his or her assigned passage.*

"The first category: **Belief in God.**"
(Reader 1 reads Exodus 20:1-2.)

"The second category: **Prohibition of improper worship.**"
(Reader 2 reads Exodus 20:3-6.)

"The third category: **Prohibition of oaths.**"
(Reader 3 reads Exodus 20:7.)

"The fourth category: **Observance of holy times.**"
(Reader 4 reads Exodus 20:8-11.)

"The fifth category: **Respect for parents and teachers.**"
(Reader 5 reads Exodus 20:12.)

"The sixth category: **Prohibition of harming a person physically.**"
(Reader 6 reads Exodus 20:13)

"The seventh category: **Prohibition of sexual immorality.**"
(Reader 7 reads Exodus 20:14)

"The eighth category: **Prohibition of theft.**"
(Reader 8 reads Exodus 20:15.)

"The ninth category: **Prohibition of harming a person by words.**"
(Reader 9 reads Exodus 20:16.)

"The tenth category: **Prohibition of coveting.**"
(Reader 10 reads Exodus 20:17.)

Excerpt from a traditional hand-scribed Hebrew Torah scroll. This passage shows the Ten Utterances, Exodus 20:1-17.

The Leader may choose three more readers to read spiritually coordinated passages from the Prophets and the New Testament: **Ezekiel 36:25-27** (a Spirit-filled, new heart); **Jeremiah 31:31-36** (the Torah to be written on Israel's hearts); and **Acts 2:1-4** (The fulfillment of the "promise of the Father").

Tissue Paper Flower Garland
Craft for Children

Real roses for Shavuot are expensive, but this DIY craft is both fun for the kids and easy on your wallet!

You will need: Tissue paper – bright colors are best • Pipe cleaners • Scissors

1. Cut your tissue paper into squares and stack 4, 5 or 6 of them together. (You can cut one large sheet easily into four big squares for children with little hands to manipulate.)

2. Take the entire stack and fold it back and forth accordion-style. You should end up with a slender rectangle when you are through:

Fold entire stack back and forth "accordion style" (like this):

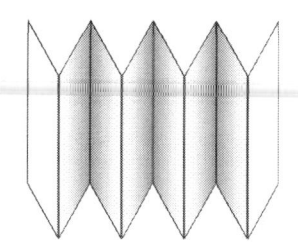

Once folded, the stack should look like a slender rectangle:

3. Fold the slender rectangle in half, then twist the end of a pipe cleaner around the fold to cinch it tightly. Leave some length on the other end of the pipe cleaner to be the flower's "stem".

Fold in half like this:

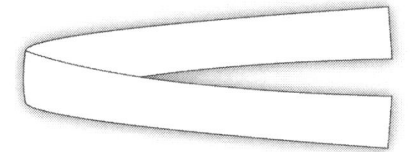

Twist the pipe cleaner around the fold, good and tight.

4. Fluff out the folds of the tissue gently, pulling at the layers until they form a nice blossom. Use the long "stem" end of the pipe cleaner to tie it to the next flower, repeating to make a garland.

The simple blossom above was made using only four large squares of tissue paper, and by following the directions on this page.

To make a more complex blossom, you can experiment by using more layers of tissue paper or different sized squares, or by shaping the ends of the folded rectangle with scissors before fluffing the petals out. The one shown at right uses more than four squares of tissue paper. It was also trimmed with scissors to create a curvy wave on the ends of the folded rectangle.

Blintzes

Delicious crepes filled with cheese, then fried and drizzled with toppings

Crepe (shell):
1 ½ cups milk
4 eggs
1 ½ cups flour
2 tbsp sugar
½ tsp salt

Filling:
2 eight-oz. packages
    cream cheese
2 egg yolks mixed well
3 tsp melted butter
6 tsp sugar
¼ tsp vanilla extract
pinch of salt

Toppings:
sour cream
pie filling (any flavor)
Other options:
chocolate sauce or
    chocolate drizzle
fresh berries or fruits
sugar and cinnamon
whipped cream

Prepare the filling first. Mix all filling ingredients together until smooth. Set aside.

Make the crepe batter: Beat eggs and milk together. Gradually sift in the flour, salt and sugar, beating well. The mixture must be fairly thin, so you can always add more milk if you find it necessary during the crepe-making part of the process.

Make the crepe: Melt some margarine in a large frying pan (a non-stick pan is best, if you have one). Stir the batter, then spoon ¼ cup of it into the hot pan, tilting the pan to allow batter to spread out thinly and cover the bottom of the pan. Cook the crepe until it just begins to brown (check the underside of the edges with a pancake turner). Slide the crepe out of the pan and onto a plate or parchment paper, cooked side up.

Make the blintz: Place a heaping tablespoon of filling in the center of the crepe. Fold the four sides up and over the filling to completely enclose it. To keep the blintz from unfolding, flip the whole thing over onto its belly. If you are ready to serve the blintz, you'll need to fry it. (If you are *not* ready to serve it, you can freeze it at this point to save it for cooking at a later time.) Return the blintz to a hot frying pan with some melted margarine in it. Sauté the blintz in the margarine, turning it until both sides are golden brown. Serve the blintz immediately, "hot off the griddle." **Toppings:** Sour cream and pie filling are popular toppings, but you might like to serve your blintzes with some of the other optional ingredients listed above.

Yields 15 to 18 blintzes.

יום תרועה

Trumpets

The Translation of Believers

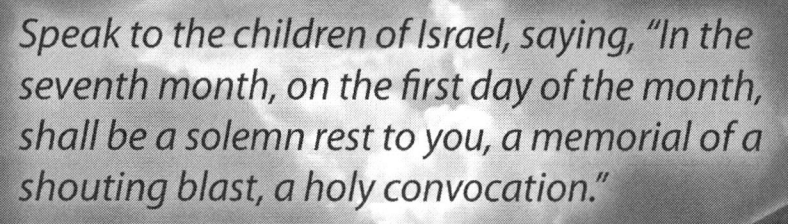

Speak to the children of Israel, saying, "In the seventh month, on the first day of the month, shall be a solemn rest to you, a memorial of a shouting blast, a holy convocation."

The words of God, Leviticus 23:24

For the Lord himself will descend from heaven with a shout, with the voice of the archangel, and with God's trumpet. The dead in Christ will rise first, then we who are alive, who are left, will be caught up together with them in the clouds, to meet the Lord in the air. So we will be with the Lord forever.

1 Thessalonians 4:16-17

Trumpets

In the previous chapters, we learned about the **spring** feasts: Passover, Unleavened Bread, Firstfruits, and Weeks. These feasts are memorials of the things Yeshua accomplished for us during the time period of His **first** coming.

Now, we will jump ahead to the seventh month of the biblical calendar where we find the **fall** feasts: Trumpets, Atonement and Tabernacles. These feasts are memorials of the things Yeshua will accomplish during the time period of His **second** coming. The first of these feasts occurs on the first day of the seventh month, and it is called the **Day of Trumpets.**

The **Feast of Trumpets** (as it is most often called in Christian circles) should more accurately be translated the **Day of a Shout** or the **Day of a Blast,** based on its actual Hebrew title throughout the Bible – **Yom Teruah*** יוֹם תְּרוּעָה *(yōm t'-roo-AH)*. The word *teruah* means "a loud noise of a shout or a blast." This Hebrew word is used throughout the Bible to represent a shout of joy, a loud voice in worship, a war cry, an alarm, or the blast of an instrument like a ram's horn (*shofar*) or brass bugle. This versatile word is translated in Scripture by many interesting phrases: *a great sound of rejoicing; a loud shout of worship; a signal of warning, a battle cry, a joyful sound.*

Yom Teruah is about all of those things. The shouts of angels and the blasts of the shofar or trumpet in the end times act as both **a shout of joyful victory** for believers and a battle cry of warning – **a dire call to repentance** – for unbelievers. Yom Teruah is a memorial of the future **restoration of God's creation** to a state of immortal perfection. The first phase of this multi-step restoration process will be the **translation of believers** from mortality to immortality. The instantaneous "translation of believers" – a miraculous transformation directly from mortal to immortal bodies as described in the New Testament – is sometimes called "the rapture" (a theological term which comes from the Latin *rapio*, meaning "caught up" or "carried off").

Jewish tradition states that this date, Tishri 1, is the **memorial of the creation of God's perfect, unspoiled world** – a sort of "birthday" of the world, so to speak. Because it precedes the Day of Atonement (Yom Kippur) by only ten days, the shofar blast of Tishri 1 serves as an **annual call to repentance.** The ten days between the two events are a solemn period of introspection and repentance which Jewish tradition has termed "The Days of Awe."

"Behold, I tell you a mystery. We will not all sleep, but we will all be changed, in a moment, in the twinkling of an eye, at the last trumpet. For the trumpet will sound, and the dead will be raised incorruptible, and we will be changed."

1 Corinthians 15:51-52

*Pronunciation note: the Hebrew word *yom*, meaning "day" or "day of," is not pronounced so it rhymes with *mom*. Instead, the "o" is a long *ō*, so it rhymes with *dome* or *roam*. It is important to make this distinction, because there is another Hebrew word, *yam*, which *does* rhyme with *mom*, and it does not mean "day." It means "sea."

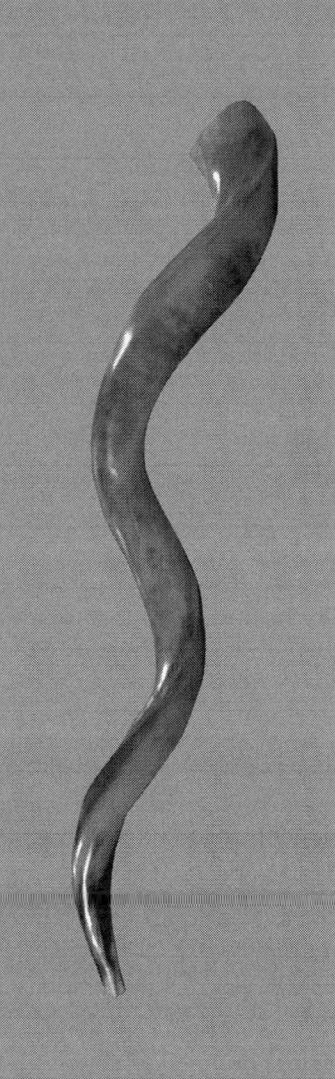

The commandment to observe Yom Teruah

Let's read what God Himself has to say about Tishri 1. We've highlighted some important points in bold.

> ²³The Lord spoke to Moses, saying, ²⁴"Speak to the children of Israel, saying, 'In the seventh month, on the first day of the month, shall be a **sabbath** to you, a **memorial** of a **shout/blast** [*teruah* תְּרוּעָה], a **holy convocation**. ²⁵You shall **do no regular work**; and you shall offer an offering made by fire to the Lord'" (Lev. 23:23-25).

> ¹ "In the seventh month, on the first day of the month, you shall have a **holy convocation**; you shall **do no servile work**: it is a **day of a shout/blast** [*Yom Teruah* יוֹם תְּרוּעָה] to you" (Num. 29:1).

Most translations attempt to clarify the meaning of the Hebrew *teruah* by adding the extra words "ram's horn" or "trumpet" – for example, "it is a day of blowing *the trumpets*," or, "it is a day for you to sound *the ram's horn*." The words "ram's horn" or "trumpets" are not present in the original Hebrew text in these particular verses.

Other verses which include *teruah*

The concept of *teruah* – "shout" or "blast" – is found many times throughout the Bible. The Hebrew word *teruah* is deeply associated with the **kingly reign** of our Lord, the King of the Universe.

For example, God put the following prophecy in the mouth of Balaam:

> ²¹He has not seen iniquity in Jacob. Neither has he seen perverseness in Israel. The Lord his God is with him. The **shout** [*teruah* תְּרוּעָה] of a King is among them (Num. 23:21).

The people brought up the ark of the covenant, representing God's kingly presence, with a **shout** and the **sound** of the **shofar**:

> ²⁸ Thus all Israel brought up the ark of the covenant of the Lord with a **shout** [*teruah* תְּרוּעָה] and with the voice/sound of the ram's horn [*shofar* שׁוֹפָר]... (1 Chron. 15:28)

The verb form of *teruah* is used by the psalmist in commanding God's people to "shout" to God, "the great King over all the earth," who "reigns over the nations" and who "sits on his holy throne." In fact, **God Himself "ascends with a *teruah*."**

> ²⁸ Oh clap your hands, all you nations. **Shout** to God with the voice of triumph! ... ⁵God has gone up with a **shout** [*teruah* תְּרוּעָה], the Lord with the sound of a ram's horn [*shofar* שׁוֹפָר] (Psalm 47:1,5).

"In the seventh month, on the first day of the month, you shall have a holy convocation; you shall do no servile work: it is a Yom Teruah to you."

The words of God, Num. 29:1

Themes repeated in the New Testament

Notice the New Testament's repetition of the themes of *teruah* (a shout or blast of a horn), ascending in triumph, and God's kingly reign.

> ⁵⁰I declare to you, brothers and sisters, that flesh and blood cannot inherit the **kingdom of God**, nor does the perishable inherit the imperishable. ⁵¹Listen, I tell you a mystery: We will not all sleep, but we will all be changed— ⁵²in a flash, in the twinkling of an eye, at the last **trumpet**. For the **trumpet will sound**, the dead will be **raised** imperishable, and we will be changed. ⁵³For the perishable must clothe itself with the imperishable, and the mortal with immortality. ⁵⁴When the perishable has been clothed with the imperishable, and the mortal with immortality, then the saying that is written will come true: "Death has been swallowed up in **victory**" (1 Cor. 15:50-54)

> ¹⁵For this we tell you by the word of the Lord, that we who are alive, who are left to the coming of the Lord, will in no way precede those who have fallen asleep. ¹⁶For the Lord himself will descend from heaven with a **shout**, with the voice of the archangel, and with **God's trumpet.** The dead in Christ will rise first, ¹⁷then we who are alive, who are left, will be **caught up** together with them in the clouds, to meet the Lord in the air. So we will be with the Lord forever (1 Thess. 4:15-17).

> ¹After these things I looked and saw a door opened in heaven, and the first voice that I heard, like a [loud] **trumpet** speaking with me, was one saying, "Come up here, and I will show you the things which must happen after this." ²Immediately I was in the Spirit. Behold, there was a **throne** set in heaven, and **one sitting on the throne** ³that looked like a jasper stone and a sardius. There was a rainbow around the throne, like an emerald to look at (Rev. 4:1-3).

The passage of 1 Thessalonians 4 is fascinating. The translation of *teruah*, "shout" in verse 16 is a Greek word connoting *a shout of command, a call, an arousing cry*. This Greek word, κέλευσμα, is used to describe how a commander musters soldiers, how the master of a ship calls his rowers into action, how charioteers spur on their horses, or how hunters urge their hounds. Rabbi Dr. Hillel ben David (Greg Killian), writing about the commanding call of the shofar in his article "The Significance of the Shofar," describes its incisive intensity:

> The sound of the shofar was more than a mere horn blast to the ancient Hebrews, to earn a name that signified a cutting or burning into the heart and soul of the people... While the harp is used to calm and soothe the spirit and soul, the shofar is constantly used to grab hold of the attention and spirit of the people. The harp is a consoler while the shofar is a preparer.

The spiritual themes of the Feast of Trumpets – God's eternal reign as King of the Universe, a heavenly shout of triumph, an arousing and commanding blast of the horn, an ascension in victory, the restoration of all creation from decay to immortality – all reverberate like the sounding of the shofar throughout New Testament Scripture.

The powerful symbolism of the shofar

God commanded that the shofar (ram's horn) be sounded to **herald the beginning of each month** (i.e., "new moon"), and this included the date of Tishri 1, Yom Teruah. The shofar has been the traditional instrument to commemorate the holy day of Yom Teruah for thousands of years.

> ¹Sing aloud to God, our strength! Make a joyful **shout** to the God of Jacob! ... ³Blow the **ram's horn** [*shofar* שׁוֹפָר] at the new moon... ⁴For it is a statute for Israel, an ordinance of the God of Jacob (Psalm 81:1,3-4).

It's not as though the shofar is the *only* type of horn God prescribed for Israel's communal life. God also commanded that silver trumpets be made for other uses (Numbers 10). Why, then, is the ram's horn specifically used to commemorate Yom Teruah? Scripture doesn't spell out the exact significance of the ram's horn, but we can catch a glimpse with some research into the name itself.

The Hebrew word *shofar* שׁוֹפָר seems to have roots in several sources. Some Bible dictionaries trace it to a root meaning "a sense of incising," as a horn gives a clear, "cutting," attention-getting sound. Others suggest more ancient roots, as in the Akkadian *shapparu*, meaning "wild goat" (the Arabic cognate is *sawafiru*, "ram's horns"). Such horns can indeed "cut" another animal in conflict, and the acute edges of their curves imply a certain "sharpness." Over the centuries, another word which shares the same root letters in Hebrew has come to mean "goodly, bright, shining, pleasing, beautiful." So, a possible composite symbolism of the shofar on Yom Teruah might be defined as **a ram's horn played as an instrument with an incisive, clear blast to arouse man's attention toward the holiness of God the King, Who is good, shining, bright, pleasing and beautiful.** The solemn repentance within any receptive person who is "cut to the heart" by the symbolic sound of the shofar is the natural result of turning spiritual eyes once again upon the dazzling holiness of God.

Michael Strassfeld (a traditional, non-Messianic Jew), speaks of the *groaning, sobbing* sound of the shofar and its *incisive call to repentance*:

> The blowing of the shofar is the only special biblical ritual for Rosh ha-Shanah... Whether it is meant to arouse our slumbering souls or as a clarion call to war against the worst part of our natures, the primitive sound of the shofar blast stirs something deep within us... On its most basic level, **the shofar can be seen to express what we cannot find the right words to say**. The blasts are the wordless cries of the people of Israel... One [traditional rabbinic] opinion is that [the call of teruah] should sound like **groaning**; another is that it should sound like sobbing; and a third opinion is that it should sound like both together (*The Jewish Holidays: A Guide and Commentary*).

This reminds us of the New Testament passage of Romans 8:26-27 which states, "In the same way, the Spirit also helps our weaknesses, for we don't know how to pray as we ought. But the Spirit himself makes intercession for us with groanings which can't be uttered. He who searches the hearts knows what is on the Spirit's mind, because he makes intercession for the saints according to God." In fact, **the shofar, being a wind instrument, is traditionally said to symbolize the "breath of God" and the "Spirit of God."** The shofar calls us to return to God in repentance and reminds us of Yeshua's return – **a symbol of the ongoing ministry of the Holy Spirit.**

ram's horn
cochlea of human ear
galaxy

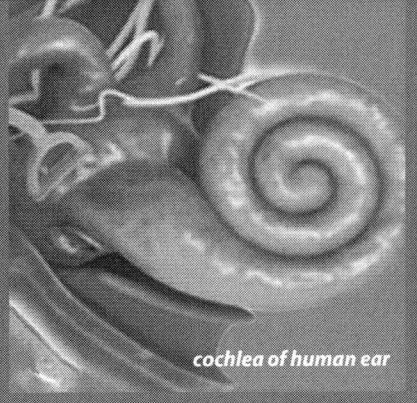

Always returning, ever expanding

The repetitious turns of the shofar's spirals are found throughout all of God's creation. These spirals are found everywhere – in galaxies and hurricanes, the Fibonacci sequence and logarithmic spiral, the shells of the nautilus and snails, the growth patterns of pine cones, dandelion seeds and sunflower seeds, the tails of sea horses and iguanas, the unfurling of ferns, flower petals, needles and leaves, the spiral staircase of DNA and the curling spirals of a Torah scroll.

Even the cochlea of the human inner ear, which transforms the sound vibration energy of the shofar blast into nerve impulses for the brain to receive as "hearing," was designed by God in the shape of this very spiral!

It is no coincidence that the Hebrew word for **repentance**, *teshuvah*, literally means "**return**," and its root comes from the Hebrew verb *shuv*, "to turn back, turn again."

A spiral signifies a **circular returning** (a cycle), as well as a **moving forward** (a progression), all at once. The annual feasts of the Lord return year after year along with the seasons – a *circular returning*. Yet, the years stretch onward, one adding to another to become epochs and ages – a *moving forward*. The spindles of the Torah scroll are turned in a circular motion as each portion is read every week of the year – a *circular returning*. Yet, as the year passes, the spindle holding the completed side builds one layer upon another – a *moving forward*.

The spiral is one of God's preferred symbols of growing life. The spiral shape of the ram's horn is a shape that ever grows (expands), yet is rooted in its concentric circles (ever returning.) Our own spiritual growth is similar to the growing spiral shape of the shofar, which begins with a small radius but ends with a wide one. By returning again and again in repentance to the sure foundation of God's Word and His Holy Person, we grow in our capacity to love God and others, year after passing year. What a powerful symbol of spiritual life is the shofar!

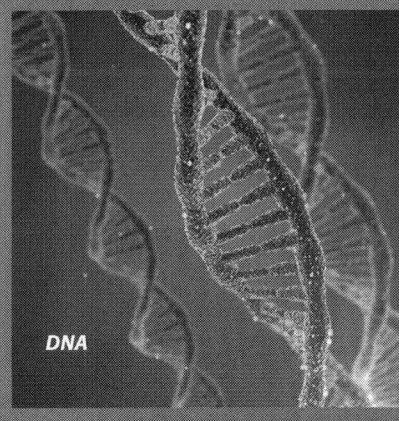

Torah scroll

snail shell

DNA

fern

The "four calls" of the shofar – God's plan of the ages

We have already learned much about the word *teruah*, meaning "a shout or a blast." Traditionally, the blast known as *teruah* is played on the shofar as a series of **nine staccato notes**, blasted quite loudly, sharply and in quick succession. The resulting sound is absolutely electrifying, which is appropriate, for the *teruah* is intended to be an arousing shout of joy and cry of alarm. However, there are additionally two other types of sounds made on the shofar. One is called *tekiah*, which is **one long, full, uninterrupted note**. The other is called *shevarim*, which is comprised of **three short, whooping blasts**.

Jewish tradition uses a particular order for sounding these blasts. In a religious service, the worship leader will loudly call out the name of the blast to be sounded, and the person blowing the shofar will respond by playing the correct melody. The worship leader calls each in a specific order, as shown in the table below. **The symbolism of the order of the four calls is striking. It tells the story of God's plan of the ages, from Creation to our final redemption in the Eternal State.**

Shofar Call	Meaning of the Call's Hebrew Name	Quality of the Call's Melody	Prophetic Significance
First Call: TEKIAH תְּקִיעָה *t'-KEE-ah*	"a blow or blast"	One long, full, uninterrupted blast; a **WHOLE** note	The state of **wholeness** of God's creation (and of mankind) before sin entered the world through Adam
Second Call: SHEVARIM שְׁבָרִים *sh'-vah-REEM*	"to destroy, to break into pieces"	Three short, whooping blasts, together lasting as long as one tekiah blast; a **BROKEN** note	Sin's breaking power; the **brokenness** of mankind and of creation as a result of sin entering the world
Third Call: TERUAH תְּרוּעָה *t'-ROO-ah*	"shout of joy or alarm, a war cry"	Nine staccato blasts, together lasting as long as one tekiah blast; a **SEVERELY BROKEN** note	The call of alarm (and joy) believers will hear at the translation of our sin-ridden bodies to immortal bodies; also signals a time of **severe brokenness** of unsaved mankind and all creation during the last days
Final Call: TEKIAH G'DOLAH תְּקִיעָה גְדוֹלָה *t'-KEE-ah g'-do-LAH*	"a great blast"	One long blast, held out as long as possible, a very long **WHOLE** note	The redemption of all believers' bodies from mortality to immortal wholeness, and the restoration of creation to perfect **wholeness**, with a new heavens and new earth

Other titles and traditional concepts of Yom Teruah

Jewish tradition uses other titles for Tishri 1 that will be helpful for you to know – not because they are all to be found in Scripture, although *some* are – but because they are commonly used by observant Jews. If you are a Gentile who loves Jewish people, you will probably agree that is *always* good to understand the lingo and mindsets of the various people you love and pray for, and that includes the traditional beliefs surrounding one of the holiest days of the biblical year. In fact, we're pretty sure you've heard one particular title for the Day of Trumpets, and maybe you've even used it yourself in casual conversation: the term "Rosh Hashanah." But do you know what it means? Let's find out!

Below is a table of various terms used by observant Jewish people for the date of Tishri 1.

Term	Translation	Meaning / Symbolism / Source
Rosh Hashanah* רֹאשׁ הַשָּׁנָה (rōsh hah-shah-NAH)	Head of the Year (i.e., "first" of the year)	First day of the Jewish civil calendar. Traditionally commemorates God's creation of the world. *Source: tradition*
Yom Teruah יוֹם תְּרוּעָה (yōm t'-roo-AH)	Day of a Shout/Blast	Holy day of commemoration that is to be accompanied by a shout/blast (i.e., of the shofar). A reminder of the translation of believers (i.e., "rapture"). *Source: Scripture*
Yom HaZikaron יוֹם הַזִּכָּרוֹן (yōm hah-zih-kah-RŌN)	Day of Remembrance (or Day of Memorial)	Holy day of commemoration. A remembrance of God's faithfulness to His people in spite of our many sins. *Source: Scripture*
Yom HaDin יוֹם הַדִּין (yōm hah-DEEN)	Day of Judgment (a.k.a. the Day of the Lord)	Tishri 1 ushers in a time of judgment on the world. This is a time of introspection and repentance. *Source: tradition, and various hints in New Testament Scripture*

The themes of the trumpet/shofar, remembrance, judgment, repentance and the sovereignty of God are prevalent in the chart above. However, **there are marked differences between the traditional Christian and traditional Jewish understandings of these concepts, especially the Day of Judgment and the Book of Life.** We will discuss these on the following page.

---

*Pronunciation note: the Hebrew word *rosh*, meaning "head" or "head of," is not pronounced so it rhymes with *squash*. Instead, the "o" is a long ō, so it rhymes with *brioche* or *gauche*. Note, too, that the *last* syllable of the word Hashanah is emphasized. If you pronounce this term correctly in Hebrew, you will probably say it differently from some of your secular Jewish friends who never studied Hebrew and who picked up an Americanized or Anglicized pronunciation by rote.

Yom Teruah is also called "Rosh Hashanah," the "Head of the Year." The date marks the beginning of the civil year, not the religious year.

What is a "civil" calendar year?

The chart on the preceding page states that Rosh Hashanah marks **the first day of the Jewish civil year.** We hope you also noticed two important things. The first is that, although Rosh Hashanah may be considered a "New Year" of sorts for Jewish people, it's certainly not a festive "hats, horns and confetti" type of celebration like New Year's Eve on December 31. Instead, **Rosh Hashanah is a solemn and holy time**. The second thing we hope you noticed is that there are *two* kinds of years for Jewish people: the *civil* year and the *religious* year.

What's the difference between a religious and civil year? For Jewish people, the *religious* year is none other than the *biblical* year. It is the exact same one that you have been studying in this book. Its first month is Nisan, and its last month is Adar. In contrast, the *civil* calendar year starts in Tishri, which happens to be the seventh month of the biblical calendar.

Why do they even have such a thing as a civil year? Well, it's not as though all the Jewish people suddenly decided to *ignore* the biblical calendar by making Tishri 1 be the start of their year; no, not at all. The date of Tishri 1 is merely a convenient demarcation for a particular kind of "fiscal" year; it arose purely from practical needs to keep track of certain things. In fact, Jewish tradition has *four* such fiscal/civil new years, each with its own unique purpose. Shevat 15 is the new year for trees, to separate their fruits for tithing. Nisan 1 is indeed the first day of God's biblical year, but it also doubles as the first day of a fiscal year for the half-shekel contribution to the temple. Elul 1 is the new year for the tithing of cattle. Tishri 1 happens to be the "new year for years"; it was set in order to count the sabbatical and jubilee years (and to figure the annual tithe on vegetables and grains).

This concept of multiple civil years is not peculiar to Jewish culture. We all observe many civil "new years" in modern life. For example, Americans know all too well the annual date of April 15 – the IRS "new year" for collecting income tax. Employers who provide health insurance often set some arbitrary annual date for open enrollment, which serves as the "new year" for employees to renew, change or begin their insurance. A municipal government maintains multiple fiscal years: they have one annual date for their fire department tax assessments, another annual date for reporting on water quality, yet another annual date for local elections, and so on. School districts, too, set dates in mid or late August to mark the first day of the school year – yet another example of a civil "new year."

The concept of a civil year is important to understand whenever you are using the term "Rosh Hashanah." Just keep this one thing in mind: When your Jewish friends speak of Rosh Hashanah as the "Head of the Year," they don't mean the beginning of the *biblical* year, Nisan 1. They mean the beginning of the *civil* year, Tishri 1.

Traditional Jewish concepts of Yom Teruah

There are some similarities, but also several major differences, between the traditional Jewish understanding and Christian understanding of Yom Teruah's themes of repentance and judgment. Here are the traditional Jewish understandings.

Rosh Hashanah and the Messiah's coming – Yom Teruah has always held deep Messianic significance. The rabbis taught that one day the shofar would sound and the Messiah would come. When he came, the dead would rise (*Daily Prayer Book*, Joseph Hertz). About a decade after Yeshua's earthly ministry, Rav Shaul (the apostle Paul) affirmed this belief when he wrote that the trumpet would sound with a shout, and Yeshua would return for His followers (upon which the translation of believers would occur). Following this, after a certain prescribed time, Jesus would begin His rule on earth as King.

The Book of Life – Traditional Jews hold that, on Rosh Hashanah, the names of the righteous are written in a Book of Life for the upcoming year and the names of the wicked in a Book of Death, but all those who are neither righteous nor wicked have ten days until Yom Kippur, the Day of Atonement, to repent before their judgment is sealed. A traditional Rosh Hashanah greeting is "May you be inscribed for a good year." This "book of life" is not necessarily considered a record of *eternal* life by most modern rabbis; the majority think of it as merely a list of those who will not die a physical death during the upcoming year. Contrary to this doctrine, Messianic Jews and Gentile believers in Yeshua believe in *complete and everlasting atonement* by the blood of Yeshua the Messiah. They do believe it necessary to continually repent of one's sins, but also that one's righteous standing depends only upon God's gift of grace, merited *not* by the believer's good works or repentance, but by the good work of Jesus performed on the execution stake, the cross. Messianic/Christian theology teaches that the "book of life" referred to in Scripture is not a list of those who will live during the upcoming year, but rather a record of those who have *eternal* life. "He that overcomes shall be clothed in white raiment, and I [Yeshua] will not blot his name out of the book of life…" (Rev. 3:5).

Crowns of reward – Traditional Jews use circular shapes for sabbath bread and cakes on Yom Teruah, not only to remind themselves of God's sovereignty, but also in the hope of a coming reward (i.e., a "crown of reward") for their righteous deeds during the year. Messianic/Christian theology recognizes these concepts too, but with the additional emphasis that God will reward our deeds not *because* of our goodness, but in *spite* of our inherited depravity. Everything righteous about us has been *imparted* to us by grace, including the very desire to repent and do good works! Therefore, our good works are just the grateful, outward expressions of our inward condition – a condition in which we are *already* considered righteous because of the free gift of God's grace. "Henceforth there is laid up for me a crown of righteousness, which the LORD, the righteous judge, shall give me at that day, and not to me only, but to all them also who love His appearing" (2 Tim. 4:8).

> *The traditional Jewish concept of the Book of Life differs significantly from that of Messianic/Christian theology.*

Other traditions of Yom Teruah

There are other traditions associated with Yom Teruah. As noted earlier, some traditions are in complete accordance with the fullness of Old and New Testament Scripture, while some are decidedly not. The day's major themes of sovereignty *(malkhuyot)*, remembrance *(zikhronot)* and the shofar *(shofarot)* are emphasized. "Remembrance" has both past and future significance. Yom Teruah is a *memorial* of God as Judge, who has always *remembered* His people with graciousness in spite of our failings. He has *remembered* those He has redeemed, even writing our names in His book of life. Yet, Yom Teruah is also a *memorial* of a time to come, urging us to *keep in mind / remember* the future time when Messiah will come to judge and rule in righteousness.

- The **sabbath bread** called *hallah* (or *challah*) is ordinarily shaped like a long, braided loaf. On Yom Teruah it is formed in a special circular shape to **resemble a crown**, as a reminder of God's eternal reign. Special holiday **cakes** are baked in rings or circular shapes to **resemble a crown** for the same reason.

- Foods, like *hallah* or apples, are **dipped in honey** to express the desire that God bring a new year that is "good and sweet." Honey is a scriptural symbol of the Word of God; Messianic believers find this sweetness in the person of Yeshua the Messiah, our Rock. Psalm 81 describes blowing the shofar on the new moon, in the time appointed. It goes on to speak of the need for Israel's repentance, and ends with God stating He would satisfy His people with His Messiah: "the finest of the wheat, and **honey** out of the rock."

- In certain orthodox settings, people come to religious services wearing **white** as a symbol of the need for humility and repentance.

- In addition to sounding the **four calls of the shofar**, special Scripture readings and liturgy are performed. Two important traditional hymns of the day are **"Melech Ozer"** (O King, O Helper), which speaks of God raising the dead and saving them by His might, and **"Adon Olam"** (Lord of the Universe/Eternity), which speaks of God's unparalleled majesty. These songs are included in the observance section at the end of this chapter.

Traditions of Yom Teruah reflect the day's three major themes: sovereignty, remembrance and the shofar.

Loaves of hallah are shaped like circular "crowns" for Yom Teruah.

Note the shofar-like spiral in the loaf at right.

Apples dipped in honey signify the sweetness of God's Word.

THE DAY OF TRUMPETS | 129

This piece of Messianic art depicts the four calls of the shofar and their representation of the stages of God's plan of the ages. On the art, Old Testament Scripture declares the commandment to sound the shofar; New Testament verses describe the shofar-like groaning of the Holy Spirit and our innermost selves (along with all of creation) as we await the day that the mortal shall be clothed in immortality and all creation shall be restored. The planet earth is centered behind the shofar, symbolic of God's creation. The four corners of the art hold symbols of Yom Teruah: three crowns for the majesty of the Triune Sovereign One (Father, Son, Holy Spirit), the scroll (i.e. "book") of life in heaven, the honey of the Word of God, and the sabbath bread (challah), shaped as a crown in honor of the holy day. Along the borders of the art, Yeshua (Jesus) is extolled as Messiah, The Living Word, The King of Kings, and Judge of the Living and the Dead. (Ink and acrylic on goatskin parchment by Lisa Cummins.)

This section includes two of the traditional hymns of Yom Teruah, having themes of the sovereignty of God and His remembering His people to raise them from the dead. Although the words of these hymns are the traditional ones of Judaism, we did add our own Messianic final verse to the hymn "Adon Olam" to bring specific honor to the Messiah, Yeshua. There are many other prayers, songs and traditions which accompany these two hymns in the Yom Teruah temple service, of course – not the least of which is the sounding of the shofar using the "four calls" described earlier in the chapter.

If you are interested in learning more about the hymns and prayers of Judaism which accompany God's feast days, you may obtain a "machzor." A machzor is a book or booklet that contains the psalms, hymns and scriptures that are traditionally sung on a given feast day. Interestingly, "machzor" is a transliteration of a Hebrew word which literally means "cycle," referring to the annual cycle of God's feasts to which we are privileged to be invited to attend, year after year.

Trumpets

**Hymns, Recipes
and Crafts for Children**

Melech, Ozer

O King, O Helper   מֶלֶךְ עוֹזֵר

In a traditional Yom Teruah service, the worship leader (chazzan) precedes the following hymn with a prayer: "Remember us for life, O King Who desires life, and inscribe us in the Book of Life, for Your sake, O Living God." We who have placed our faith in Messiah Yeshua already rest in the certain knowledge that we are eternally inscribed in the Lamb's Book of Life. Thank you, Lord Jesus!

מֶלֶךְ עוֹזֵר וּמוֹשִׁיעַ וּמָגֵן. בָּרוּךְ אַתָּה, יהוה, מָגֵן אַבְרָהָם.

Melech, Ozayr, oo-Mo-shee-ah oo-Ma-gayn; Melech, Ozayr, oo-Mo-shee-ah oo-Ma-gayn,
Baruch Atah, Adonai; Baruch Atah, Adonai, Magen Avraham!
Baruch Atah, Adonai; Baruch Atah, Adonai, Magen Avraham!

O King, O Helper, Savior and Shield; O King, O Helper, Savior and Shield,
Blessed are You, O Lord; Blessed are You, O Lord, Shield of Abraham!
Blessed are You, O Lord; Blessed are You, O Lord, Shield of Abraham!

You are the Mighty One, forever, O Lord; You are the Mighty One, forever, O Lord,
You raise the dead, sleeping in their tombs; You are mighty to save!
You raise the dead, sleeping in their tombs; You are mighty to save!

Adon Olam

Lord of the Universe (Eternal Lord) אֲדוֹן עוֹלָם

Adon Olam is a traditional hymn which is usually sung by the cantor entirely in Hebrew. We wrote an English translation of the traditional Hebrew verses so that you can enjoy the meaning of this beautiful hymn. We also created a brand new verse, the very last one on this page. You won't find this last verse in a traditional Yom Teruah machzor (order of service), because the verse extols Jesus as Messiah and Lord of the Universe.

A- don o- lam a- sher ma- lah b' ter- em kol y' seer niv- rah L'- et nah- sah v'- ħef tso- kol a- zai meh- leh sh'- mo nik- rah---

אֲדוֹן עוֹלָם, אֲשֶׁר מָלַךְ, בְּטֶרֶם כָּל יְצִיר נִבְרָא, לְעֵת נַעֲשָׂה בְחֶפְצוֹ כֹּל, אֲזַי מֶלֶךְ שְׁמוֹ נִקְרָא.

Adon Olam, ah-shayr mah-lach, b'-teh-rem kol y'tseer niv-rah,
L'ayt nah-sah, v'chef-tso kol, a-zai meh-lech sh'-mo nik-rah.

Eternal Lord, He reigned alone, before the earth was ever formed,
when by His will all things were born; the Name of our King was then made known.

And when, in time, this age shall cease, He still will reign in majesty.
He was, and is, and e'er shall be, glo-rious in, e-ter-ni-ty.

Beyond compare, the Lord is One. His nature can be shared with none,
With no be-gin-ning and no end, and His is the majesty and strength.

He is my living God Who Saves, My Rock when griefs or trials befall,
My Banner and my Refuge strong, my cup overflowing when I call.

I place my soul into His hand, awake or sleeping, under His command;
my body, too, for God is near, and therefore I will have no fear.

O Word Made Flesh, O Light of men, through Whom all things created were made,
Unblemished Lamb, Whose cleansing blood is offering eternal for our sin.
Yeshua HaMashiach come again! *(this line repeats the last phrase of the melody to end the song)*

Paper Crown
Craft for Children

Cut out (or trace over) the template at right.

Trace around the template onto cardboard or sturdy construction paper and cut out the shape. You'll need at least two cutouts of the shape to create one crown.

Tape the shapes end to end:

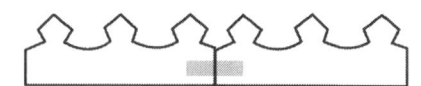

Then tape the ends together to make a circular crown, overlapping them as much as needed for a comfortable fit to the child's head:

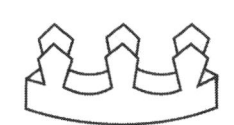

Optional: After measuring the length of the crown to the child's head, draw a pencil line right where the ends overlap and cut the excess off at about an inch longer than that line – you want to leave a little extra length for overlapping when it comes time to tape the crown together – but don't tape it just yet. Lay the paper flat on the table again and let the child decorate his or her crown with glitter, lace, or stick-on "gems." Instruct the child to avoid decorating the "overlap" excess area demarcated by your pencil line. Tape the crown together once all the glued-on decorations are good and dry. While children decorate their crowns, you can talk to them about the crowns of rewards for believers (1 Cor. 9:25, James 1:12, 2 Tim. 4:8, Rev. 2:10, 1 Pet. 5:4), how Yeshua wore a crown of thorns for us (John 19:2), and how the twenty-four elders will cast down their crowns before Yeshua (Rev. 4:10).

Get creative! Craft stores sell great stick-on gems and fancy lace.

OBSERVANCE OF THE DAY OF TRUMPETS | 135

Party Horn Shofar
Craft for Children

You will need: • Cheap party horns • Cardboard tubes from empty paper towel roll, wrapping paper roll, or toilet paper rolls (you'll need three or four small tubes per shofar) • Masking tape • White Elmer's school glue • White tissue paper (or brown, if you happen to have it) • Inexpensive acrylic craft paint (brown)

1. If the kind of party horn you buy is like the one shown, you can build the cardboard right around the metallic bell. We prefer using this kind. But if you bought the kind with the curled tube of paper that unfurls as you blow it, you'll need to cut the paper part completely off, so that you are left with just the plastic noisemaker part.

2. Gently unravel your roll or rolls of cardboard, or, if you prefer, just cut them lengthwise with scissors. Some people don't cut them lengthwise, but instead cut them into 5-inch sections of tube and then just crimp the cardboard into the desired shape. Be creative and experiment with the method you like best!

3. Using masking tape, affix one end of the cardboard to the noisemaker part and then continue to wrap cardboard around the entire party horn, expanding as you go, into the general shape of a shofar. One way to build the shofar shape is to insert the crimped end of a section of tube into the open end of the next one, as shown. Let the shofar bend itself into a curvy shape however it wants to go. It doesn't need to be perfect, because you will be covering it all with tissue paper. Blow into the noisemaker to test it from time to time (make sure you haven't crimped everything so much that no noise can get through). You can make a short, simple shofar, like the one shown at right, or a long, curly shofar if you want to get really creative.

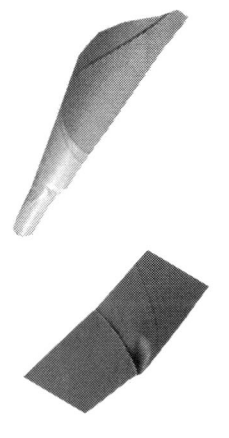

4. Once your general shofar shape is made, dilute some Elmer's glue with water and apply tissue paper and glue to the surface of the shofar, using a paper mache technique. This will give the horn some texture and strength, and it will smooth over any "joints" where you may have inserted one tube inside another. Let the whole thing dry, then paint it with brown craft paint.

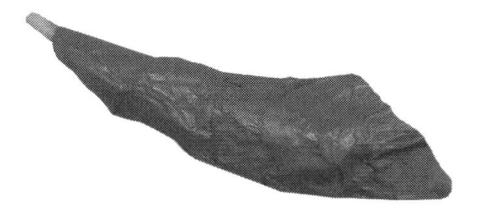

5. *Tekiah! Shevarim! Teruah! Tekiah G'dolah!* You are now ready to practice the four calls with the kids!

Easy Apple Bundt Cake

Crown shaped for Yom Teruah, in honor of the King, Messiah Yeshua

6 cups Granny Smiths*, peeled & thinly sliced
1 ½ cups sugar
5 tbsp sugar
4 tsp cinnamon
3 cups flour
1 tbsp baking powder
½ tsp salt
4 eggs
½ cup light brown sugar
1 cup vegetable oil
½ cup orange juice
2 ½ tsp vanilla extract
confectioners sugar (optional)

Preheat oven to 350. Grease, sugar, and flour a 10" tube pan. We like to use a non-stick Bundt pan like the one shown at right; it results in an elegant "crown" shape for the cake.

Combine apple slices with 5 tbsp sugar and the 4 tsp cinnamon, set aside.

Combine flour, baking powder and salt in a bowl and set aside.

In a large mixing bowl, beat eggs with 1 ½ cups sugar and ½ cup brown sugar. Add vegetable oil, orange juice and vanilla; beat well. Gradually add the flour mixture to it, blending continually. Mix until well blended, about 1 minute.

Pour a third of the batter into the pan. Top with a layer of half of the apple slices, first draining off any liquid from the apples. Pour in half the remaining batter and top with remaining apple slices. Top off the cake with all the remaining batter, making sure the apple layer is covered completely.

Bake 55 to 60 minutes, until the top turns golden brown and a knife inserted near the center comes out clean. Let cool 10 minutes in pan. Turn out onto a wire rack and let cool completely. Optionally, you may drizzle the cooled cake with a glaze made of confectioners sugar and milk. (We always do!)

Serves 16.

*This cake is also excellent if you use other types of apples. You may successfully substitute dark brown sugar for the light brown sugar as well.

OBSERVANCE OF THE DAY OF TRUMPETS | 137

Apple Bundt Cake   *(See recipe at left)*

Round Challah

Apples and Honey

Enjoy a blessed Yom Teruah!

Atonement

The Atonement
of All Israel

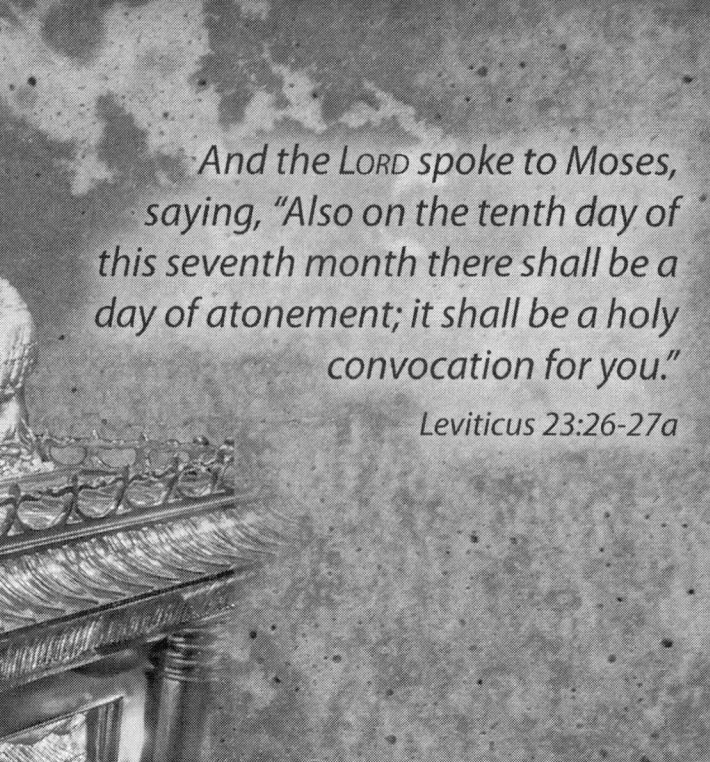

*And the L*ORD *spoke to Moses, saying, "Also on the tenth day of this seventh month there shall be a day of atonement; it shall be a holy convocation for you."*

Leviticus 23:26-27a

And I will pour out on the house of David and on the inhabitants of Jerusalem the Spirit of grace and of supplication, so that they will look on Me whom they have pierced; and they will mourn for Him, as one mourns for an only son...

Zechariah 12:10

Atonement

The second of the fall holy days occurs on the tenth day of the seventh month of the biblical year. In the Hebrew of the Old Testament, it is called **Yom Kippur*** יוֹם כִּיפּוּר *(yōm kee-POOR)*, meaning the **Day of Atonement**.

Since this day is the holiest of God's holy days, it is no wonder that the ten days leading up to it have been dubbed "the Days of Awe" by Jewish tradition. Yom Kippur was the day that the High Priest entered the most holy part of the temple to make an offering for all Israel's atonement. Only the High Priest could enter – a symbol of our Messiah being the only person fit to enter the Holy of Holies on our behalf. After offering a sacrifice for himself, the High Priest would bring forth the blood for the sacrifice made for the people. This blood was God's requirement for the "covering" or "propitiation" for the people's sins. God commanded that this be done yearly, on the date of Tishri 10.

We have seen that God's appointed times hold prophetic meaning on multiple levels. There is always at least one "near" fulfillment and one "far" fulfillment – some events happening earlier, the others happening later. One near fulfillment of Yom Kippur was God's annual provision of atonement for the sins of His people through animal sacrifices within His established temple system. A farther fulfillment was the atonement accomplished once and for all through Jesus' act of shedding His own blood, which is the ultimate and eternal propitiation for sin. An even farther fulfillment, which is yet to occur, will be a special time in which **"all Israel" – a believing remnant of Jewish people – will be saved, as they receive the atonement provided through Messiah Yeshua's sacrificial death.**

Today, there are rumblings throughout the world of many Jews becoming "born again" – that is, receiving their Messiah's atoning sacrifice. Messianic congregations, cropping up everywhere and growing in strength and number, are some of the forerunners (and catalysts) of a miraculous change of heart within the believing remnant of Israel – a change which will one day culminate in a magnificent future event of national salvation foretold by the prophet Zechariah and confirmed by Rav Shaul (the apostle Paul). Yom Kippur, the Day of Atonement, is the symbolic representation of this event. As we await this future time of salvation for all Israel, we can observe the holy day of Yom Kippur by thanking God for the atonement available to us today in Messiah Jesus. We can fast and pray that more people, Jew and Gentile alike, come to receive Him as their own atonement.

And thus all Israel will be saved; just as it is written, "The Deliverer will come from Zion; He will remove ungodliness from Jacob."

Romans 11:26

*Pronunciation note: Recall that the Hebrew word *yom*, meaning "day" or "day of," has a long *ō*, so it rhymes with *dome* or *roam*. The Hebrew word *kippur* should be pronounced so it rhymes with *allure*, not *skipper*. The emphasis should be on the second syllable of the word, which is pronounced like *poor*.

The commandment to observe Yom Kippur

Let's read what God Himself has to say about Tishri 10, the Day of Atonement. We've highlighted some important points in bold.

> ²⁶The Lord spoke to Moses, saying, ²⁷ "However on the **tenth day of this seventh month is the day of atonement**: it shall be a **holy convocation** to you, and **you shall afflict yourselves**; and you shall offer an offering made by fire to the Lord. ²⁸**You shall do no kind of work in that same day; for it is a day of atonement, to make atonement for you before the Lord your God**... ³¹You shall do no kind of work: **it is a statute forever throughout your generations in all your dwellings**. ³²It shall be a **sabbath of solemn rest** for you, and **you shall deny yourselves**. In the ninth day of the month at evening, from evening to evening, you shall keep your sabbath" (Lev. 23:26-28,31-32, cf. Num. 29:7-11).

"Afflicting" and "denying" oneself

Although the English translation in the passage above chooses to use two different terms – **afflicting** oneself and **denying** oneself – the exact same Hebrew verb is used both times in the passage: ע.נ.ה *ah-nah*, coming from a root meaning *to be made low, to be humbled, to be afflicted* or *to become submissive*. The verb has a wide range of meanings depending on context, but in this particular context of "afflicting oneself" as an act of worshipful obedience, it means *to chasten oneself toward repentance and to humble oneself before God*. The exact Hebrew wording is "you shall afflict your souls," which also may be rendered "you shall afflict yourselves."

How is this "afflicting of the soul" accomplished? It appears that a dual response is required: a humbling of the *inner* man through repentance, and a humbling of the *outer* man through physically abstaining from certain things; in other words, **a fast**. Jonathan ben Uzziel, a student of Hillel and doctor of the Torah at Jerusalem during the time of King Herod, described the term "afflicting one's soul" as "abstaining from eating and drinking, and the advantage of bathing and wiping, and the use of the bed and sandals" (Targum Jonathan). *Any* form of abstinence which is done with the intention of seeking God and humbling one's heart in repentance can be a Godly fast. The most common form of fasting for Yom Kippur is abstaining from food and perhaps only drinking a little water that day (to the extent that one's medical situation allows).

"The Fast" – Yom Kippur in the New Testament

The fact that Yom Kippur is a solemn fast day makes it unique from the other six "feast" days. The New Testament encourages us to fast and pray as often as we feel led and for many reasons, but the fast of Yom Kippur is special. **The fast of Yom Kippur is the only fast that God specifically commanded.** That's why, for thousands of years, Yom Kippur has simply been called "The Fast." Luke used this shorthand term, "the Fast," as he recorded the book of Acts between 80 and 90 CE. **Believers in Jesus were likely still observing Yom Kippur fifty years after Jesus' resurrection,** for Luke presumed his reader understood the term without need for explanation: "...much time had passed and the voyage was now dangerous, because **the Fast** had now already gone by..." (Acts 27:9)

The meaning of "atonement"

At the first mention of the word *atonement* in Scripture in Exodus 29:33, we find the Hebrew word כֻּפַּר *koo-PAR*. This term is one particular noun spelling of the verb כ.פ.ר *kah-far*, which can mean *to cover, forgive, cleanse, be merciful, pardon, reconcile,* or *make atonement*. It also means *to pacify, appease, make propitiation*. This verbal root is the origin of the noun *kippur* in the name "Yom Kippur."

Atonement is *not*, as some might say, "an Old Testament concept" which has been "done away with." It is an ongoing, eternal ministry carried out by Jesus the Savior on our behalf. Atonement is one of the most wondrous miracles of almighty God, granted to those who, by faith in true repentance, have received Yeshua as Savior and Messiah. This is the reason that God's Day of Atonement on Tishri 10 serves as such a perfect memorial of the work Yeshua did (and continues to do) to cover our sins and cleanse us of all unrighteousness.

Atonement and the ark's "mercy seat": the *kapporet*

The roots of the Hebrew word for *atonement* may be seen within the very name for the lid of the sacred ark which stood in the holy of holies in the tabernacle and temple. The Hebrew name for this lid, also called "the mercy seat," is the **kapporet** כַּפֹּרֶת *kah-PO-ret*, meaning *a propitiation*. Notice the similarity between this word, *kapporet*, and the word *kippur*. It was over this slab of gold that the very presence of God rested in glory amid the cloud of incense that the priest provided. The high priest would sprinkle the blood of the sin offering for atonement upon this "mercy seat" or "propitiation."

The symbols of the Day of Atonement

Leviticus 16 describes how the priest made the offerings on Yom Kippur. There are many wonderful symbols of our Messiah throughout the passage. It is well worth a read-through. Please take a moment now to read the entire chapter, then study the graphic on the following two pages.

The Holy of Holies, illustration, The Phillip Medhurst Picture Torah. Note the cloud above the *kapporet,* or mercy seat. This Hebrew term for the lid of the ark also means "atonement" or "propitiation."

The procedures of the high priest on Yom Kippur (Leviticus 16) and their symbolic meaning

This graphic, while by no means an exhaustive list of the procedures involved, provides at least a basic overview.

casting off ornate garments and putting on linen

The high priest **removed his usual ornate garments** (the colorful ones covered with precious stones) and washed himself, then put on **plain, white linen garments,** symbolizing humility, repentance, and unity with the rest of the people in representing them all.

White linen is used in both the funeral shroud (death) and the man's traditional marriage garment (purity and the hope of resurrection). **Yeshua put off his glory and put on a mortal body**, demonstrating great humility and unity with humanity in representing us all, even to the point of wearing a linen shroud in death.

sin offering for the priest and his household

The high priest went **out to the outer court** to sacrifice a bull at the altar of burnt offering. This **sin offering** was for himself and the other priests. The bull's carcass would be later burned **outside the camp.**

Jesus became our sin offering and **suffered outside the city gate**, just as the bodies of the sin offering were burned outside the camp (Heb. 13:11-13). Being **a perfect and eternal high priest**, He did not need to offer a sin offering for Himself, for He was holy, blameless and pure (Heb. 7:22-28).

sprinkling the bull's blood on the mercy seat amid a cloud of incense

The high priest then entered the holy of holies for the first time with some of the blood from the sin offering from the altar. He also carried some of the coals and incense from the altar. The smoke from the burning incense hid the ark of the covenant from view as **he sprinkled the blood on and in front of the mercy seat of the ark**.

Yeshua's blood is sprinkled as the mediator of a new covenant (Heb. 12:24). Since He is the great High Priest who ascended into heaven, we are now able to **approach God's throne of grace boldly** (Heb. 4:14-16)

THE DAY OF ATONEMENT

"Therefore, since we have a great high priest who has ascended into heaven, Jesus the Son of God, let us hold firmly to the faith we profess. For we do not have a high priest who is unable to empathize with our weaknesses, but we have one who has been tempted in every way, just as we are—yet He did not sin. Let us then approach God's throne of grace with confidence, so that we may receive mercy and find grace to help us in our time of need" (Heb. 4:14-16).

Old Testament Practice	Step	New Testament Fulfillment
The high priest went outside the tabernacle and **cast lots for two goats** to see which would be sacrificed as a sin offering for the people. At the altar, the high priest killed the goat as the sin offering for the people, then returned to the holy of holies **to sprinkle the blood of the goat on behalf of the people.**	**sprinkling the goat's blood on the mercy seat for the people**	**Yeshua's blood is sprinkled** as the mediator of a new covenant (Heb. 12:24).
The high priest then went back outside to the altar and **sprinkled the altar itself with the blood** of the bull (for himself) and the goat (for the people).	**sprinkling the blood on the altar**	**Yeshua's blood is sprinkled** as the mediator of a new covenant (Heb. 12:24).
While in the courtyard, **the high priest laid both of his hands upon the second goat**, thus symbolizing the transfer of Israel's sins, and **sent it away into the wilderness.**	**the scapegoat, or "azazel" (dismissal)**	Just as the *azazel* signified the *removal* of sin and guilt from an entire community, so **Jesus served as azazel,** taking on the sin and guilt of humanity. He who knew no sin was made to be sin on our behalf (2 Cor. 5:21).
The high priest entered the holy place (not the holy of holies) where **he removed the linen garments.** He bathed and put **back on his ornate garments.**	**removing the linen garments**	After removing the linen shroud of death, Yeshua was resurrected and ascended into heaven, where **He now sits restored in His full glorious raiment** (Rev. 4:1-3).
As a final sacrifice, the high priest offered a ram for himself and a ram for the people. **The sacrificial carcasses were burned outside the camp.**	**final sacrifice and burning outside the camp**	**Jesus suffered outside the city gate**, just as the bodies of the offerings were burned outside the camp (Heb. 13:11-13).

> *"For the life of the flesh is in the blood, and I have given it to you on the altar to make atonement for your souls."*
>
> *God's words in Leviticus 17:11*

Why "blood"?

We see the prevalence of the term "blood" in the preceding graphic about the priestly procedures of Yom Kippur. Why **blood**? The Bible explains.

> "For the life of the flesh is in the **blood**; and I have given it to you on the altar **to make atonement for your souls**: for **it is the blood that makes atonement by reason of the life**" (the words of God, Lev. 17:11).
>
> ...and without the shedding of **blood**, there is no **remission** [of sin]... (Heb. 9:22b)
>
> "For this is My **blood** of the new covenant, which is **poured out for many for the remission of sins**" (the words of Jesus, Matt. 26:28).

There are many other passages from both the Old and New Testaments which speak of **the blood requirement for the remission of sin. This requirement is eternal and has never changed.** It is crucial to keep this in mind, especially as we later explore the modern Jewish understanding of Yom Kippur.

> *Yeshua's blood, the blood of the renewed covenant, was poured out for many, for the remission of sins.*

Why have daily *and* yearly sin offerings?

Most believers, upon reviewing the wonderful details of the high priestly offerings on the Day of Atonement, find themselves scratching their heads. **Why was there a need for those special prescribed sacrifices on Yom Kippur, when an elaborate ritual of *daily* sacrifices for the atoning of sin already existed?** (See Leviticus chapters 1-7 for details on the daily sacrifices.)

The answer is found in the difference between **unintentional** and **intentional** sins. **The daily sacrificial system covered only unintentional sins**, also known as "sins of ignorance" (Lev. 4:2,13,22,27; 5:15,18; Num. 15:24-29).

Intentional sins (those done with a "high hand") **were not covered by the daily sacrifices.** These were covered only on Yom Kippur. Leviticus 16:16 says the animal was sacrificed "because of the uncleanness of the children of Israel, and because of their transgressions in **all** their sins," literally, "whatever their sins have been." And in Leviticus 16:21, there is a repetition of this inclusive language.

> And Aaron shall lay both his hands upon the head of the live goat, and confess over it **all the iniquities** of the children of Israel, and **all their transgressions in all their sins...** (Lev. 16:21).

How great a grace, how miraculous a mercy, was granted by this loving God in providing an annual covering – an atonement – for willful, treacherous rebellion!

However, the offerings of Yom Kippur were never designed to provide a permanent and lasting answer to the problem of sin. The whole reason that the sacrifices of Yom Kippur needed to be done annually was to "roll forward" the "covering/atonement" of the sins of Israel, year after year. The intent was a "looking forward" to that one, promised, perfect, eternal high priest who could offer a *lasting* sacrifice, and that was the Messiah who would "save Israel from their sins" (cf. Mt. 1:21).

After centuries of waiting, the wondrous grace of Yom Kippur was finally extended. It was extended into all eternity, and it was extended even to other peoples (the Gentiles), who can now join with believing Jewish people in faith to receive an *eternal* atonement provided by the Jewish Messiah, the *perfect* high priest. What a blessing!

> Now there have been many of those priests, since death prevented them from continuing in office; but **because Jesus lives forever, He has a permanent priesthood.** Therefore He is able to save completely those who come to God through Him, because He always lives to intercede for them. Such a high priest truly meets our need—one who is holy, blameless, pure, set apart from sinners, exalted above the heavens. Unlike the other high priests, He does not need to offer sacrifices day after day, first for His own sins, and then for the sins of the people. **He sacrificed for their sins once for all when he offered Himself** (Hebrews 7:23-27).

How beautiful a memorial is Tishri 10, the day of Yom Kippur. It is no wonder that God commanded it be observed as a "statute forever" (Lev. 16:29,31,34), for it is the very picture of Yeshua's role as High Priest, who makes continual and eternal atonement for our souls.

> *Jesus is the only perfect High Priest – blameless, pure, holy, set apart from sinners and exalted above the heavens.*

Looking forward... looking backward

The biblical concept of *yizchor*, memorial, is bi-directional in time. Biblical memorial is just as often *forward* looking – to the future – as it is *backward* looking – to the past. Nowhere is this more true than on the holiest yizchor date on the calendar: Yom Kippur.

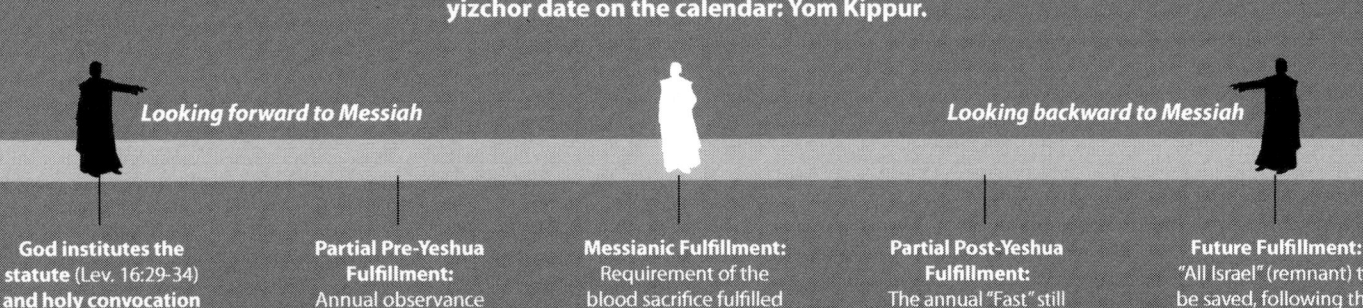

Looking forward to Messiah | *Looking backward to Messiah*

God institutes the statute (Lev. 16:29-34) and holy convocation (Lev. 23:26-32) **of Yom Kippur, the Day of Atonement**

Partial Pre-Yeshua Fulfillment: Annual observance throughout Israel's history as they await the coming Messiah in faith

Messianic Fulfillment: Requirement of the blood sacrifice fulfilled eternally (not annually) by Yeshua's sacrifice (Heb. 9:12,14,22,26)

Partial Post-Yeshua Fulfillment: The annual "Fast" still observed by Rav Shaul (Paul) and Messianic believers, as a holy memorial (Acts 27:9)

Future Fulfillment: "All Israel" (remnant) to be saved, following the "fullness of the Gentiles" (Rom. 11:25-32, Zech. 13:1,8-9, Isa. 59:20,21, cf. Acts 15:14)

Eternal Fulfillment: Zech. 14:21, Rev. 21:1-4, 27

> *In rationalizing away God's system of sacrificial atonement with its required blood offering, Judaism has come to regard the idea of a Messiah who sheds blood in sacrifice as somehow alien.*

Traditional Jewish understanding

There are many beautiful traditions associated with the Day of Atonement which we would like to share with you. Believers in Jesus will find these songs and practices deeply holy and inspiring, especially given the significance we believers would attach to their meanings. However, it is very important to understand that modern-day traditional Judaism has a very different understanding of sin and atonement than that of Christianity/Messianic Judaism.

Modern Jews who believe in God but don't believe in Yeshua as Messiah (a group which is often dubbed "traditional Judaism," for lack of a better term) have **drifted away from the scriptural concept that blood sacrifice is a requirement for the remission of sin**, and have since replaced the blood requirement with three new requirements: **repentance, prayer** and **righteous deeds.** The reason (they claim) such replacement was necessary was the physical destruction of the temple (and along with it, its priestly sacrificial system).

In the Yom Kippur *machzor* (prayerbook for the Day of Atonement), there is evidence that there once was a time that Jewish people looked forward to a day that their Messiah would be wounded on their behalf and thus provide pardon from their intentional sin (iniquity), just as the Yom Kippur sacrifices did.

> Our righteous anointed is departed from us, and we have none to justify us. He has born the yoke of our iniquities and our transgression, and is wounded because of our transgression. He bears our sins on his shoulder that we may find pardon for our iniquities. We shall be healed by his wound, at the time that the Eternal will create Him [the Messiah] as a new creature (*Form of Prayers for the Day of Atonement, Revised Edition,* pp. 287-8, Rosenbaum & Werbelowsky, New York, 1890).

Why, then, has the concept of a sacrificial Messiah become such a strange and foreign thing for Jewish people today? When did these changes occur?

The answer lies partly in how the rabbis chose to rationalize the loss of the temple. The ancient biblical practice of presenting the blood of the sacrificial animal (the *kapporah*) ceased shortly after the time that Yeshua gave His life as a sacrifice for mankind. The *kapporah* – the sacrificial atonement by the shedding of the blood of the sacrificial animal – is intrinsic and essential to biblical Judaism, yet is nowhere to be found in modern Judaism. **Traditional Judaism substituted a humanist value system for God's truth regarding the only way to make atonement for sin: the blood sacrifice.**

This substitution has had dismal consequences. In rationalizing away God's system of sacrificial atonement with its required blood offering, Judaism has come to regard Yeshua's atoning work in His shedding of blood as somehow alien.

Jewish tradition now states that three things – **teshuvah** תְּשׁוּבָה, *repentance*, **tefillah** תְּפִלָה, *prayer*, and **tsedakah** צְדָקָה, *righteous deeds* are replacements for the required blood sacrifice for the remission of sin.

> "Repentance (Teshuvah) and works of charity (Tsadakah) are man's intercessors before God's throne" (Talmud, Shab. 32a).

> "Sincere repentance (Teshuvah) is equivalent to the rebuilding of the temple, the restoration of the altar, and the offering of all sacrifices" (Talmud, Pesik; ed. Buber 24:158; Lev. R.7; Sanh. 43b).

On the other hand, Messianic Jews (born-again Jews who regard Jesus to be the promised Messiah) believe that the death of Messiah provided an eternal sacrificial blood offering, once and for all time, as the remission of our sins.

> *Traditional Judaism now teaches that repentance, prayer and righteous works are the replacement for God's required blood sacrifices.*

The "pure soul" and "sealing" the book

Traditional Judaism has another major difference from Messianic Judaism. This is the prevalent belief within traditional Judaism in the "pure soul." This doctrine teaches that there is no such thing as original sin or an inherited sin nature (i.e., inherited depravity). Just as we learned in the last chapter that "the book of life" holds a different meaning for traditional Jews than it does for born-again people, so, too, the term "atonement" holds a different meaning.

So, the "soul" is not considered to be in need of "salvation," according to much of traditional Judaism. Sure, people sin every day, that much is admitted. But those sins are considered atoned for by repentance, prayer and righteous deeds. Too, the Day of Atonement is considered the day on which God *seals* the names of the faithful in the book of life. According to most of modern-day traditional Judaism, this book is not a listing of those having *eternal* salvation, just of those who will remain physically alive during the coming year. It is believed that on Rosh Hashanah, "It is written," while on Yom Kippur, "It is sealed." The gates of heaven close at the end of Yom Kippur services, just as the gates of the temple closed after the conclusion of religious services on the Day of Atonement long ago. In contrast to this belief, a Messianic Jew views God's "sealing" as the "sealing of the Holy Spirit," the "earnest" of eternal salvation – a salvation *already* bought and paid for by Messiah's blood sacrifice. Born-again people are *already* written in the Lamb's Book of Life and have been sealed in it *forever*.

As you visit traditional temples and synagogues, especially during the high holy days of Yom Teruah and Yom Kippur, it is crucial to be aware of these doctrinal differences. There is much richness and beauty in the traditions of the day; much Scripture is sung aloud. As a believer in Messiah Yeshua, you cannot help but recognize layer upon layer of beautiful symbolism about Him embedded in every prayer, hymn and practice. But, remember: it is not so easy for the average Jewish person in attendance to see Him there like you do... largely because of rabbinical substitutions which have clouded the pure Word of God.

Traditions of Yom Kippur

Since the Day of Atonement is a solemn fast day, there are no special foods associated with it. However, there are many beautiful traditions which have been done for centuries, and which you may feel called to do yourself.

White linen – It is a custom for women to wear white dresses and men to wear white *kittels*, symbolic of purity. The *kittel* is a white cotton or linen robe, traditionally worn by the men on their wedding day. It is also used as their burial shroud. The memorial of Aaron's simple linen robes on Yom Kippur is unmistakable. The simplicity of the kittel and its humble material reminds the wearer that, stripped of all symbols of status and wealth, all humans are equally lowly before God, judged on an equal basis, and destined to return to the dust. The white robes, too, are reminders of holy, heavenly garbs of purity. Some congregations even dress the Torah scroll in a pure white cover on Yom Kippur. Yeshua Himself wore white linen as His shroud, after taking on the lowly form of mortal humanity and being sacrificed for us.

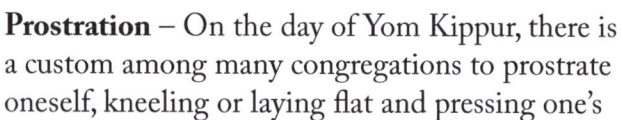

On the eve of Yom Kippur (Prayer), oil on canvas by Jakub Weinles, circa 1900. Note the long white robes (kittels) worn by the men beneath their prayer shawls.

Prostration – On the day of Yom Kippur, there is a custom among many congregations to prostrate oneself, kneeling or laying flat and pressing one's forehead almost to the ground, during the words of certain prayers. This is viewed as the natural response of a penitent heart before the presence of God. It is also a humbling, pleading posture which many people say evokes a greater sensitivity to God's presence.

The book of Jonah – Among many other passages of Scripture, the book of Jonah is read on the Day of Atonement due to its themes of repentance (both Jewish and Gentile) and God's forgiveness. The book also holds the reminder that the Jewish nation, like Jonah, cannot flee the service of God without His drawing them back to it.

The shofar – The shofar is blasted on Yom Kippur, not only as a signal of the closing of the ten days of awe which began on Yom Teruah, but also as a reminder of the great shofar blast of the Jubilee year, which was blown every fifty years on Yom Kippur.

The fast – Observant Jews fast from sunset to sunset, the entire biblical day. Many deny themselves not only food but water as well. There are other areas which may be denied in addition to food, such as bathing or marital relations, but not all congregations observe these other areas.

Kol Nidre – "All Vows"

There are many traditional liturgies for Yom Kippur, several of which you can learn about in the "observance" section following this page. One in particular requires some sensitivity in explaining: *Kol Nidre*, "All Vows." This is an old piece of liturgy which is actually sung in Aramaic rather than Hebrew.

The utmost goal of the Day of Atonement is seeking reconciliation with God. However, petitioning God for His forgiveness involves recognizing that we often say we will do things that we later fail to carry out for one reason or another. These spoken statements may be viewed from a scriptural standpoint as vows, or promises. Some of our broken vows are formal – signed and spoken before witnesses of family members, congregations, social groups or government agencies.

For centuries, Jewish people have used the statements of the Kol Nidre liturgy as a sort of formal renunciation of any vows made during the year. Kol Nidre is an important portion of the surrounding liturgy which asks for God's pardon for any rash, unintended or false promises made, as well as any vows made in sincerity that were unintentionally broken. Kol Nidre holds a long-established historical position as an acceptable (though man-made) rite appropriate to the supreme holiness of the Day of Atonement.

Kol Nidre has held prominence over the years for another reason, though. That reason will break your heart. If you are a Gentile Christian, the next few paragraphs will be very disturbing for you to read, but they are absolutely necessary for you to learn about if you aren't already aware of them. They describe the historical facts of **"Christian" antisemitism** and **forced conversion**.

> The Kol Nidre liturgy is an important traditional element of Yom Kippur... and has a horrifying history.

Historical "Christian" antisemitism

Today, Jewish people who come to faith in Yeshua as Messiah and are actively involved in the ministry of a Messianic congregation are encouraged to continue to participate in the culture of biblical Judaism. This includes all the Bible-based practices which God invented and/or approves, such as observing the biblical calendar, circumcising one's sons, *bar/bat mitzvah* (son/daughter of the commandment) ceremonies, and many other elements of Jewish culture which express the grace of God as recorded in both the Old and New Testaments.

But this relatively recent encouragement for Jewish believers to participate in biblical culture didn't always exist. The long history of the so-called "Christian" church is completely riddled with systemic, unbridled antisemitism. (We truly felt compelled to put the term "Christian" in quotation marks here. Once you read some of the horrific statements on the next page which were authored and sanctioned by the official bodies who called themselves "the Church," we think you will agree that no true, born-again believer could ever have conceived them.)

In centuries past, even the holy days and customs which God Himself had commanded to be observed as "permanent and eternal" ordinances – like Passover – were strictly forbidden by the Church to all Jews who came to faith in Christ.

Forced vows of renunciation

Jewish people who willingly came to faith in Jesus as the long awaited Messiah of Israel, especially during the persecutions of the fourth and fifth centuries, were **legally required to separate themselves utterly from any association with Judaism, the Jewish people** (including their extended family)**, and any customs viewed as "Jewish" – even those customs which God Himself commanded in the Bible.** Below is a vile "profession of faith" which Messianic Jews who loved Jesus were forced to recite in order to be accepted into the Church body.

> I renounce all customs, rites, legalisms, unleavened breads and sacrifices of lambs of the Hebrews, and all other feasts of the Hebrews, sacrifices, prayers, aspersions, purifications, sanctifications and propitiations, and fasts, and new moons, and Sabbaths, and superstitions, and hymns and chants and observances and synagogues, and the food and drink of the Hebrews; in one word, I renounce absolutely everything Jewish, every law, rite and custom... and if afterwards I shall wish to deny and return to Jewish superstition, or shall be found eating with Jews, or feasting with them, or secretly conversing and condemning the Christian religion instead of openly confuting them and condemning their vain faith, then let the trembling of Cain and the leprosy of Gehazi cleave to me, as well as the legal punishments to which I acknowledge myself liable. And may I be anathema in the world to come, and may my soul be set down with Satan and the devils.*

This profession is not unusual; its phrasing is similar to other professions employed in various countries throughout Church history. In places where such professions were not legally required, the attitudes *behind* them nevertheless prevailed. Simply put, this was the behavior expected of Jews worldwide – if they had any hopes of becoming part of the Church. You may easily verify this fact for yourself with just a little research. Just open up any book on the history of antisemitism and the Church. As a beginning point for study, we highly recommend the book *Our Hands Are Stained With Blood* by Michael L. Brown.

We strongly encourage you to invest the time to study this topic if you haven't already. A thorough understanding of the Church's historical, systemic antisemitism is absolutely crucial if you hope to reach out with any sensitivity toward your unsaved Jewish friends, who are acutely aware of the centuries of hateful acts perpetrated against their people in the name of Christianity.

---

*From *Codex Liturgicus Ecclesiæ Universæ, Liber I* (The Vatican, Rome, 1749-1766), p. 105, by Joseph Aloysius Assemanus (Giuseppi Luigi Assemani, appointed by Pope Benedict XIV as professor of liturgy and member of the Vatican's academy for historic research); as quoted by James Parkes in his book *The Conflict of the Church and the Synagogue: A Study in the Origins of Antisemitism* (Meridian Books/The World Publishing Company, New York / The Jewish Publication Society of America, Philadelphia, 1961) in Appendix 3, "Professions of Faith Extracted from Jews on Baptism," Section B, "Profession of Faith, from the Church of Constantinople," p. 397.

Say it... or die

If you were forced at the point of a sword to swear that you were a Buddhist, or a Hindu – or a believer in any other religion – and if you decided you'd better just say it because it would save the lives of your children and all your extended family, would that suddenly make you a *true* Buddhist or Hindu? Of *course* it wouldn't. This is a phenomenon called "forced conversion." Forced conversion was a quandary Jewish people have had to face over and over, all over the world, through many centuries.

You see, the words of the "profession of faith" on the previous page were not only reserved for Jewish people who had *decided* to accept Messiah Yeshua as savior and Lord. Many Jews who did *not* believe in Messiah Yeshua were *also* required to say these vows – just to stay alive. In other words, they were given a simple choice by the Gentile "Christian" religious system of their day: "Say it, or die."

That's why the recitation of Kol Nidre became an even stronger tradition on Yom Kippur. Here are the words to Kol Nidre in English:

> *Every vow forced upon us and every oath sworn to by us,*
> *Every denial and every word that we promised,*
> *All we swore, every promise we made,*
> *All renunciations that we have professed on our very souls,*
> *From this until the next Atonement Day shall all be held void.*
>
> *Blessings will come to us, absolved of such vows.*
> *We deny and renounce all such vows; they shall not take root.*
> *They shall be canceled; they shall all be null and void.*
> *They shall have no strength, no power to bind us,*
> *For such vows are not vows, and such promises are not promises,*
> *Since, forced on us, they have no power.*

If you are a Gentile, a wonderful opportunity lies ahead for you. By studying the truth about the history of Church-fostered antisemitism, you can better demonstrate love for your Jewish friends, because you'll become highly sensitive to the centuries of abuse their families have suffered in the name of "Christianity." We, the authors of this book (who happen to both be Gentiles), think it's crucial to admit that these atrocities did occur under the banner of "Christianity." We personally use this admission as a beginning point for confession – asking forgiveness. This serves as a starting point for real healing between the two communities. What better day to acknowledge these ancient wounds and to ask for God's healing and forgiveness than on the Day of Atonement – Yom Kippur.

In the Synagogue – Kol Nidre, oil on cardboard by Wilhelm Wachtel, circa 1900. This painting depicts a man wearing a tallit (prayer shawl), surrounded by candles on the eve of Yom Kippur during the chanting of the Kol Nidre rite.

The hymns of Yom Kippur are filled with heart-wrenching melodies and soul-baring confessions. Those who have faith in Yeshua as Messiah and Savior are able to confess our sins to a High Priest who understands all our weaknesses. He has been tempted like us in every way possible, yet has never sinned. It is wonderful to immerse ourselves in the words and melodies of the hymns on the following pages, knowing that our atonement has been achieved once and for all through His eternal sacrifice.

Atonement

Hymns and Rites

Avinu, Malkeinu

Our Father, Our King   אָבִינוּ מַלְכֵּנוּ

The prayer of Avinu Malkeinu is said during services on Yom Teruah and Yom Kippur. Joseph Hertz, one-time chief rabbi of the British Empire, described it as "the oldest and most moving of all the litanies of the Jewish year." According to the Talmud, a prayer beginning with the words "Our Father, Our King" was recited by Rabbi Akiva, who lived between 50 and 135 CE (Talmud, Taanit 25b). This was an era in which many thousands of Yeshua's disciples were still alive and worshiping together. It is not unreasonable to suppose that these disciples recited certain verses of this liturgy as they observed the fast of Yom Kippur in obedience to Scripture. Over the centuries, this prayer has expanded to include forty-four verses; only one is shown below. Avinu Malkeinu has been set to a variety of melodies; the tune below is just one of them.

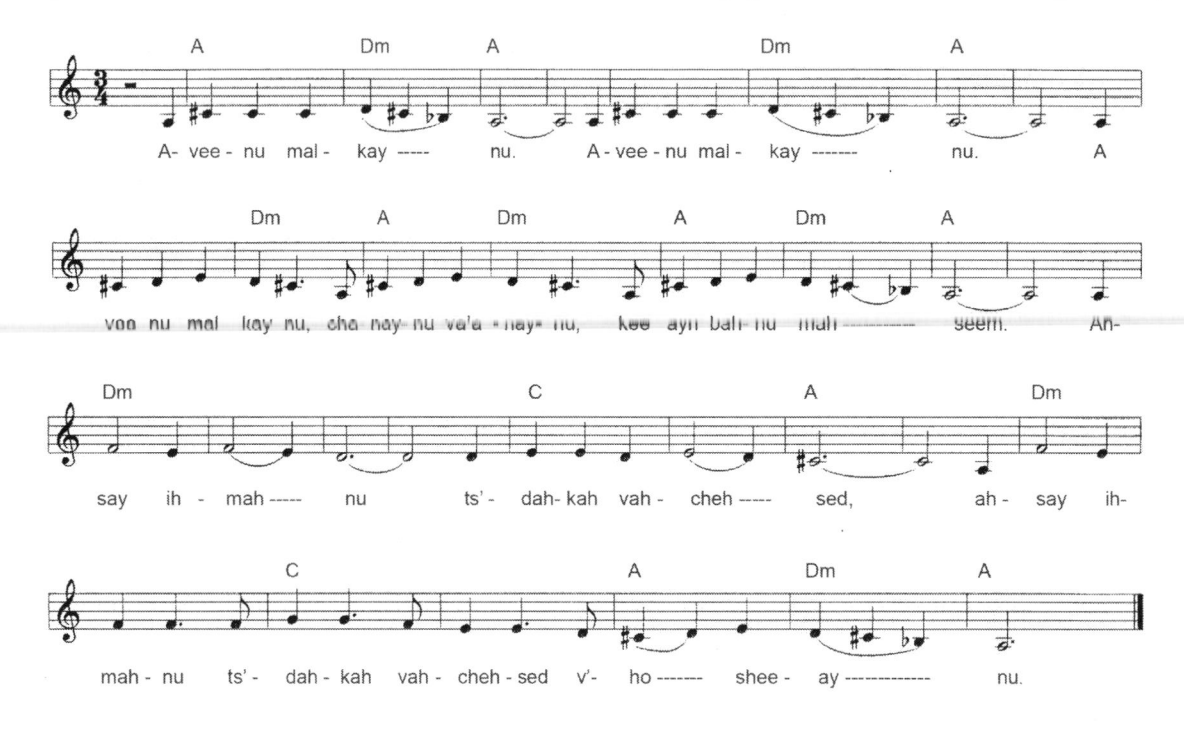

אָבִינוּ, מַלְכֵּנוּ, חָנֵּנוּ וַעֲנֵנוּ, כִּי אֵין בָּנוּ מַעֲשִׂים.
עֲשֵׂה עִמָּנוּ צְדָקָה וָחֶסֶד וְהוֹשִׁיעֵנוּ.

Ah-vee-nu mal-kay-nu... Ah-vee-nu mal-kay-nu...
Ah-vee-nu mal-kay-nu, chah-nay-nu vah-ah-nay-nu, kee ayn bah-nu mah-ah-seem.
Ah-say ih-mah-nu ts'-dah-kah vah-cheh-sed... Ah-say ih-mah-nu ts'-dah-kah vah-cheh-sed,
v'-ho-shee-ay-nu.

Our Father, our King, be gracious unto us and answer us, for we have no righteous deeds [of our own]. Perform righteousness and mercy upon us, and save us.

Kol Nidre

All Vows   כָּל נִדְרֵי

There are several traditional chants for this litany, but the one below is possibly the most well known. There are, of course many variations of this basic melody; the one shown here is by no means the "definitive" melody. The music we included below is for only Kol Nidre's initial phrases, to give you a taste of its mournful quality; the full Kol Nidre continues for several more lines. The significance of Kol Nidre as it relates to Yom Kippur is described on pages 151-153.

כָּל נִדְרֵי וֶאֱסָרֵי וּשְׁבוּעֵי וַחֲרָמֵי וְקוֹנָמֵי וְקִנּוּסֵי וְכִנּוּיֵי.
דְאִנְדַּרְנָא וּדְאִשְׁתַּבַּעְנָא וּדְאַחֲרִימְנָא וּדְאָסַרְנָא עַל נַפְשָׁתָנָא...

Kol nid-ray veh-eh-sa-ray oo-sh'-voo-ay va-cha-ra-may v'-ko-na-may v'-kee-noo-say v'-chee-noo-yay d'-een-dar-na oo-d'-eesh-ta-ba-na oo-d'-ah-cha-reem-na oo-d'ah-sar-na al naf-sha-tah-na...

All vows: prohibitions, oaths, consecrations, vows that we may vow, swear, consecrate or prohibit upon our souls...

For the remainder of this litany's translation, please see page 153.

Al Chet

For the sin   עַל חֵטְא

Al Chet (pronounced "ahl ḥayt") is a corporate confession, which is chanted with a traditional melody in the synagogue. Why is Al Chet a "corporate" litany? Why not recite it silently to oneself, before the L<small>ORD</small>, during the service? Although no one individual is guilty of every one of these sins, we confess them aloud as a group because each of us bears some responsibility, at least in part, for the sins of the group and for the spiritual health of every member. "Do you not know that you (plural) are a temple of God, and that the Spirit of God dwells in you (plural)?" The Greek words for "you" in this verse (1 Cor. 3:16) are in the plural form, indicating both corporate responsibility for sin and corporate blessing for obedience for those in the Body of Messiah. Later in the letter, Paul writes, "If one part of the body suffers, every part suffers with it; if one part is honored, every part rejoices with it. Now you are the body of Christ, and each one of you is a part of it" (1 Cor. 12:26-27).

The phrases below represent an excerpt of Al Chet. They have been modified in translation with abbreviated phrasing to better fit the space; they provide only a brief introduction to the prayer. We have also added a our own, non-traditional conclusion to the liturgy here – a proclamation of Messiah Yeshua's role in the acts of confession and forgiveness.

Leader   For the sin we committed before You...
> under duress or willingly,
> with hard heartedness,
> without knowing it,
> by the idle things we have said,
> in public or in private,
> through immorality,
> knowingly and with deceit,
> by offensive speech,
> by wronging others,
> through our inner thoughts,
> by association with vice or lewdness,
> by insincere confession,
> willfully and carelessly,
> by contempt for parents and teachers,
> by exercising power or violence,
> by desecrating Your Name,
> by foolish talk,
> by impure speech,
> with the Evil Inclination,
> against those who know and against those who do not know...

All   ...For them all, O God of forgiveness, forgive us, pardon us, atone for us.

Leader: For the sin we committed before You…
> by fraud and false promises,
> by bribery,
> by scornful mocking,
> by slanderous evil talk,
> in business dealings,
> in food and drink,
> through usury and interest,
> through haughty pride,
> with prying eyes,
> with idle chatter,
> with arrogant eyes,
> with brazen defiance…

All: …For them all, O God of forgiveness, forgive us, pardon us, atone for us.

Leader: For the sin we committed before You…
> by shirking responsibility,
> in judgment,
> by plotting against others to entrap,
> by a begrudging selfishness,
> by foolish light-headedness,
> by being stubborn,
> by running to do evil,
> by gossip-mongering,
> by taking false oaths,
> by groundless hatred,
> by breach of trust,
> through confusion of heart…

All: …For them all, O God of forgiveness, forgive us, pardon us, atone for us.

Leader

For the sins requiring...
    a burnt offering,
    a sin offering,
    varying offerings,
    guilt offerings for a definite or a possible sin,
    lashes for rebelliousness,
    forty lashes,
    premature death at the hands of the Heavenly Court,
    spiritual excommunication and childlessness,
    the four death penalties of the human court...

For sins against a positive commandment and a negative commandment, whether it can be remedied by a positive action or not,
For sins which are revealed to us and those which are not revealed to us...

Those sins which are revealed to us we have declared and confessed to You. Those sins which are not revealed to us are known to You.
For You are the Forgiver of Israel and the Pardoner of the tribes of Jeshurun in every generation, and beside You we have no king Who pardons and forgives – only You.*

All

Forgive us for all these sins, O God of forgiveness. In place of our own punishment which we rightly deserve, You have accepted the perfect sacrifice of your Servant, our Messiah, Yeshua, for...

> He was wounded for our transgressions, He was bruised for our iniquities, the chastisement of our sins was on Him, and with His stripes we are healed. All we like sheep have gone astray, we have turned every one to his own way, and the LORD has laid on Him the iniquity of us all (Isaiah 53:5-6).

---

*From this point forward, we depart from the traditional Jewish liturgy and introduce a set of Yeshua-honoring responsorial verses of Scripture concerning atonement.

Leader: There is no remission of sin other than by the shedding of blood, as it is written:

All: "without the shedding of blood there is no forgiveness" (Heb. 9:22)
"for it is the blood by reason of the life that makes atonement" (Lev. 17:11)

Leader: In the past, God provided atonement for willful sins through His sacrifice system. It is written:

All: "Then [the high priest] shall slaughter the goat of the sin offering which is for the people, and bring its blood inside the veil, and do with the blood as he did with the blood of the bull, and sprinkle it on the mercy seat and in front of the mercy seat. And he shall make atonement... because of [Israel's] transgressions" (Lev. 16:15-16).

"Then the Lord spoke to Moses, saying, ... the life of the flesh is in the blood, and I have given it to you on the altar to make atonement for your souls; for it is the blood by reason of the life that makes atonement" (Lev. 17:1,11).

Leader: Now, He provides that atonement through the eternal sacrifice of Yeshua our Messiah:

All: "The blood of bulls and goats and ashes of a heifer sprinkled on the unclean sanctified them so that they were ceremonially clean. How much more then will the blood of Messiah, who, through the eternal Spirit of God, offered Himself unspotted to God, cleanse your consciences from worthless deeds, that we may serve the living God?" (Heb. 9:13-14)

"But when this priest had offered one sacrifice for sins for all time, He sat down at the right hand of God... For by one sacrifice He has perfected forever those who are being made holy" (Heb. 10:12, 14).

סוכות

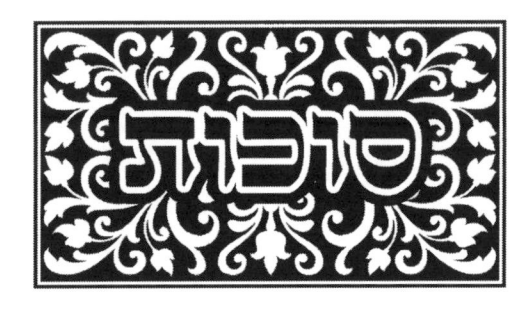

Tabernacles
The Millennial Kingdom

"If any man thirsts, let him come to Me and drink.
...He that believes in Me, as the scripture has said,
out of his heart shall flow rivers of living water."

Jesus at the Feast of Tabernacles, John 7:37b-38

"With joy you will draw water out
of the springs of y'shua (salvation)."

Isaiah 12:3

"And on that day living
water will flow out from
Jerusalem, half of it toward
the eastern sea and the
other half toward the
western sea, in summer
and winter alike."

The end times – Zechariah 14:8

"Then all the survivors from the nations that came
against Jerusalem will go up year after year to
worship the King, the Lord of Hosts, and to celebrate
the Feast of Tabernacles."

The end times – Zechariah 14:16

Tabernacles

On the fifteenth day of Tishri – fifteen days after Yom Teruah (the Day of the Shouting Blast) and five days after Yom Kippur (the Day of Atonement) – the magnificent, joyful **Feast of Tabernacles** commences, when the moon is at its fullest and brightest. This final feast of the fall season is a glorious seven days long (plus an extra, eighth day, an added day of rest). When coordinated with the modern western calendar, Tabernacles usually falls in late September or early October. Coming as it does at the close of the harvest, Tabernacles has always been associated with great gratitude and overflowing joy.

Tabernacles, or "Booths" as it is sometimes called, is the last of the seven appointed times which our Lord describes in Leviticus 23. For this reason, the Feast of Tabernacles will be the concluding chapter of this book you are holding. In the following pages, you will see how appropriate it is that our chapter on Tabernacles is the *last* chapter, for in many ways the Feast of Tabernacles symbolizes a unique "final chapter" of human history on this fallen planet: the **Millennial Kingdom – a thousand-year-long period of worldwide peace.**

In the Hebrew of the Old Testament, Tabernacles is called **Sukkot*** סֻכּוֹת *soo-KŌT*, which literally means "thicket shelters" and is usually translated **booths** or **tabernacles**. Sukkot (also transliterated *succot, succoth* or *sukkoth*) is the plural form of the word **sukkah** סֻכָּה *soo-KAH*, meaning "thicket shelter." But the booth used during the Feast of Tabernacles is not like the richly adorned "tabernacle" which housed the glory of God during Israel's wanderings. *That* tabernacle, which was the dwelling place of God's glory and the resting place of the covenant, employs a different Hebrew word (*mishkan*, "residence"). When God describes the booth to be used in His Feast of Tabernacles, He uses the term *sukkah:* a **humble, impermanent, fragile shelter** – a hut tacked together out of temporary materials, vulnerable to the elements of wind, sun and rain, having a leafy "roof" so permeable that the light of the moon and stars may be seen through the thatching laid loosely overhead.

God initially commanded that His people "dwell in booths" in order that their descendants would remember how He had "caused them to live in booths when He had brought them out of Egypt" (Lev. 23:42-43). But that is just one of Sukkot's "near" fulfillments. Sukkot also represents the time that **Messiah took on a human body**, a frail, mortal, temporary "tabernacle," when He came to dwell among us. A yet further fulfillment of Sukkot is when **He will return in glory to dwell among humanity** *again*, this time to reign for a thousand years.

> "And they found written in the Law, which the Lord had commanded through Moses, that the Israelites were to dwell in booths during the feast of the seventh month."
>
> *Nehemiah 8:14*

*Pronunciation note: The last syllable of *sukkot* has a long *ō*, so it rhymes with *coat*, not *hot*. The final syllable is emphasized, so the word *sukkot* almost rhymes with "remote."

The commandment to observe the Feast of Booths

Let's read what God Himself has to say about the Feast of Tabernacles, or Booths. We've highlighted some of the important points in boldface type.

> [33]The Lord spoke to Moses, saying, [34]"Speak to the children of Israel, and say, '**On the fifteenth day of this seventh month is the Lord's feast of booths for seven days.** [35]On the **first day** shall be a **holy convocation**: you shall do no regular work. [36]Seven days you shall offer an offering made by fire to the Lord. On the **eighth day** shall be a **holy convocation** to you; and you shall offer an offering made by fire to the Lord. It is a solemn assembly; you shall do no regular work... [39]So on the fifteenth day of the seventh month, **when you have gathered in the fruits of the land, you shall keep the feast of the Lord seven days: on the first day shall be a solemn rest, and on the eighth day shall be a solemn rest.** [40]You shall take on the first day the **fruit of goodly trees, branches of palm trees, and boughs of thick trees, and willows of the brook**; and **you shall rejoice** before the Lord your God seven days. [41]You shall keep it a feast to the Lord seven days in the year: **it is a statute forever throughout your generations**; you shall keep it in the seventh month. [42]You shall **dwell in booths seven days.** All who are native-born in Israel shall dwell in booths, [43]**that your generations may know that I made the children of Israel to dwell in booths, when I brought them out of the land of Egypt.** I am The Lord your God'" (Lev. 23:33-36, 39-43; compare Num. 29:12-40).

> [13]You shall keep the **feast of booths seven days, after you have gathered in from your threshing floor and from your winepress:** [14]and **you shall rejoice in your feast, you, and your son, and your daughter, and your male servant, and your female servant, and the Levite, and the foreigner, and the fatherless, and the widow, who are within your gates.** [15]You shall keep a feast to the Lord your God seven days **in the place which the Lord shall choose;** because the Lord your God will bless you in all your increase, and in all the work of your hands, and you shall be **altogether joyful.** [16]**Three times in a year** shall all your males appear before the Lord your God in the place which he shall choose: **in the feast of unleavened bread, and in the feast of weeks, and in the feast of booths;** and they shall not appear before the Lord empty: [17]every man shall give as he is able, according to the blessing of the Lord your God which he has given you (Deut. 16:13-17).

As you can see from the text in boldface type above, God made *many* important declarations as He invented this particular feast. Some of these important points are probably starting to sound very familiar to you; they have much in common with the other six appointed times of the Lord which you have already studied in this book. The following paragraphs will explore some of them.

"Book-ended" by two special sabbaths

We see in the quote from Leviticus on the previous page that God set the first and eighth days of this feast to be special sabbaths – holy convocations – upon which no regular work was to be done. Does this "book-ending" remind you of another biblical feast? If you are thinking of the spring feast of Unleavened Bread, you are correct! The difference is that the special sabbaths of Unleavened Bread are held on its first and *seventh* days, whereas the special sabbaths of Tabernacles are held on its first and *eighth* days.

A joyful time of ingathering

Both the Leviticus and the Deuteronomy portions on the previous page mention the connection between Sukkot and the gathering of the harvest. The words *joy* or *joyful* appear three separate times in those passages. According to the traditions of Judaism, Tabernacles has always been the most joyful of all God's feasts.

A feast for eternity

Sukkot's scriptural symbolism of the Messianic Kingdom is outlined on the following pages, so it will soon become evident to you why God has commanded that the Feast of Booths be an eternal, everlasting observance (Lev. 23:41). Like all of God's appointed times, Sukkot is commanded as a "statute forever."

A tabernacle in Jer. [Jerusalem], Quarter of European Jews, Rehavia, Mr. Bassam's flat. Photographic negative, 1939, from the G. Eric and Edith Matson Photograph Collection, Library of Congress.

One of the three pilgrimage feasts

We've already studied two of the three pilgrimage feasts which required a visit to Jerusalem: Passover/Unleavened Bread and Weeks. In Deuteronomy 16:16, God also lists Tabernacles as one of the *shalosh regalim* (literally, "three feet", i.e., journeys made on foot).

For the foreigner and the homeless, too

God made it clear that *everyone* –native-born Israeli or traveling stranger, well-to-do businessman or homeless orphan – is called to participate in His Feast of Tabernacles. Living in a fragile hut for seven days has always been a reminder of Israel's one-time plight as wandering, homeless foreigners. Today, continuing to "dwell in booths" for seven days can engender empathy toward those in our society who feel isolated or are without a permanent home.

Sukkot is a foreshadowing of world peace and prosperity – a symbol of the Messianic age when Yeshua will come to physically "dwell among us" once again.

The Messianic age of worldwide peace

Of the seven Levitical appointed times, Sukkot is the last to occur in the biblical year. As such, **Sukkot is a symbol of the Messianic age** – the time period when Yeshua will come to dwell again among us here on earth and establish His kingdom. True peace will reign for the first time since mankind's fall in the garden of Eden. This reign of peace will extend from Jerusalem and will bless **all the nations of the world**, which are recorded in the book of Genesis as having sprung from **seventy** clans. In fact, there is an amazing hint of these "seventy nations" within the very number of bulls God commanded to be sacrificed during each day of the seven-day-long Feast of Sukkot:

> [12]On the fifteenth day of the seventh month you shall have a holy convocation; you shall do no servile work, and you shall keep a feast to the Lord seven days: [13]and you shall offer a burnt offering, an offering made by fire, of a pleasant aroma to the Lord; **thirteen** young bulls... [17]On the second day you shall offer **twelve** young bulls... [20]On the third day **eleven** bulls... [23]On the fourth day **ten** bulls... [26]On the fifth day **nine** bulls... [29]On the sixth day **eight** bulls... [32]On the seventh day **seven** bulls... (Num. 29:12-32, excerpted.)

Adding the numbers of bulls all together makes a grand total of **seventy**, which is Scripture's symbolic number for "the nations of the world." God's eternal intent to extend His blessing first to Israel, then additionally to the nations, is beautifully expressed by this early set of commandments concerning the sacrifices of Sukkot.

As further evidence of God's intent, the very portion which is read from the prophets during Sukkot – according to rabbinic tradition – includes this passage from Zechariah 14 which describes the end times, when Messiah will reign:

> [8]It will happen in that day, that **living waters will go out from Jerusalem**; half of them toward the eastern sea, and half of them toward the western sea; in summer and in winter will it be. [9]**The Lord will be King over all the earth.** In that day the Lord will be one, and His name one... [16]It will happen that everyone who is left of **all the nations** that came against Jerusalem will go up from year to year to worship the King, the Lord of hosts, and **to keep the feast of Tabernacles**. [17]Whoever of **all the families of the earth** doesn't go up to Jerusalem to worship the King, the Lord of hosts, on them **there will be no rain** (Zech. 14:8-9, 16-17).

The mentions of *living waters* and *rain* in this passage are also crucial. Later, we will demonstrate how they relate to New Testament passages about Sukkot.

The Feast of Ingathering

God sometimes employs an intriguing synonym for the Feast of Tabernacles: the **Feast of Ingathering** (or Feast of Harvest), which He uses in Exodus 23:16 and 34:22. In the passages on the previous pages, we see that God set His Feast of Sukkot to occur "after you have gathered in the fruits of the land" and "after you have gathered in from your threshing floor and from your winepress." Tabernacles is indeed a fall feast, and that is one explanation for its timing after the "ingathering." But why did God set the timing for this particular feast in just this way?

> *The Feast of Tabernacles is also the "Feast of Ingathering" – symbolic of the ingathering of a harvest of <u>people</u>.*

Often, when Scripture speaks of harvests (in both Old and New Testaments), it symbolizes *the ingathering of people*. The scriptural concept of "ingathering" can have many facets: God's ingathering of Israel back to her land out of the four corners of the world to which she has been dispersed; God's gathering of those who love Him out of the polluted, corrupted world; the end-time gathering of people from all nations to Jerusalem to hear and obey the word of God; the final gathering of the Gentiles who would be saved; the angels' harvesting of souls for presentation before God's throne.

> ¹²I will surely **assemble**, Jacob, all of you; I will surely **gather** the remnant of Israel... (Micah 2:12a)

> ⁵Don't be afraid; for I am with you. I will bring your seed from the east, and **gather** you from the west. ⁶I will tell the north, 'Give them up!' and tell the south, 'Don't hold them back! Bring My sons from far, and My daughters from the ends of the earth—⁷everyone who is called by My name, and whom I have created for my glory, whom I have formed, yes, whom I have made (Isa. 43:5-7).

> ³¹He will send out his angels with a great sound of a trumpet, and they will **gather** together his chosen ones from the four winds, from one end of the sky to the other (Matthew 24:31).

> ¹But in the latter days, it will happen that the mountain of the LORD's temple will be established on the top of the mountains, and it will be exalted above the hills; and **peoples will stream to it.** ²**Many nations** will go and say, "Come, and let us go up to the mountain of the LORD, and to the house of the God of Jacob; and he will teach us of His ways, and we will walk in His paths." For out of Zion will go forth the law, and the word of the LORD from Jerusalem; ³and He will judge between many peoples, and will decide concerning strong nations afar off. They will beat their swords into plowshares, and their spears into pruning hooks. Nation will not lift up sword against nation, neither will they learn war any more (Mic. 4:1-3).

Sukkot, coming as it does at the end of the agricultural cycle and being the last of the seven appointed times, is a wonderful picture of all these facets of *ingathering*.

The four species

Here's a peculiar commandment God made concerning His Feast of Ingathering: "On the fifteenth day of the seventh month, when you have gathered in the fruit of the land, you shall keep the feast of the LORD for seven days... And you shall take for yourselves on the first day **the fruit of beautiful trees, branches of palm trees, the boughs of leafy trees, and willows of the brook**, and you shall rejoice before the LORD your God for seven days" (Lev. 23:39-40).

Traditional Jews call these four items **the four species**, or *arba'at ha-minim* in Hebrew. You'll probably also hear the species referred to by the term **lulav** לוּלָב *(loo-lahv)*, literally meaning *palm leaf* or *palm twig*. Modern Jews will use this term to refer to the three species which are "branches of trees" and which are kept bundled together. (The bundle is called a "lulav" because the palm frond happens to be the largest, most prominent of the three.) As you can see in the photograph below, those three species which are "branches of trees" are traditionally kept together in a neat sort of "holder" consisting of two tubes woven from the leaves of a palm. This bound bunch of branches is held in one hand, while the fruit is held in the other. All are "waved" in a special ceremony symbolic of God's "ingathering" of His people (described on the next page). The traditional choices for the four species are described below.

"lulav" לוּלָב *loo-lahv*
palm

Traditionally, this is preferred to be a ripe, green, straight, closed frond of the date palm tree. It is said to symbolize the human spine; the prayer is that one would walk uprightly before God.

"aravah" עֲרָבָה *ah-rah-vah*
willow

Traditionally, it is preferred to use two fresh branches of the willow, typically one that grows along a river, although they grow in people's backyards all over Israel. The willow leaf is said to symbolize the lips; the prayer is that one's speech would always be pleasing to the LORD.

"hadass" הֲדַס *hah-dahss*
myrtle

Traditionally, it is preferred to use three fresh branches from the myrtle tree of the kind that grows in Israel. Its leaf is said to symbolize the eyes; the prayer is that one's eyes would only desire to look upon God's holiness.

"etrog" אֶתְרוֹג *eh-trōg*
citron

Traditionally, the fragrant fruit of the yellow citron is preferred. The stem on top should be intact. The etrog is said to symbolize the human heart; the prayer is that the meditation of one's heart be acceptable to God.

Some see Abraham, Isaac and Jacob symbolized in the three binding strips. Others see Father, Son and Holy Spirit.

Note that the branches are selected from the kinds of trees that are very reliant on water in order to flourish. Sukkot's emphasis on water will be further explored on the following pages.

Waving the branches

Traditionally, the worshipper at Sukkot will hold the lulav in one hand and the etrog in the other and participate with the rest of the family or congregation in a "waving ceremony." A traditional blessing is recited (which you can learn in the "observance" section of this chapter), followed by a **gentle waving of the lulav three times toward each of the four directions of the compass:** north, south, east and west. This symbolizes the repeated promises of God throughout Scripture to **gather His people from the four corners of the earth.** Finally, **the lulav is gently waved in an up-and-down motion,** attesting to **God's sovereignty over all creation.** This also looks forward to the promise of a **future earthly Messianic kingdom,** one in which God's will is enacted on earth just as it is in heaven.

Messianic believers and Gentile Christians see additional layers of symbolism in this wonderful rite. As we wave the lulav together – Jew and Gentile under one tabernacle, one *sukkah*, in one accord – we see not only the ingathering of God's cherished people Israel, but the ingathering of His elect from among *all* nations, *all* those who love God and are called according to His purpose. We see the coming future Messianic age, not governed by some unknown Messiah, but by One with whom we are already intimately familiar and deeply in love: Yeshua ha Mashiach, Jesus the Christ, God's own beautiful and glorious Branch.

> ²In that day, **the branch of the Lord will be beautiful and glorious, and the fruit of the land will be the beauty and glory of the surviving remnant of Israel.** ³It will happen, that he who is left in Zion, and he who remains in Jerusalem, shall be called holy, even everyone who is written among the living in Jerusalem; ⁴when the Lord shall have washed away the filth of the daughters of Zion, and shall have purged the blood of Jerusalem from its midst, by the spirit of justice, and by the spirit of burning. ⁵The Lord will create over the whole habitation of Mount Zion, and over her assemblies, a cloud and smoke by day, and the shining of a flaming fire by night; for over all the glory will be a canopy. ⁶There will be a **sukkah*** for a shade in the daytime from the heat, and for a refuge and for a shelter from storm and from rain (Isaiah 4:2-6).

---

*Astonishingly, this word in the original Hebrew is the actual word **sukkah** סֻכָּה "thicket shelter, booth." In Christian translations of the Bible, however, the word in this verse is translated all kinds of different ways: *shelter, booth, tabernacle, pavilion, covering*. Some Bible versions seem to be better than others at conveying the word's true meaning. God chose the word *sukkah* here for a reason: to express the spiritual connection between His Feast of Sukkot and the glorious reign of Messiah.

The waving ceremony symbolizes God's ingathering of souls from the four corners of the earth, as well as His sovereignty over all creation. It looks ahead to the Messianic age of peace.

The humble, fragile, temporary sukkah of sticks and thatch which we build during the Feast of Tabernacles is a strong reminder of the contrast between man-made provisions and God's brilliant glory which shelters His people in perfect and permanent peace.

The sukkah as a symbol of God's glory

On the previous page, we read a beautiful passage from Isaiah 4, in which God says His cloud and smoke (by day) and flaming fire (by night) will be over all of Mount Zion and its assemblies. His glory will be like a wedding canopy, and He will provide his own *sukkah* to shelter His people – and *sukkah* is the actual Hebrew word used there in verse 6. **The stick-and-thatch sukkah that humans build during the Feast of Tabernacles is just a humble copy – a shadow – of God's glorious, supernatural shelter over His people.**

The sharp contrast between our own temporary, stick-and-thatch shelters and God's shining eternal glory serves as a reminder that **we must look to God as our provider for true sustenance and shelter in life.** No matter how often humanity strives to build its own "shelters" of peace and security, they will all be temporary, unable to weather any storms. The only *real* source of permanent security and peace is God Himself.

In 1 Kings 8, we find another significant scriptural connection between the concepts of the booth or tabernacle (sukkah), God's manifest glory, and God's timing in His decision to dwell among men during the first temple period. Solomon finished building the temple nearly *eleven months prior* to the Feast of Tabernacles, but he purposely *waited* until the feast arrived before officially consecrating the temple.

> ⁸And all the men of Israel assembled themselves to King Solomon [for the dedication of the temple] at the **feast** in the month Ethanim [Tishri] which is **the seventh month**... ¹⁰When the priests withdrew from the Holy Place, **the cloud filled the temple of the LORD.** ¹¹And the priests could not perform their service because of the cloud, for **the glory of the LORD filled His temple** (1 Kings 8:2,10-11).

So preeminent was the Feast of Sukkot during and after the era of Solomon's temple that it was simply called "the feast" (verse 8). How significant that God came to **dwell among His people** – by presenting **His manifest glory** in the holy of holies in the temple – **during the Feast of Sukkot!**

Peter, a Jew who was well familiar with the Feast of Sukkot and who must have observed it annually along with the rest of the nation of Israel, made an instant connection between God's manifest glory and the sukkah. Dazzled by the **shining glory** of Jesus during the transfiguration on the mount, Peter **suggested three *sukkot* be built**: one for Jesus, one for Moses and one for Elijah (Mt. 17:4, Mk. 9:5, Lk. 9:33). The actual Greek word used in that passage for booths or tabernacles is **skēnē** σκηνή *(skay-NAY)*, meaning "sukkah." **Skēnē** is the same root used John chapter 7 for the "Feast of Tabernacles" – **skēnopēgia** σκηνοπηγία *(skay-no-pay-GHEE-ah)* – literally, "the setting up of booths."

The sukkah as a symbol of a dwelling

We have learned that the sukkah we build during Tabernacles is meant to be *temporary*. God stated the reason for this is to remind Israel that they once were foreigners passing through foreign lands as they journeyed toward the promised land. The spiritual truth underlying this concept remains as strong as ever: we born-again people of God are temporary travelers, passing through this earth with our eyes fixed on the glory of eternal life ahead. We make no special effort to put down roots or build permanent structures within the corrupt world system in which we find ourselves. For we are "in this world" but not "of this world." We live our lives in accordance with the words of the famous hymn: "This land is not my home. I'm just a-passing through."

The New Testament sometimes employs the Greek word, *skēnē*, sukkah, to mean more than just an earthly thicket shelter. In the writings of the apostles, **the sukkah is often a symbol of a *dwelling*,** evoking both earthly shelters and heavenly dwellings alike. Unlike the Hebrew scriptures, in which two different Hebrew words are used for God's tabernacle in the wilderness and the humble sukkah built during the feast, the New Testament connects the two separate concepts with the single word *skēnē*. In a single word, they contrast the passing, temporary shelter of our lives here on earth against the eternal dwelling awaiting the believer on high. This is demonstrated by the use of the Greek word *skēnē* in its various forms, which we show in boldface type in the English passages below.

> I tell you, make for yourselves friends by means of unrighteous mammon, so that when it fails, they may receive you into the eternal **dwellings** (σκηνάς) (Luke 16:9).

> ...we have such a high priest, who sat down on the right hand of the throne of the Majesty in the heavens, a servant of the sanctuary, and of the true **tabernacle** (σκηνῆς), which the Lord pitched, not man... But Christ having come as a high priest of the coming good things, through the greater and more perfect **tabernacle** (σκηνῆς), not made with hands, that is to say, not of this creation... (Hebrews 8:1-2, 9:11)

> By faith, Abraham, when he was called, obeyed to go out to the place which he was to receive for an inheritance. He went out, not knowing where he went. By faith, he lived as an alien in the land of promise, as in a land not his own, dwelling in **booths** (σκηναῖς) with Isaac and Jacob, the heirs with him of the same promise (Hebrews 11:8-9).

> After these things I looked, and the temple of the **tabernacle** (σκηνῆς) of the testimony in heaven was opened... I heard a loud voice out of heaven saying, "Behold, God's **dwelling** (σκηνή) is with people, and He will dwell with them, and they will be His people, and God Himself will be with them as their God" (Rev. 15:5, 21:3).

The New Testament employs the symbol of the sukkah to represent both the temporary shelter of this present life and the eternal, glorious dwelling we believers will enjoy in the life to come.

> *"You will joyously draw water from the springs of y'shua [salvation]!"*
>
> Isaiah 12:3

> *"He who believes in Me, as the scripture has said, out of his heart will flow rivers of living water."*
>
> The words of Jesus as He attended the Feast of Tabernacles, John 7:38

Water and light: Jesus in the Feast of Tabernacles

In this portion of the chapter we will finally enter into the mind-blowing significance of the Feast of Sukkot as it portrays our beautiful Messiah. Two key aspects of its celebration, **water** and **light**, are perfect symbols of Yeshua.

The Feast of Sukkot was the first festival observed in the new temple which Solomon had built in Jerusalem. For the dedication ceremonies, all the elders and leaders of Israel came up to Jerusalem. The new structure must have struck awe into the hearts of the worshippers as they caught sight of the **dwelling place of the glory of God**.

During biblical times, the temple was kept **brightly lit**, and "there was not a courtyard in Jerusalem that did not reflect its **light**," state the rabbis in the traditional Jewish writings of the Talmud. Describing the temple during the Feast of Tabernacles, they write:

> The Levites played on harps, lyres, cymbals and trumpets and countless instruments of music, standing on the fifteen steps leading down from the courts of the Israelites to the Court of the Women, corresponding to the fifteen Songs of Ascent in the Psalms [120 to 134] (Talmud, Suk. 51:a-b). **He that has never seen the joy of this festival has never in his life seen joy... It was so bright that a woman would be able to sort wheat by the light of the celebration** (Suk. 53a).

Yeshua – the water of Sukkot

Every morning during the festival, the priests would perform a ceremony of **drawing water** to pour out on the altar. During the ceremony, they sang the words of Isaiah 12:3: "With joy **you shall draw water** out of the wells of salvation!" (Talmud, Suk. 48b). The Hebrew word used for *salvation* in this verse is **y'shua** יְשׁוּעָה *(y'-shoo-ah)*, the feminine noun meaning *salvation*. The obvious similarity to our Savior's name is evident here, for His name, Yeshua, shares the same Hebrew root letters and comes from the same verb which means *to save*. Since Jesus is indeed our "salvation" (He is the only means of eternal salvation), Messianic believers see a dual meaning in this verse from Isaiah: We draw living water from the wells of *Salvation / Jesus*.

In fact, it was **during the very Feast of Sukkot** that Jesus stood in the temple complex and cried out,

> "He who believes in Me, as the scripture has said, out of his heart will flow **rivers of living water**" (John 7:38).

Yeshua – the light of Sukkot

As evidenced by the quotes from Talmud on the previous page, **light has traditionally been a central theme of the Feast of Tabernacles.** In fact, one reason the thatched roof of the sukkah is built with many openings to the sky is so that the worshipper can see the stars and moon of God's heavens and be cognizant of **"the light of His presence."** The openings of the semi-permeable roof are symbolic reminders that God's eyes are always upon His people to protect them, and, in return, our eyes should always be upon *Him*, seeking **His light** and direction.

During the festival of Sukkot, light was an important part of the ceremonies and celebration. Young priests would light four golden *menorot* ("menorahs," or lampstands), each about 75 feet tall. According to rabbinic sources,

> There was not a courtyard in Jerusalem that was not **lit up by the light of it [the place of the water ceremony]**. Pious men... would dance around [the **lampstands**] with **lit torches** in their hands, singing songs and praises, while the Levites played... musical instruments (Mishna, Sukkah 5:3-4).

It was during the Feast of Tabernacles – menorahs and torches blazing – that Yeshua stood up and proclaimed,

> **"I am the light of the world.** Whoever follows me will never walk in darkness, but will have **the light of life**" (John 8:12).

A remarkable connection between the Light of the World and the Feast of Tabernacles could possibly be hidden in the words of Psalm 118:27. This Psalm is part of the *Hallel*, which is traditionally sung during Sukkot. Here's the interesting verse:

> The LORD is God and He has made His **Light** [i.e., Messiah Yeshua] shine upon us. With **boughs*** in hand, join the **festival**** procession up to the horns of the altar (Psalm 118:27).

"There was not a courtyard in Jerusalem that was not lit up by the light of the festivities."

Mishnah, Sukkah 5

"I am the light of the world. Whoever follows Me will never walk in darkness, but will have the light of life."

The words of Jesus as He attended the Feast of Tabernacles, John 8:12.

*The "boughs," possibly those of the three species of the lulav, are carried during the "festival."

**Usually when Scripture uses the stand-alone phrase "the feast" or "the festival," it is understood to refer to the pre-eminent Feast of Tabernacles. Several of our most heralded and authoritative Christian commentaries maintain that "the feast" in Psalm 118:27 does indeed refer to the Feast of Tabernacles.

> "Blessed is He who comes in the name of the LORD" is just Jewish "code" for "Blessed is the Messiah who will come save us!"

Hoshana Rabbah – The "Great Save Now"

The last day of the seven-day Feast of Tabernacles is called by several different names in traditional Judaism: the "Last Day," the "Great Day," the "Last Great Day" or "the Great Hosanna." In Hebrew, it is called "Hoshana Rabbah."

To understand the astounding hidden references to Jesus the Savior in the day called "the Great Hosanna," it's imperative to have a working definition of the word "Hosanna."

Hosanna is an English word which derives from the Greek **hosanna** ὡσαννά *(ho-sah-NAH)*, which itself originated from the Hebrew term **hoshana*** הוֹשַׁע נָא *(ho-shah NAH)*, literally meaning "save now!" (i.e., *please deliver!* or *save, I pray!*) It is simultaneously a desperate cry for help and a shout of worshipful acclamation toward the God the Savior.

And what about the word **Rabbah**? That word is just a phonetic spelling of a Hebrew term meaning "great." So, the traditional Jewish title of the last day of Sukkot, *Hoshana Rabbah*, means the "Great Hosanna" or the "Great Save Now!"

As we mentioned in earlier paragraphs, the group of Psalms known as the *Hallel* is sung at Sukkot, and has been traditionally sung each year at Passover and Tabernacles since before the time of Yeshua. It is within one of these Psalms (Psalm 118) that we find the primary reference to the Hebrew term behind the word *Hosanna*. It is crucial for you to know **that the words of this psalm were traditionally understood to be a prayer for a coming Messiah who would save the house of Israel and were always sung with this intention clearly in mind.** Here is the exact quote of those verses:

> O LORD, **please save us** [literally, "Hosanna"]! O LORD, please prosper us! Blessed is He who comes in the name of the LORD! We have blessed you from the house of the LORD. The LORD is God, and He has given us light (Psalm 118:25-27).

Another important thing to understand is that "Blessed is He who comes in the name of the LORD" is the traditional Jewish "code phrase" for "Blessed is the Messiah." It was a code phrase used for centuries to cry out in faith and hope, looking for the Messiah who would save God's people.

---

*Some scholars believe the term may have originated from a slightly different alternate Hebrew spelling, *Hoshianu*, which would sound more like "ho-shee-ah-nah." The general meaning of "save now!" or "please, save!" is the same in either spelling.

Yeshua – fulfillment of Hoshana Rabbah

John 7:2 begins with the words, "Now the feast of the Jews [or, the Judean feast], the feast of Booths [Sukkot] was at hand." A few verses later, we see that Yeshua attended this feast. On the seventh day of the feast, the Great Day, Hoshana Rabbah – the day in which everyone was singing the traditional prayer for the Messiah to come and save them all – Yeshua made the earth-shaking declaration right there in front of everyone that He was indeed that Messiah!

> Now on the **last day**, the '**Great Day**' [i.e., Hoshana Rabbah] of the **Feast** [Sukkot, or Tabernacles], Jesus stood and cried out, saying, "If any man is thirsty, let him come to Me and drink. He who believes in Me, as the scripture has said, from his innermost being shall flow rivers of living water." But this He spoke of the Holy Spirit, whom those who believed in Him were to receive... (John 7:37-39).

Picture the scene. Massive crowds of people were gathered in Jerusalem, waving the branches of the lulav and singing the words of Psalm 118, "Save us, we beseech you! Blessed is He who comes in the name of the LORD!" The priests were pouring water at the foot of the altar, praying for rain (God's outpouring of His spirit and salvation). The traditional thinking at the time was that, through these songs and prayers of joyous celebration, the people would be "drawing" down upon themselves, like water, the very Holy Spirit of God. Everyone present understood that this feast wasn't just about physical water. The whole day was an obvious act of symbolism of the outpouring of the Holy Spirit and the saving of Israel.

So, when Yeshua stood up and made His declarations in *this* context, His statements were crystal clear to everyone. He was saying unmistakably that *He* was the source of living water. *He* was the source of the outpouring of the Holy Spirit. *He* was the one who had come from heaven to save them. *He* was Messiah!

Was it really that clear to everyone? Much of the crowd's response in John 7:40-53 proves that everyone understood the observance of Hoshana Rabbah to be about looking for the coming Messiah. They understood exactly what Jesus meant when He made his symbolic statements about being the source of "living water." Read John 7:40-53 again right now. They all understood, all right.

Even to this very day, throughout places of Jewish worship the world over, lulavs are waved, willow branches are beaten on the ground, and the Hallel is sung on Hoshana Rabbah as the people look for a coming Messiah and pray for God's dual gifts of rain and Spirit. In Messianic circles, though, this celebration is held with the knowledge of who this Savior actually is: Jesus the Christ.

When Jesus stood up on Hoshana Rabbah and declared Himself to be the source of "living water," He was declaring Himself to be the long-awaited Messiah... and everyone in Jerusalem knew it.

A Sukkot-like event – though not at Sukkot

If you are anything like us, as you pictured the scene on the previous page, your mind probably jumped immediately to the time that Jesus made His triumphal entry into Jerusalem. As Jesus rode into Jerusalem on the donkey and colt, there were people all over the city waving tree branches, just like they would usually do at Sukkot. They were even shouting "Hosanna" to "the son of David" (code for "Messiah"), just as they would ordinarily do on the "last great day" of the Feast of Sukkot. The entire city was stirred up, because everyone knew that *anyone* who would be riding in a procession and permitting the Hallel to be shouted to Him like this would be claiming to be the Messiah. Here's a description of the triumphal entry:

> ⁶The disciples went, and did just as Jesus commanded them, ⁷and brought the donkey and the colt, and laid their clothes on them; and he sat on them. ⁸A very great multitude spread their clothes on the road. Others cut branches from the trees, and spread them on the road. ⁹The multitudes who went before him, and who followed kept shouting, "Hosanna to the son of David! Blessed is he who comes in the name of the Lord! Hosanna in the highest!" ¹⁰When he had come into Jerusalem, all the city was stirred up, saying, "Who is this?" (Matthew 21:6-11)

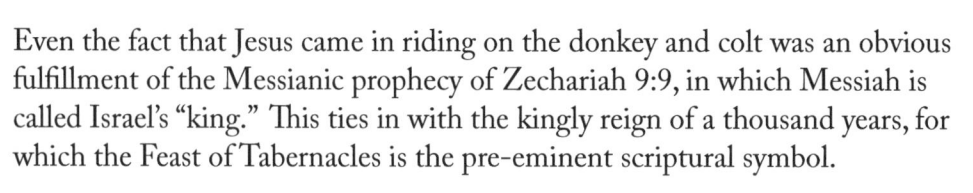

The Procession in the Streets of Jerusalem (Le cortège dans les rues de Jérusalem), opaque watercolor over graphite on paper, by James Tissot, circa 1886-1894, Brooklyn Museum collection. Note the erect, slender palm branches, similar to those used in traditional *lulavs* for Sukkot, being carried by the people following Jesus in the procession.

Even the fact that Jesus came in riding on the donkey and colt was an obvious fulfillment of the Messianic prophecy of Zechariah 9:9, in which Messiah is called Israel's "king." This ties in with the kingly reign of a thousand years, for which the Feast of Tabernacles is the pre-eminent scriptural symbol.

But there's only one problem with all of this. The triumphal entry did *not* occur at Sukkot. It occurred around Passover. Not in fall, but in spring. So, this otherwise "Sukkot-like" event happened at a very strange time! No Bible scholar we know of has been able to categorically answer this seeming disparity, but we do have our own theory (and it is *just* a theory). We think that the people welcoming Jesus during the triumphal entry desired a purely *human, earthly* king – a *political* savior who would save them from a physical overlord, Rome. The people were either unable or unwilling to accept that the first coming of Jesus was *not* to establish His earthly kingdom, but rather – as He repeatedly proclaimed – to give His life as a Servant and establish His heavenly kingdom in the hearts of men. The *first* coming (that of the "suffering Servant") is represented by the *spring* feasts. It won't be until the *second* coming (represented by the *fall* feasts) that Jesus will establish His physical reign on earth. So, one possible reason for the strange timing of the triumphal entry is that it may serve as an object lesson. Our Lord may have permitted it to occur "out of sequence" as a real-life parable, illustrating the fact that all events must align to *His* timetable, not man's.

Eighth Day of Assembly – Shemini Atzeret

At the beginning of this chapter, we learned that God established an additional day, an "eighth day" of "assembly," which closes out the seven-day Feast of Tabernacles with a holy, special sabbath (Lev. 23:33-34,36). Judaism's term "Shemini Atzeret" or "eighth day of assembly" comes from Leviticus 23:36, where we find the Hebrew words **Shemini Atzeret** שְׁמִינִי עֲצֶרֶת *shih-mee-NEE ah-TSAY-rayt*, literally "eighth [of] assembly."

In Scripture, the number **eight** symbolizes "one step beyond perfect completeness." It embodies the concept of one's cup flowing over with goodness. The Hebrew word for *eight* has a root related to *oil*, so the idea of abundant fatness – prosperity – seems to be associated with it. Because eight represents a sort of "beyondness past completeness," it often represents *new beginnings*, as in the "eighth day of circumcision." Bible scholars point to the number eight as being associated time after time in Scripture with *renewal, regeneration* and *resurrection*. How appropriate that the eighth day concludes the Feast of Tabernacles, whose seven days symbolize Yeshua's thousand year reign, for at some point following this reign begins a *brand new era* – the "eternal state."

There is a wonderful symbolism of the word **atzeret**, too. This spelling only occurs eleven times in Scripture, and in every case it refers to a solemn, sacred assembly. Three of those solemn instances even refer to a fast. *Atzeret* is really just a noun form of the Hebrew verb **atsar**, ע.צ.ר, meaning *restrain, retain, hold back, restrict, stop, prevent, prevail, confine*.

Of all the Hebrew words which God could have chosen to describe the eighth day following the most joyous feast of the biblical year, why, then, choose *atzeret*? Clearly, the very holiness of this special sabbath would require festival goers to "dial it back" a little from the great revelry and merriment of the preceding seven days. This involves a level of self *restraint*. Also, one could imagine that God, desirous of extending this time of dwelling among His people just one day longer, would lovingly want to *restrain* His people just one more day for a last sabbath gathering before they must embark on their long journeys homeward from Jerusalem. Perhaps you've experienced this longing to *restrain* a beloved friend or relative to stay just one day longer at the end of a cherished visit.

Messianic believers recognize an additional layer of symbolism in the term *atzeret*. We know that Sukkot is a picture of the Messianic Age of worldwide peace under King Yeshua, during which Satan will be *bound, restrained, restricted, confined*. Yeshua's very government and the Holy Spirit, too, will *restrain* the self-centered, evil instincts of humanity – which will permit peace to flourish.

Shemini Atzeret is a symbol of the restraining ministry of the Holy Spirit to bring about peace. It also speaks of the overflowing abundance of life which we enjoy as reborn, regenerated people in Christ.

Megillat Kohelet, the scroll of Ecclesiastes, is traditionally read during the Feast of Tabernacles. Its heavy, philosophical tone balances the levity of Sukkot with a sobering restraint. The overarching message is that, whether we enjoy the prosperity of a bountiful harvest or not in life, the only true reason for our existence is to love and serve the LORD.

Simchat Torah – Rejoicing in the Torah

At the close of Sukkot comes a traditional Jewish celebration called **Simchat Torah*** שִׂמְחַת תּוֹרָה *(sim-HAT tōh-RAH)*, literally meaning "rejoicing of the Torah." The celebration is held either on Shemini Atzeret or the day after, depending on the local tradition. Since Shemini Atzeret is understood to represent "one day past complete fulfillment" as well as "the day of new beginnings or renewals," it marks the time that the synagogue's annual cycle of readings from the Torah (Genesis through Deuteronomy) is concluded and begun anew.

The word *torah* in Hebrew simply means *instruction, direction*, hence *teaching*, although in many passages it seems to express God's commandments for proper living; hence the popular English translation "law." The widely accepted "automatic" translation of "law" for *torah* in English Bibles today is rather unfortunate; it is almost too restrictive a word for the Hebrew *torah*, whose root letters come from a verb meaning *pointing, directed* or *shooting forth*. The broad implication is the *shooting forth* of light, life and blessing that results when any believer heeds the *clear direction* of God's wisdom.

Soviet Jewry rally on Simchat Torah, 1983, black and white photograph, American Jewish Historical Society collection on the American Soviet Jewry Movement, photographer unknown. Note the long line of dancing participants amid the festivities.

Depending on the context, when a traditional Jew says the word "Torah," he may either be referring to *all* of God's written instruction (the entire Old Testament, including the prophets and other writings), or just a certain portion (such as the first five books – Genesis through Deuteronomy – all written on a single scroll called a "Torah scroll"). Messianic Jews (who believe in Jesus) often expand their usage of "Torah" to include the New Testament, for it, too, contains God's words of *instruction* – His loving *direction*, given to us for our good.

---

*Pronunciation and definition notes: The "ch" of *simchat* is pronounced like a rough "h," like the *ch* in *Bach*. The Hebrew word *torah* is properly pronounced with two distinct syllables, first, "toe" (like the one on your foot) and then "rah" (with the emphasis on "RAH"). The correct Hebrew pronunciation of *torah* does not rhyme with "Laura" or "Bora Bora," but instead rhymes more with "faux pas," "Ohm's Law" or "scroll saw." *Torah* generally means *instruction* but can be extended to mean *law* under certain circumstances. An excellent example of its extended meaning is that of a human father giving strict "instruction" to his sons that they must "never play ball out in the busy street." One could rightly say that the father is "laying down the law." However, the intent of this "law" is not to catch his sons in the act so he can gleefully prosecute them; it's simply to preserve their well being. In exactly the same way, the true intent of God's *torah* is His protective, loving instruction (which only seeks the very best for us in a life of freedom) – not harsh, dictatorial domination (which seeks enslavement, subservience and oppression).

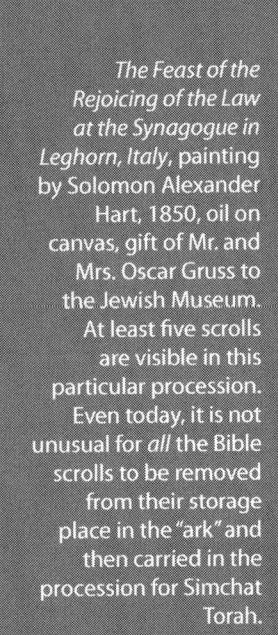

The Feast of the Rejoicing of the Law at the Synagogue in Leghorn, Italy, painting by Solomon Alexander Hart, 1850, oil on canvas, gift of Mr. and Mrs. Oscar Gruss to the Jewish Museum. At least five scrolls are visible in this particular procession. Even today, it is not unusual for *all* the Bible scrolls to be removed from their storage place in the "ark" and then carried in the procession for Simchat Torah.

Jewish congregations have some wonderful traditions for celebrating Simchat Torah. In the temple or synagogue, they joyfully carry the Torah scroll around the assembled people seven times, singing boisterous hymns and clapping along. People will leap out of their chairs and form a long line behind the Torah, dancing to the music. In orthodox communities, this dancing and singing procession may continue for some time, spilling out into the neighborhood and going all up and down the streets.

Rejoicing in God's instruction (i.e., His Word) is something we are commanded to do frequently throughout Old and New Testaments. In fact, it comes naturally to those of us who have benefited from the born-again experience. After all, Jesus is God's incarnate Word, the Torah made flesh (John 1:14). By dwelling in us, He instills His *instruction* supernaturally within us, writing all of His laws upon our hearts (Jer. 31:33). When we rejoice in the *Torah*, we are actually rejoicing in *Him*.

A closing thought – the timing of Jesus' birth

Some Bible commentators speculate that the Feast of Tabernacles not only symbolizes the *future* coming of Christ as King, but also may mark the time of His *first* coming thousands of years ago. In other words, they theorize that **the baby Jesus may have been born during the Feast of Sukkot**. The theory is based upon determining Elizabeth's husband Zechariah's assigned weeks to serve in the temple according to Scripture's account of the courses of the temple priesthood. If you are interested in learning more about this theory, read the article entitled "When was Jesus born?" in the appendix.

Build a sukkah. Wave a lulav. Eat, drink, sing, and dance around with the Torah scroll. All are invited to the festivities!

*The harvest feast of Tabernacles is a symbol of the great gathering of all nations – not just Jewish people – to love and worship the L*ORD*. The following activities for the whole family (and all your invited guests) can make the celebration that much more fun and inclusive.*

Tabernacles

**A song for Sukkot
Lulav waving ceremony
Ideas for building a sukkah
Children's crafts**

"To the sukkah"
A song about the Feast of Tabernacles

This good old traditional song is a great tune to teach the children all about Sukkot. Adults love it, too!

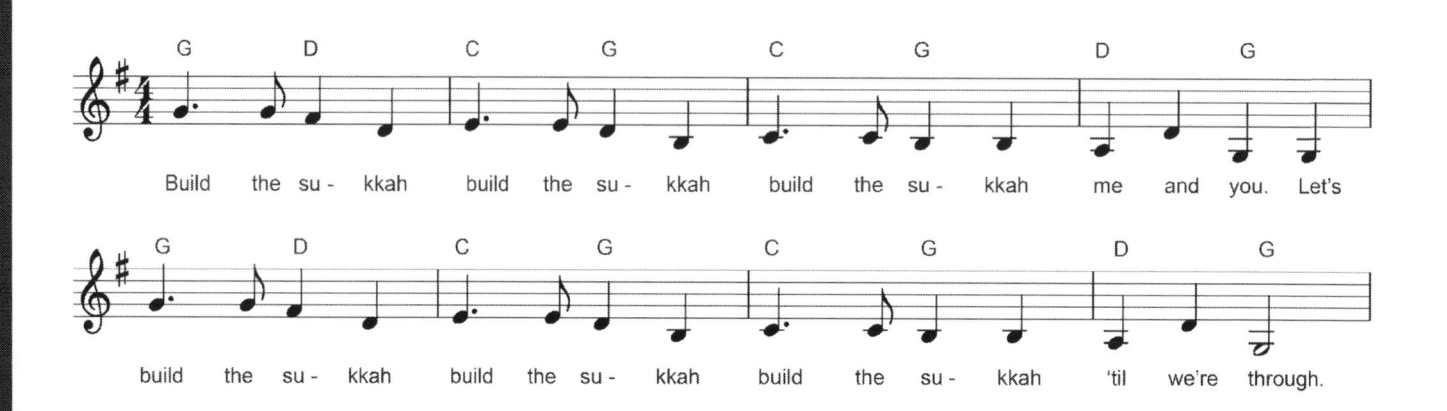

Build the su-kkah build the su-kkah build the su-kkah me and you. Let's build the su-kkah build the su-kkah build the su-kkah 'til we're through.

Let's build the sukkah, build the sukkah,
build the sukkah, me and you.
Let's build the sukkah, build the sukkah,
build the sukkah 'til we're through.

To the sukkah, to the sukkah, to the sukkah we will go.
Wave the lulav, wave the lulav, wave the lulav to and fro.

In the sukkah, in the sukkah, in the sukkah we will be.
Wave the lulav, wave the lulav,
wave the lulav because we're free.

Lulav waving ceremony

When we wave the lulav, we stand and face the east to remember Jerusalem, the holy city. While waving, we silently thank God for continuing to love His people Israel and desiring to bring them back to their land and to Himself.

All — *Saying the blessing before waving the lulav:*

Blessed are You, Lord our God, King of the Universe, Who has instilled within us the holiness of His commandments and has commanded us regarding the taking up of the lulav.

בָּרוּךְ אַתָּה, יהוה, אֱלֹהֵינוּ מֶלֶךְ הָעוֹלָם,
אֲשֶׁר קִדְּשָׁנוּ בְּמִצְוֹתָיו,
וְצִוָּנוּ עַל נְטִילַת לוּלָב.

Ba-ruch a-tah Adonai, El-o-hay-nu Meh-lech ha-O-lam, a-shayr kid-shah-nu b'-mitz-vo-tahv, v'tsih-va-nu al n'-tee-lat loo-lav.

Leader — As we wave the lulav three times in each of the four directions of the compass, let us silently petition the Lord to remember those who are His – both Jew and Gentile – who are scattered to the four corners of the earth. As we reach out and draw in with each motion, we silently thank the Lord for His desire to reach out and draw us to Himself. We lift up a silent prayer on behalf of someone who doesn't yet know the Lord, that he or she may be drawn to God and find salvation.

Face east. Hold the lulav and etrog so both hands are touching together. With a slow, gentle, waving shake, reach out and draw in. Each time you draw in, let the bottom part of lulav to touch your chest (your heart). You may follow this order:*

1 EAST: Reach out straight <u>ahead</u> of you, draw in, three times.

2 SOUTH: Reach to your <u>right</u>, draw in, three times.

3 WEST: Reach <u>behind</u> you <u>over the shoulder</u>, draw in, three times.

4 NORTH: Reach to your <u>left</u>, draw in, three times.

5 UP: Reach up <u>above</u> you and draw down, three times.

6 DOWN: Lower your hands <u>below</u> your chest and draw back up, three times.

*Another tradition uses a different order: south, north, east, up, down, west. There's also a tradition to sing the Hebrew of Psalm 118:1-4 of the Hallel along with the Hebrew "Hoshianna" – "We implore you, Lord, save us" – during the waving.

Sukkah building ideas

There are a variety of traditions in Judaism concerning the "appropriate" way to build a sukkah. Some consider it okay to decorate them; some insist that the sukkah itself should be the point of focus – its beauty is enough decoration on its own. There are, of course, many rules about minimum heights and widths if you want to go the "traditional, observant" route, but we suggest you build your first Sukkah more casually, and just allow the Holy Spirit to direct you in what is right for you and your family. We compared the "minimum requirements" of the customs throughout Judaism and arrived the following:

Build the sukkah **outdoors** under the **open sky**. Try not to have any other roof or any canopy overhanging it; you need to be able to see the stars through the roof. Keep the structure *simple* and *humble;* that is the point of a sukkah.

Walls can be any material sturdy enough not to blow away in a normal wind. This includes wood, fiberglass panels, or waterproof fabrics attached to a metal or PVC pipe frame. Pre-existing walls (like those of your home, patio or garage) can serve as one or more of the sukkah's walls.

Make a sturdy **roof** framework (wood, metal, etc) over which to lay your *sechach* (any raw, unfinished material produced by plants or trees). The *sechach* can be straw, bamboo, tree branches, palm fronds, etc. Lay them densely enough to provide daytime shade, yet sparsely enough to see the stars at night.

The tradition is to **eat all your meals** in the sukkah for the entire duration of the feast – *and* to invite guests! For this reason, you might make your sukkah more pleasant by adding lighting, chairs and tables. Some people hang colorful posters, fresh fruits, flowers or other decorations from the beams and walls.

A pergola like this one can make an excellent sukkah. Simply tack pieces of lattice around it and cover the top with sechach. Hang curtains or cloth to cover the sides to further "enclose" the walls (curtains not shown).

Jewish Family in a Sukkah, artwork, January 1882, The National Library of Israel collection. This sukkah was built of wooden boards. Note the raised floor of wooden boards, candle chandelier, table and chairs, wooden hinged doors, *sechach* roof covering, floral garlands and curtains.

This sukkah is outside Beith Yossef synagogue in Paris, France. Lattice and bamboo fencing was used for the sukkah's roof and its three temporary walls; the fourth wall is just the exterior of the existing building. Curtains hang at the entrance (the retractable "door" is a rich velvet curtain embroidered in gold with the Star of David). The interior and exterior are decorated with branches of foliage. Inside, a simple fluorescent tube fixture illuminates two folding tables. (*Français: Soucca, Synagogue Beith Yossef, Pletzl, Marais, 18 rue des Ecouffes, IVe arrondissement, Paris, France,* October 2009, photograph by Djampa.)

Children's crafts

Edible sukkah

You can help the kids make their own edible sukkah! Like those of a traditional gingerbread house, the sukkah walls may be made from gingerbread or graham crackers and held together with stiff frosting (cheap frosting from a can works fine if you don't want to bother making Royal icing; just dab some into the bottom corner of a Ziplock freezer bag, seal the top, and snip off a bit of the corner for a no-muss, no-fuss icing squeeze bag. Kids can easily "pipe" the frosting while keeping the waste and mess to a minimum). The roof rafters may be made from cinnamon sticks or pretzel sticks. The sukkah pictured at right uses cinnamon sticks, which really do look like wooden rafters. Lay pieces of parsley or cilantro across the top as the *sechach*. We've begun decorating the sukkah at right with some Jelly Belly raspberry and blackberry candies, which are attached with dots of stiff chocolate frosting. They look a little like grape clusters. We also made a table from two stacked Rolo candies topped with a pretzel square, but you could use crackers or slabs of chocolate for your furniture. You can get really creative with the furnishings and decor, perhaps even making some candy "people" to sit inside the sukkah.

Kids' craft lulav

Kids' craft lulavs can be made from just about any material. No matter *what* materials you choose, the kids are going to have lots of fun making lulavs. We've seen children's craft lulavs made from things as simple as celery sticks, parsley and string. Some people make them out of balloons (the long ones like those used for balloon animals). They can also be made from craft felt, construction paper, folded cloth napkins, painted popsicle sticks, or pens and pencils covered in silk leaves attached with green florist's tape. (Lulav pens/pencils make "doing homework" during the fall season a little more fun and a little less tedious.) A play-dough lulav, shown at right, is suitable project for kids of all ages. Play-dough lulavs are even fun for the adults to make; you might make it an all-ages activity at your next Sukkot party, with awards for "silliest lulav," "smallest lulav," "biggest lulav" or "prettiest lulav," etc. There are no limits on lulav crafts, so use your imagination! We bet you'll come up with your own unique material for making craft lulavs with your kids.

Thy Word is a lamp unto my feet and a light unto my path.

Psalm 119:105

Helpful Resources

You've just completed your study of the Feast of Tabernacles – the seventh appointed time of the LORD – which brings us to the conclusion of *Messiah's Calendar Book 2*. Before we part, we'll leave you with this appendix containing some helpful articles and a glossary/index.

May our LORD bless you as you persist in the study of His Holy Word.

Contents

Article: "Did Jesus die at the third or the sixth hour?"

Article: "Did Jesus spend 72 full hours in the grave?"

Article: "When was Jesus born?"

Glossary and Index

Indexes of Recipes, Children's Crafts and Activities, Songs and Liturgy

Other Books By James T. and Lisa M. Cummins

Did Jesus die at the third or the sixth hour?

The following article by Trevor Major, M.Sc., M.A. is reprinted by permission, courtesy of Apologetics Press (www.apologeticspress.org). It answers a common question about an apparent discrepancy in the gospels that arises upon comparing the "third hour" of Mark 15:25 with the "sixth hour" of John 19:14.

Q.

A skeptic argued the following: Mark 15:25 says that Jesus was crucified at "the third hour," but John 19:14 says that Pilate presented Jesus to the Jews at "about the sixth hour." Thus it appears that Jesus was on the cross three hours before His trial. How do we resolve this alleged biblical discrepancy?

A.

The Jews and the Romans used different standards for reckoning the hours of the day, although both systems split the day into two periods of 12 hours. A new day for the Romans began at midnight (as it does for us today), whereas a new day for the Jews began in the evening at what we would call 6 p.m.

Various clues within the fourth gospel indicate that John was using the Roman system (Geisler and Howe, 1992, p. 376). This makes sense given that John was writing outside of Palestine to a Hellenistic audience. That Mark used a Jewish system makes sense in light of the strong tradition that his gospel account follows sermons delivered by the apostle Peter (Eusebius, *Ecclesiastical History*, 3.39). As always, we have to take into account the context, as well as cultural differences between the Jewish and Gentile worlds.

Given this distinction, the problem disappears. John has Pilate handing Jesus over for crucifixion at 6 a.m., and Mark has Jesus on the cross three hours later at 9 a.m. (i.e., "the third hour"). In fact, John begins his whole account of Jesus' audience with Pilate by noting that it was "early morning" (18:28). This reference follows immediately after Peter and the rooster crowing incident. Roosters, of course, can crow at any time, but are most famous for signaling the beginning of a new day.

This is perfectly consistent with Mark's account. The previous evening, Jesus and the disciples traveled from the upper room to the Mount of Olives and then to Gethsemane. The disciples fell asleep, and Jesus had to wake them in order to meet the arresting mob. Mark records the rooster crowing incident, and notes that the Jews delivered Jesus to Pilate "in the morning" (15:1). A skeptic might doubt that the events at the Prætorium took place at such an early hour (i.e., before 6 a.m.), but there is no evidence for this objection, and there is no inconsistency in the Gospel accounts.

I would like to end with a word of warning. Skeptics are notorious for raising a dozen objections in as many minutes. As you can see, it takes a lot more time and work to answer an objection than it does to raise it. And yet, if we do not answer every objection, no matter how frivolous it may be, the skeptic claims victory. We should recognize that most skeptics have no interest in making sense out of Scripture. The powers of comprehension and interpretation they would bring to an average newspaper are left behind in the case of the Bible. Perhaps this uneven treatment should not be surprising. After all, the skeptic has much to lose if the Bible is right.

REFERENCES

Geisler, Norman and Thomas Howe (1992), *When Critics Ask* (Wheaton: IL: Victor).

Did Jesus spend 72 full hours in the grave?

The following excerpt about the reckoning of Jesus' three days in the tomb is from an article entitled "Reasoning About the Resurrection of Christ" by Eric Lyons, M.Min., as published by www.apologeticspress.org.

While statements such as "on the third day," "after three days," and "three days and three nights" may appear contradictory at first glance, in reality they harmonize perfectly if one understands the more liberal methods ancients used to reckon time. In the first century, any part of a day could be computed for the whole day and the night following it (cf. Lightfoot, 1979, pp. 210-211). The Jerusalem Talmud quotes rabbi Eleazar ben Azariah, who lived around A.D. 100, as saying: "A day and night are an Onah ['a portion of time'] and the portion of an Onah is as the whole of it" (Shabbath ix. 3, as quoted in Hoehner, 1974, 131:248-249, bracketed comment in orig.). Azariah indicated that a portion of a twenty-four hour period could be considered the same "as the whole of it." Thus, in Jesus' time one would have been correct in teaching that Jesus' burial would last "three days and three nights," even though it was not three complete 24-hour days.

Scripture is peppered with references which demonstrate that a part of a day was oftentimes equivalent to a whole day.

- According to Genesis 7:12, the rain of the Noahic Flood was upon the Earth "forty days and forty nights." Verse seventeen of that same chapter says it was on the Earth for just "forty days." Obviously, "forty days" and "forty days and forty nights" refer to the same time period in this context.

- During the reign of King Ahab, Israel and Syria "encamped opposite each other for seven days" (1 Kings 20:29). Yet, "on the seventh day the battle was joined" and Israel killed 100,000 Syrian foot soldiers (20:29). Clearly, the two armies did not occupy their camps for a full seven days, but for six days and a part of the seventh. The remainder of day seven was spent in battle.

- When Joseph's brothers came to visit him for the first time since selling him into Egyptian bondage more than a decade earlier (Genesis 37:12-36), Joseph incarcerated them for "three days" (Genesis 42:17). The text then reveals that he spoke to them "the third day," and 42:18-24 represents them as being released that day— i.e., the third day. If Joseph's brothers (with the exception of Simeon, 42:24) were released on day three of their imprisonment, then the "three days" they spent in the prison (42:17) are not equivalent to three 24-hour periods, but rather parts of three days.

- When the Israelites visited King Rehoboam and asked him to lighten their burdens (2 Chronicles 10:3-4), he wanted time to contemplate their request, so he instructed Jeroboam and the people of Israel to return "after three days" (10:5). Verse twelve of that chapter indicates that Jeroboam and the people of Israel came to Rehoboam "on the third day, as the king had directed, saying, 'Come back to me the third day.'" Fascinating, is it not, that even though Rehoboam instructed his people to return "after three days," they understood him to mean "on the third day" (cf. 1 Kings 12:5,12).

- When Queen Esther was about to risk her life by going before King Ahasuerus uninvited, she instructed her fellow Jews to follow her example by not eating or drinking "for three days, night or day" (Esther 4:16). Yet, the text then tells us that Esther went in to the king "on the third day" (5:1).

By studying these and other passages, one can see clearly that the Bible uses expressions like "three days," "the third day," "on the third day," "after three days," and "three days and three nights" to signify the same period of time. Again, "[a]ccording to the Oriental mode of reckoning, three consecutive parts of days were counted three days" (Jamieson, et. al., 1997).

From Acts 10, we can glean further insight into the ancient practice of counting consecutive days (in part or in whole) as complete days. Luke recorded how an angel appeared to Cornelius at "about the ninth hour of the day" (approximately 3:00 p.m.; 10:3). "The next day" (10:9) Peter received a vision from God and welcomed visitors sent by Cornelius. "On the next day" (10:23) Peter and the servants of Cornelius departed for Caesarea. "And the following day they entered Caesarea" where Peter taught Cornelius and his household the Gospel (10:24). At one point during Peter's visit, Cornelius spoke about his encounter with the angel of God. Notice carefully how he began the rehearsal of the event. He stated: "Four days ago to this hour, I was praying in my house during the ninth hour..." (10:30, NASB). Although the event really had occurred only 72 hours (or three literal days) earlier, Cornelius spoke of it as taking place "four days ago to this hour." Why four days instead of three? Because according to the first-century method of reckoning time, a part of the first day and a part of the fourth day were counted as whole days. Surely one can see how this information aligns itself perfectly with Jesus' burial taking place on Friday and His resurrection occurring on Sunday. A part of Friday, all day Saturday, and a part of Sunday would be considered three days in ancient times, not one or two.

Even though in 21st-century America some may find this reasoning somewhat confusing, similar idiomatic expressions are used frequently today. For example, we consider a baseball game that ends after only completing 8½ innings a "9-inning game." And even though the losing pitcher on the visiting team only pitched 8 innings (and not 9 innings like the winning pitcher from the home team), he is said to have pitched a complete game. Think about the college student who explains to his professor that he worked on a research project "day and night for four weeks." He obviously does not mean that he worked for a solid 672 hours (24 hours x 7 days x 4 weeks) without sleeping. It may be that he worked from 6:00 a.m. to 12:00 a.m. for four weeks on the project, but not 672 sleepless hours. If he only slept five or six hours a night, and worked on the project nearly every hour he was awake, we would consider this person as one who truly did work "day and night for four weeks." Finally, consider the guest at a hotel who checks in at 5:00 p.m. on Wednesday, and checks out at 3:30 p.m. Thursday—less than 24 hours later. Did the man stay one day or two days at the hotel? Technically, the guest was there for less than one full day (24-hour period), yet the hotel legally can charge him for two days since he did not leave before the mandatory 11:00 a.m. checkout time. Considering how flexible we are in measuring time, perhaps we should not be surprised at how liberal the ancients were in calculating time.

Further evidence proving that Jesus' statements regarding His burial were not contradictory center around the fact that even His enemies did not accuse Him of contradicting Himself. No doubt this was due to their familiarity with and use of the flexible, customary method of stating time. In fact, the chief priests and Pharisees even said to Pilate the day after Jesus was crucified: "Sir, we remember, while He was still alive, how that deceiver said, 'After three days I will rise.' Therefore command that the tomb be made secure until the third day" (Matthew 27:63-64). The phrase "after three days" must have been equivalent to "the third day," else surely the Pharisees would have asked for a guard of soldiers until the fourth day. Interesting, is it not, that modern skeptics charge Jesus with contradicting Himself, but not the hypercritical Pharisees of His own day.

The idiomatic expressions that Jesus and the Bible writers employed to denote how long Jesus would remain in the grave does not mean that He literally was buried for 72 hours. If we interpret the account of Jesus' crucifixion, burial, and resurrection in light of the cultural setting of the first century, and not according to the present-day (mis)understanding of skeptics, we find no errors in any of the expressions that Jesus and the gospel writers used.

REFERENCES:

Barker, Dan (1992), *Losing Faith in Faith* (Madison, WI: Freedom from Religion Foundation).

Barker, Dan (1996), "Did Jesus Really Rise from the Dead?," Debate with Michael Horner at the University of Northern Iowa, April 2, [On-line], URL: http://www.infidels.org/library/modern/dan_barker/barker_horner.html.

Butt, Kyle (2002), "Jesus Christ—Dead or Alive?," *Reason & Revelation*, 22[2]:9-15, February.

Clarke, Adam (1996), *Adam Clarke's Commentary* (Electronic Database: Biblesoft).

Hoehner, Harold W. (1974), "Chronological Aspects of the Life of Christ—Part IV: The Day of Christ's Crucifixion," *Bibliotheca Sacra*, 131:241-264, July.

Jamieson, Robert, et al. (1997), *Jamieson, Fausset, Brown Bible Commentary* (Electronic Database: Biblesoft).

Josephus, Flavius (1987 edition), "Antiquities of the Jews," *The Works of Josephus*, trans. William Whiston (Peabody, MA: Hendrickson).

Kistemaker, Simon J. (1993), *Exposition of the First Epistle to the Corinthians* (Grand Rapids, MI: Baker).

Lightfoot, John (1979 reprint), *A Commentary on the New Testament from the Talmud and Hebraica* (Grand Rapids, MI: Baker).

McKinsey, C. Dennis (no date), "The Bible is God's Word?" [On-line], URL: http://members.aol.com/ckbloomfld/pamphlets.html.

McKinsey, C. Dennis (1983), "Commentary," *Biblical Errancy*, February.

McKinsey, C. Dennis (2000), *Biblical Errancy* (Amherst, NY: Prometheus).

Rusk, Roger (1974), "The Day He Died," *Christianity Today*, March 29.

Scroggie, W. Graham (1948), *A Guide to the Gospels* (London: Pinkering & Inglis).

When was Jesus born?

The following article is by Jim and Lisa Cummins. It presents some evidence for the theory that Jesus may have been born during the Feast of Tabernacles.

Why should we care?

Each year with the onset of Christmas, the question is inevitably raised about what was the *actual* season of the birth of Yeshua (Jesus). For people who celebrate Christmas as a mere social observance, this question is so unimportant as to be laughable. However, for people who love God's Word and seek the clearest possible understanding of it, the answer to this question can be very important. All the major events of Yeshua's life and ministry correlate with and are prophesied by God's biblical "appointed times" (i.e., "the feasts of the LORD"). Therefore, we should not be too surprised about the possibility that His birth, too, might correlate with one of God's appointed times.

Does the Bible provide a way to calculate the timing of Yeshua's birth?

The answer is a resounding YES. There are actually several biblical evidences which give clear references to the time of year, making it possible to calculate the season in which Yeshua was born.

The Rotation of the Courses of the Priesthood

The key to establishing the timing of Yeshua's birth is based in part upon establishing the time of the birth of his cousin Yochanan (John). And the key to establishing Yochanan's birth is to be found in the **rotation of the courses of the priesthood.** *Huh? The rotation of the what?* We'll explain.

In temple times, the temple tasks were assigned to the priests, and each of the priests was only responsible for his tasks for half a month. So, all the priestly families were divided into 24 groups, or *courses*, in order that everyone could take their turn doing the ministry for their assigned two weeks per year. We can find the time divisions for the courses of the priesthood in 1 Chronicles 24:1-19, where King David divided the priestly families into 24 groups. Of course, during certain times of year, *all* the priests had to show up to work at the temple, such as at Passover, Pentecost (Weeks) and Sukkot (Tabernacles), but they served to provide additional help to the priests who were *already* there, serving their appointed two weeks.[1]

The text of 1 Chronicles 24:1-19 describes how lots were drawn to determine the order of the courses. Picking up from verse 7,

> The first lot fell to Jehoiarib, the second to Jedaiah, the third to Harim, the fourth to Seorim, the fifth to Malkijah, the sixth to Mijamin, the seventh to Hakkoz, **the eighth to Abijah**, the ninth to Jeshua, the tenth to Shekaniah, the eleventh to Eliashib, the twelfth to Jakim, the thirteenth to Huppah, the fourteenth to Jeshebeab, the fifteenth to Bilgah, the sixteenth to Immer, the seventeenth to Hezir, the eighteenth to Happizzez, the nineteenth to Pethahiah, the twentieth to Jehezkel, the twenty-first to Jakin, the twenty-second to Gamul, the twenty-third to Delaiah and the twenty-fourth to Maaziah. This was their appointed order of ministering when they entered the temple of the LORD, according to the regulations prescribed for them by their ancestor Aaron, as the LORD, the God of Israel, had commanded him.

You'll notice we bolded and underlined the **eighth course, the course of Abijah** in the above text. We'll explain the significance of this phrase in the next section.

Examining the New Testament accounts

Let's turn now to the account of Luke 1:5-27, which describes the miraculous angelic prophecy announcing the future conception and birth of Yochanan (John).

> [5]In the time of Herod king of Judea there was a priest named **Zechariah, who belonged to the priestly division of Abijah;** his wife Elizabeth was also a descendant of Aaron. [6]Both of them were righteous in the sight of God, observing all the Lord's commands and decrees blamelessly. [7]But they were childless because Elizabeth was not able to conceive, and they were both very old.
>
> [8]**Once when Zechariah's division was on duty and he was serving as priest before God,** [9]he was chosen by lot, according to the custom of the priesthood, to go into the temple of the Lord and burn incense. [10]And when the time for the burning of incense came, all the assembled worshipers were praying outside.
>
> [11]Then an angel of the Lord appeared to him, standing at the right side of the altar of incense. [12]When Zechariah saw him, he was startled and was gripped with fear. [13]But the angel said to him: "Do not be afraid, Zechariah; your prayer has been heard. Your wife Elizabeth will bear you a son, and you are to call him John. [14]He will be a joy and delight to you, and many will rejoice because of his birth, [15]for he will be great in the sight of the Lord. He is never to take wine or other fermented drink, and he will be filled with the Holy Spirit even before he is born. [16]He will bring back many of the people of Israel to the Lord their God. [17]And he will go on before the Lord, in the spirit and power of Elijah, to turn the hearts of the parents to their children and the disobedient to the wisdom of the righteous—to make ready a people prepared for the Lord."
>
> [18]Zechariah asked the angel, "How can I be sure of this? I am an old man and my wife is well along in years."
>
> [19]The angel said to him, "I am Gabriel. I stand in the presence of God, and I have been sent to speak to you and to tell you this good news. [20]And now you will be silent and not able to speak until the day this happens, because you did not believe my words, which will come true at their appointed time."
>
> [21]Meanwhile, the people were waiting for Zechariah and wondering why he stayed so long in the temple. [22]When he came out, he could not speak to them. They realized he had seen a vision in the temple, for he kept making signs to them but remained unable to speak.
>
> [23]**When his time of service was completed, he returned home.** [24]**After this his wife Elizabeth became pregnant and for five months remained in seclusion.** [25]"The Lord has done this for me," she said. "In these days he has shown his favor and taken away my disgrace among the people."
>
> [26]**In the sixth month of Elizabeth's pregnancy,** God sent the angel Gabriel to Nazareth, a town in Galilee, [27]to a virgin pledged to be married to a man named Joseph, a descendant of David. And the virgin's name was Mary.

From this passage, we learn that Zechariah was a member of the **course of Abijah** (Lk 1:5), which is the **eighth course**, according to 1 Chronicles 24:10. If we begin the order of the courses starting with the first biblical month of Nisan, **then the course of Abijah would have fallen on the final two weeks of the fourth month (Tammuz).**[1] Tammuz corresponds to June/July of our western calendar. The graphic below illustrates how the priestly courses correspond to both the biblical calendar and western calendar. (Only the first eight courses are shown.)

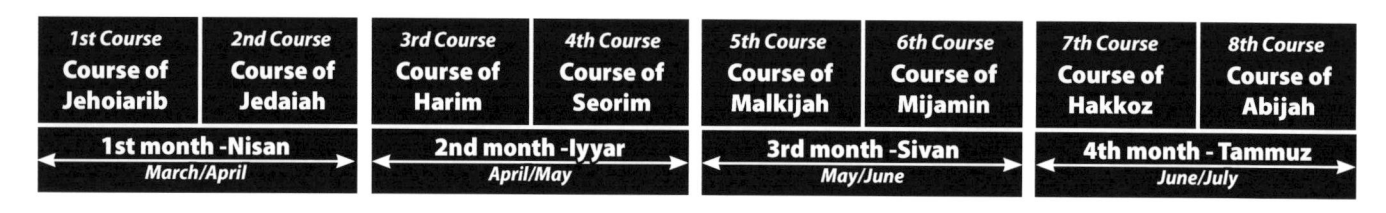

1st Course	2nd Course	3rd Course	4th Course	5th Course	6th Course	7th Course	8th Course
Course of Jehoiarib	Course of Jedaiah	Course of Harim	Course of Seorim	Course of Malkijah	Course of Mijamin	Course of Hakkoz	Course of Abijah
1st month - Nisan (March/April)		2nd month - Iyyar (April/May)		3rd month - Sivan (May/June)		4th month - Tammuz (June/July)	

This tells us that the announcement by Gabriel to Zechariah was during the latter half of the month of Tammuz, because Zechariah's course (the course of Abijah) would have been on duty at that time.

The text goes on to speak of Elizabeth's conception of Yochanan (v. 23-24). Though the words "after this" are somewhat inexact, it's not unreasonable to conclude that **the conception occurred during the month of Av** – the month coming just "after" the month Tammuz and "after" Zechariah's time of service at the temple.

Luke 1:24 then states that Elizabeth "hid herself for five months." The text goes on to say in verse 26 that **"in the sixth month (of Elizabeth's pregnancy)" the angel Gabriel was sent from God to make his announcement to Miriam (Mary) of the coming birth of the Messiah.** Luke 1:36 corroborates the fact that Elizabeth was in her sixth month of pregnancy during the angel's visit to Mary, for the angel clearly states this to Mary during his discussion with her: "Even Elizabeth your relative is going to have a child in her old age, and she who was said to be unable to conceive is **in her sixth month.**"

Calculating the probable birth month of Yeshua

From here it becomes just a matter of calculating the normal gestation periods for Yochanan and Yeshua, to arrive at the month of Yeshua's birth. Once we know what month Yochanan was born, we add six months to determine what month Yeshua was born, because we know that Elizabeth was already six months pregnant at the time of Yeshua's conception.

Yochanan was conceived in the fifth month (Av, corresponding to July/August). Counting off nine months brings us to a birth month of Nisan (March/April). Adding six months to this month brings us to the very special month of Tishri, during which occur the most holy feasts of the year according to Leviticus 23: *Yom Teruah* (Day of Trumpets), *Yom Kippur* (Day of Atonement) and *Sukkot* (the Feast of Tabernacles or Booths). Below is a graphic showing the twelve months of the biblical year, the likely months of John's conception and birth, and the likely **month of Yeshua's birth: Tishri.** For convenience in calculation, our graphic begins with the month of the year that John was conceived, and continues on through a second year to bring us to the probable birth month of Yeshua:

				Av Jul/Aug • Yochanan Conceived	Elul Aug/Sep	Tishri Sep/Oct	Cheshvan Oct/Nov	Kislev Nov/Dec	Tevet Dec/Jan	Sh'vat Jan/Feb	Adar Feb/Mar
Nisan Mar/Apr • Yochanan Born	Iyyar Apr/May	Sivan May/Jun	Tammuz Jun/Jul	Av Jul/Aug	Elul Aug/Sep	Tishri Sep/Oct • Yeshua Born	Cheshvan Oct/Nov	Kislev Nov/Dec	Tevet Dec/Jan	Sh'vat Jan/Feb	Adar Feb/Mar

The meaning of Tabernacles expressed in the birth of Yeshua

The possibility of Yeshua's birth in Tishri is all the more astounding when compared with the prophetic significance of the Feast of Tabernacles (Sukkot). In accordance with God's commandments in Leviticus 23:34-43, Jewish people continue to this day to cut branches from leafy trees and live in booths, or tabernacles, reminding them of God's shelter in the wilderness and His promise to come and dwell among them one day during the millennial reign as Messiah. They wave branches before the Lord, symbolic of the "ingathering" or harvest of all the souls who would return in repentance to the one true God. As the feast occurs at the conclusion of the harvest each year, the harvest theme of ingathering is very appropriate. The entire feast is symbolic of the coming of Messiah to dwell among His ingathered people. **What could be more fulfilling of the prophetic Feast of Tabernacles than the birth of Messiah in a temporary dwelling (a stable, a temporary dwelling for the King – a *sukkah*)?** "Emmanuel" – Hebrew for "God with us" – had come down from heaven to **dwell among us**.

Another beautiful scriptural clue to this mystery exists in Isaiah's famous Messianic prophecy (chapter 9) speaking of the never-ending reign of Yeshua, which he clearly links to the birth of a Child:

> ²The people walking in darkness have seen a great light; on those living in the land of deep darkness a light has dawned. ³You have enlarged the nation and increased their joy; **they rejoice before you as people rejoice at the harvest...** ⁶**For to us a child is born,** to us a son is given, and **the government will be on his shoulders**. And he will be called Wonderful Counselor, Mighty God, Everlasting Father, Prince of Peace. ⁷**Of the greatness of his government and peace there will be no end. He will reign on David's throne and over his kingdom, establishing and upholding it with justice and righteousness from that time on and forever.**

God presents here, as if in a single unit, the separate themes of the Feast of Tabernacles ("the harvest," "the harvest of rejoicing", or "the feast of joy," terms synonymous with the Feast of Tabernacles throughout Scripture), along with the *birth* of Messiah and the *millennial reign* to come, of which Tabernacles is the prophetic symbol.

But there is yet another clue to the Feast of Tabernacles being the likely time period of the birth of Yeshua, one which is hidden in the New Testament. A look at the Greek wording of John 1:14 brings out intriguing connections:

> The Word became flesh and **made his dwelling** among us. We have seen his glory, the glory of the one and only Son, who came from the Father, full of grace and truth.

In the original Greek language, the phrase **"made his dwelling"** is the word *eskēnōsen* εσκήνωσεν, which more accurately should be translated **"tabernacled."** This Greek verb literally means "to pitch a tent, to dwell in a tent, to encamp." (See Strong's #4636 root definition). It brings to mind the temporary, tent-like dwellings of Sukkot. In fact, the Greek root *skēnē, tabernacle* σκηνή found in the Greek word above is the very same root in the New Testament's term for the Feast of Tabernacles, *skēnopēgia* σκηνοπηγία.

Therefore, we see that **the very wording that the Holy Spirit chose to employ in John 1:14 provides a connection between the concept of the Feast of Tabernacles and the incarnation of Messiah.**

Other support for Tabernacles being the time period of Yeshua's birth

- **No room at the inn**. Apart from the census itself, the most likely cause for there being no room at the inn would have been the massive influx of Jewish people coming to Jerusalem to observe the Feast of Tabernacles, as was required by God's commandment. The bedroom community of Bethlehem, just five miles from Jerusalem, would have been flooded with visitors, both before and during the festival. According to John O. Reid (*When Was Jesus Born?*), "Joseph and Mary had to find shelter in a barn or some other kind of animal shelter like a cave or grotto because the inns were full (vs. 7). This indicates that the pilgrims from around the world had begun to arrive in Jerusalem and surrounding towns. Thus, the fall festival season had already commenced. There would have been no similar influx of pilgrims in December."

- **The timing of the census** would (most likely) have immediately followed the fall harvest. According to Reid, "The census of Quirinius [Cyrenius] that required Joseph to travel from Galilee to Bethlehem would most probably have taken place after the fall harvest when people were more able to return to their ancestral homes. Besides, it was customary in Judea to do their tax collecting during this period, as the bulk of a farmer's income came at this time."

- **The tradition that "Elijah" was expected at Passover** - A part of the traditional seder (order of the service) during the Passover meal is to open the door and look expectantly for Elijah to "return" so that he may announce the coming of Messiah. This symbolic tradition expresses the prevalent belief within Judaism that Elijah was responsible to usher in the Messiah, and that Elijah's return would occur during the season of Passover/Unleavened Bread. Yeshua addressed this very topic when His disciples asked him in Matthew 17:10, "Why then do the teachers of the law say that Elijah must come first?" Verses 11-13 state:

    > [11]Jesus replied, "To be sure, Elijah comes and will restore all things. [12]But I tell you, **Elijah has already come**, and they did not recognize him, but have done to him everything they wished. In the same way the Son of Man is going to suffer at their hands." [13]Then the disciples understood that **he was talking to them about John the Baptist**.

In Matthew 11:14, Jesus stated of John, "And if you are willing to accept it, **he is the Elijah who was to come**." Also, as we read in the preceding pages, the angel Gabriel prophesied to Zechariah that Yochanan would "go on before the Lord, in the **spirit and power of Elijah**, to turn the hearts of the parents to their children and the disobedient to the wisdom of the righteous—to make ready a people prepared for the Lord."

If we accept the calculation model that Yochanan was indeed born in the month Nisan, it means he would have "arrived" during the very month in which the Passover is celebrated. **Therefore, this "Elijah" (John) would have been born during the month Nisan, precisely when Elijah was traditionally expected to return.** If this is true, it may lend further support to the theory that the birth of Messiah actually *did* occur in the month of **Tishri,** because Nisan precedes Tishri by six months, and we know that Yochanan's birth preceded Yeshua's by six months.

---

[1]Most scholars believe the two weeks of priestly service were served *consecutively*, but a minority of scholars think the two weeks could have been split up so that the first week of service was performed in the first half of the year, and the second week was performed in the second half of the year. *All* scholars agree that all the priestly courses were present at the Temple in Jerusalem for the "shalosh regalim", the three annual feasts of Deut. 16:16 that the Lord required attendance in Jerusalem. For the purposes of our calculations in this paper, we went with the prevalent view of two *consecutive* weeks. If you are interested in discovering what other time periods might align with the birth of Yeshua, you might try writing out the priestly courses on a biblical calendar so that they would have been served *one* week at a time, and see what other possible birth months of Jesus may arise. There are *several* possible birth months, as you might expect. As in all matters "not essential to salvation," the question of the timing of Yeshua's birth must *always* be explored under the peaceable freedom of the Spirit of God, and must *never* be permitted to grow into a source of contention between believers.

Glossary and Index

Abib *ah-BEEB* • the pre-exilic name of the first biblical month. (19, 20, 52)

Adar *ah-DAR* • the post-exilic name of the twelfth biblical month. In leap years, there are two months of Adar: Adar I (also called *Adar Aleph* or *Adar Rishon*) and Adar II (also called *Adar Bet* or *Adar Sheni*.) (21, 126)

Adon Olam *ah-DŌHN o-LAHM* • a term transliterated from Hebrew meaning "Lord of the Universe" or "Eternal Lord;" the name of a traditional hymn sung during the **High Holidays**. (133)

Al Chet *ahl ḤAYT* • a term transliterated from Hebrew meaning "for the sin;" the name of a traditional liturgy of confession and repentance recited on the **Day of Atonement**. (158)

appointed time • in biblical terminology, a day or period of days which God designates for His own specific, holy purposes. See also **moadim**. (22-25)

Aseret Ha Dibrot *ah-SEH-ret hah dih-BRŌT* • a term transliterated from Hebrew meaning "ten utterances" or "ten statements," the ten basic principles of Exodus 20:1-17 encompassing all of the hundreds of God's commandments throughout the Bible. These ten statements are frequently called "the ten commandments" in western culture. (113)

Atonement, Day of • An appointed time of the Lord held on Tishri 10. See full definition under **Yom Kippur**. (21, 23, 127, 141-153)

Av *ahv* • the post-exilic name of the fifth biblical month. (20)

Awe, Days of • the ten days between Tishri 1 (Feast of Trumpets) and Tishri 10 (Day of Atonement) during which traditional Jews repent of their sins of the prior year. (119, 141)

Avinu, Malkeinu *ah-VEE-noo, mal-KAY-noo* • a term transliterated from Hebrew meaning "Our Father, Our King;" the name of a traditional hymn sung during the **High Holidays**. (156)

azazel *ah-zah-ZEL* • a word transliterated from the Hebrew for "dismissal"; the "scapegoat" which was sent into the wilderness, bearing away Israel's sins on the Day of Atonement. (145)

BCE • "before common era" – a synonym for BC ("before Christ"). Also abbreviated *B.C.E.*, *b.c.e.* or *bce*. This term is used in scientific and academic publications which attempt to maintain a neutral position with regard to religious beliefs. Also commonly used in Jewish publications. See also **CE**.

Bedikat Chametz *b'-dee-KAHT ḥah-MAYTZ* • a term transliterated from Hebrew meaning "examination for that which is leavened," i.e., the search for leaven. (56-57, 60)

biblical calendar • The calendar system devised by God in Scripture, which begins its year with the month Nisan. (15, 19, 20-21, 126)

Booths, Feast of • see **Sukkot**.

Glossary and Index, *continued*

b'rachah *b'rah-ḤAH* • a word transliterated from Hebrew meaning "blessing"; a benediction directed to the Lord. (37)

Bul *bool* • the pre-exilic name of the eighth biblical month. (21)

CE • "common era" – a synonym for AD (*Anno Domini*, Latin, "in the year of the Lord"). Also abbreviated *C.E., c.e.* or *ce*. This term is used in scientific and academic publications which attempt to maintain a neutral position with regard to religious beliefs. Also commonly used in Jewish publications. See also **BCE**.

Chag Ha Matzah *ḥag hah-mah-tsah* • a term transliterated from Hebrew meaning "feast of unleavened bread." In Hebrew Scripture it is written in plural form, Chag Ha Matsot (*ḥag hah-mah-tsōt.*) See also **Unleavened Bread.** (20, 23)

challah *ḤAH-lah* • from a Hebrew word meaning "loaf" or "cake," also transliterated *hallah* – a braided, leavened bread traditionally served on the weekly sabbath or on special sabbaths. (128-129)

chametz *ḥah-MAYTZ* • a term transliterated from Hebrew meaning "that which is leavened." (49, 56-57, 60)

Chanukah *ḥah-noo-kah* • a term transliterated from Hebrew meaning "dedication." Also transliterated *Hanukah*, *Hanukkah*, etc. Chanukah is a man-made feast (one which Jesus nevertheless attended at the temple and in no way refuted, cf. John 10:22 and context) commemorating the miraculous deliverance, cleansing and rededicating of the temple after a particular "abomination of desolation" which occurred during the Maccabean period. The entire historical event acts as a spiritual type symbolizing the ultimate fall of the coming Antichrist at the command of Messiah Yeshua. (19, 21)

charoset *ḥah-ro-set* • a sweet, chopped apple and nut mixture eaten during the Passover **seder**. (41, 45)

Cheshvan or **Marcheshvan** *ḥesh-VAHN, mar-ḥesh-VAHN* • the post-exilic name of the eighth biblical month. (21)

chodesh *ḤŌ-desh* • a word transliterated from Hebrew meaning "month." From the Hebrew root *chadash*, meaning "to renew, to repair."

civil calendar • a calendar (in any country) which is used for civil, official or administrative purposes. See also **Jewish civil calendar.** (125, 126)

Counting the Omer • a shorthand term for the activity of counting the fifty days from Firstfruits to the Feast of Weeks. "Omer" is a word transliterated from Hebrew, meaning "sheaf." See also **S'firat Ha-Omer**. (72, 74, 81-92)

Glossary and Index, *continued*

Eighth Day of Assembly • see **Shemini Atzeret.**

Elul *eh-LOOL* • the post-exilic name of the sixth biblical month. (20, 126)

Etanim *ay-tah-NEEM* • the pre-exilic name of the seventh biblical month. (21)

"Fast, The" • "The Fast" is the fast day of **Yom Kippur**, the **Day of Atonement**, the only fast commanded by God in Scripture. (142)

Firstfruits, Feast of • a feast of the LORD held Nisan 16. See also its Hebrew name, **Yom Ha Bikkurim**. Jesus was resurrected on this date. (20, 22-24, 65-75, 100, 107)

Four Species • the branches of the palm, myrtle and willow, along with the fruit of the citron, which are "taken up" (waved) during the Feast of Tabernacles. See also **lulav**. (170-171, 185)

Gregorian calendar • also called the "western calendar" – the calendar currently used in America, Europe and western society, containing the months January, February, etc. So named for Pope Gregory XIII, who decreed its use in 1582 CE. This calendar is a modification of the earlier Julian calendar, which was decreed in 46 BCE by Julius Caesar. (19)

haggadah *hah-gah-dah* • a term transliterated from the Hebrew word for "telling," a booklet containing the story of Passover and the order of the **seder**. (36, 39-44)

hallah *HAH-lah* • from a Hebrew word meaning "loaf" or "cake," also transliterated *challah* – a braided, leavened bread traditionally served on the weekly sabbath or on special sabbaths. (128-129)

High Holidays • the time of year spanning the fall feasts of the LORD, thereby including the Day of Trumpets, the Day of Atonement and the Feast of Tabernacles. Also called the "High Holy Days."

holy convocation • a day or other time period designated by God for a holy, formal assembly of the people.

Hoshana Rabbah *ho-shah nah rah-bah* • a term transliterated from Hebrew, literally meaning "save please, great!" sometimes translated "the Great Save Now" – Israel's plea to her Messiah for deliverance, a litany traditionally sung or cried out during the Feast of Tabernacles. (176-177)

Ingathering, Feast of • Another of God's names for the Feast of Tabernacles. (169)

Iyar *ee-YAR* • the post-exilic name of the second biblical month. (20, 97, 100)

Jewish civil calendar • a civil calendar developed by Jewish people (in ancient Israel, but also continuing in the modern Diaspora) initially for the purpose of keeping track of planting, harvesting, tithing and land leases. The Jewish civil calendar begins its year with the month Tishri. (125-126)

Glossary and Index, *continued*

kapporet *kah-PO-ret* • a word transliterated from Hebrew for "propitiation" – the "mercy seat" or "seat of grace"; the gold lid with two cherubim which covered the ark of the covenant and over which the glory of God would appear. (143)

Kislev *kiss-lev* • the post-exilic name of the ninth biblical month. (21)

Kol Nidre *kōl nee-dray* • a term transliterated from Hebrew/Aramaic meaning "all vows"; the name of a liturgical hymn performed on **Yom Kippur**. (151, 157)

lulav *loo-lahv* • a word transliterated from Hebrew meaning "palm leaf" or "palm twig" – a shorthand term referring to the bundle of branches of the palm, myrtle and willow, which are "taken up" (waved) during the Feast of Tabernacles. See also **four species**. (170-171, 185)

lunar calendar • a calendar in which the first day of every month is determined by the cycle of the moon. (19)

Ma Nishtanah *mah nish-tah-nah* • a term transliterated from Hebrew meaning "how different!" – the name of a song sung by a child during the Passover **seder**. The song asks four questions, providing the adults the opportunity to answer them and "tell the story" of Passover. (44)

Marcheshvan • see **Cheshvan**.

Mashiach *mah-SHEE-ah* • a word transliterated from Hebrew meaning "Anointed One" or "Messiah," often translated via Greek into English as the term "Christ." The Hebrew title of *Mashiach*, the Anointed One, may be used in conjunction with the name Yeshua as "Yeshua ha Mashiach," meaning "Jesus the Christ."

matzah • a term transliterated from Hebrew meaning "unleavened bread." Also spelled variantly as *matsah, matza*, etc. (32, 37, 43, 45, 61)

Melech, Ozer *MEH-leh, o-ZAYR* • a term transliterated from Hebrew meaning "O King, O Helper" – the name of a traditional hymn sung during the **High Holidays**. (132)

Messianic believer • a Jewish person who believes in Jesus (Hebrew, *Yeshua*) as Messiah and LORD, and who has received His free gift of salvation by grace through faith (and not by works), and who chooses to continue to embrace those elements of Jewish culture which are biblical, such as God's calendar. Also, the term "Messianic believer" may apply to a Gentile who chooses to participate in a similar style of biblical worship. "Messianic congregations" are comprised of born-again Jews and Gentiles who choose to join together in a Messianic style of worship.

moadim *mo-ah-DEEM* • a plural word transliterated from Hebrew meaning "appointed times." (22-23)

Glossary and Index, *continued*

new moon • the phase of the moon when it first becomes visible as a slender crescent (as defined by ancient Judaism for religious purposes. For the modern astronomical definition, see **waxing crescent**). The presence of the new moon signals the beginning of the biblical month. See also **Rosh Chodesh.** (19, 122, 128)

Nisan *nee-SAHN* • the post-exilic name of the first biblical month. (19-24, 29-30, 33, 51, 65-68, 70-71, 73, 97, 99-100, 126)

Passover • See also its Hebrew name, **Pesach**. It was on the date of Passover, Nisan 14, that Jesus was crucified. (20, 22-24, 27-45, 51-52, 54, 56-57, 65-66, 70, 99)

Pentecost • A word originating from the Greek meaning "fiftieth." Pentecost is a synonym for the Feast of Weeks. See also **Shavuot** and **Weeks, Feast of.** (20, 22-24, 65, 72, 74, 96-115)

Pesach *PEH-saḥ* • a word transliterated from Hebrew, meaning "Passover." Commanded by God to be held on Nisan 14, this is also the date of Jesus' crucifixion. See also **Passover.** (20, 23-24, 29-45)

pilgrimage feasts • the three feasts of the LORD which God commanded to be held in Jerusalem: Passover/Unleavened Bread, Weeks and Tabernacles. See also **shalosh regalim.** (99, 167)

post-exilic • literally, "after the exile." In the case of Israel, this refers to the time period after Israel's exile in Babylon. Post-exilic biblical month names came from the Babylonian culture and language. (19)

pre-exilic • literally, "before the exile." In the case of Israel, this refers to the time period before Israel was exiled to Babylon. Pre-exilic biblical month names came from the Canaanite culture and language. (19)

Purim *poo-REEM* • a word transliterated from Hebrew, meaning "lots" – the name of a man-made feast held in the month Adar, celebrating God's miraculous deliverance of the Jewish people as described in the book of Esther. (19, 21)

religious calendar • a calendar whose purpose is to keep track of religious observances. Also called an "ecclesiastical calendar." The Jewish religious calendar, with the exception of some additional man-made fast days and a few minor feast days, is otherwise identical to God's biblical calendar, which begins its year with the month Nisan.

Rosh Chodesh *rōsh Ḥō-desh* • a term transliterated from Hebrew meaning "head of the month" – the first day of the biblical month. See also **new moon.**

Rosh Hashanah *rōsh hah-shah-NAH* • a term transliterated from Hebrew, meaning "head of the year" – the first day of the Jewish civil year, which is Tishri 1. See also **Yom Teruah.** (125-127, 149)

sabbath • a day or other time period designated by God as a day of rest, on which no regular work is to be done. A sabbath may or may not additionally be designated as a **holy convocation,** on which assembly of the people would then be required as well.

Glossary and Index, *continued*

seder *SAY-der* • from the Hebrew word for "order, orderly arrangement" – the traditional order in which the ceremonies of Passover are performed. (36-44)

S'firat Ha-Omer *s'fee-RAHT hah-oh-MAYR* • a term transliterated from Hebrew meaning "counting of the omer" in which the fifty days from Firstfruits to the Feast of Weeks are counted. "Omer" is a word transliterated from Hebrew meaning "sheaf." See also **Counting the Omer**. (72, 74, 81-92)

shalosh regalim *sha-lōhsh r'-gah-leem* • a term transliterated from Hebrew literally meaning "the three feet" or "the three steps" – the three pilgrimage feasts which the Lord commanded to be held in Jerusalem: Passover/Unleavened Bread, Weeks and Tabernacles. See also **pilgrimage feasts**. (99, 167)

Shavuot *sha-voo-ŌT* • a word transliterated from Hebrew meaning "weeks" – an appointed time of the Lord held on Sivan 6, exactly fifty days following Firstfruits, from which is derived its Greek-based name, *Pentecost*, meaning "fifty." See also **Weeks, Feast of.** (20, 23, 97-115)

Shehecheyanu *sheh-heh-ḥeh-YAH-nu* • a term transliterated from Hebrew meaning "Who has granted us life" – the name of a blessing sung whenever enjoying something pleasant for the very first time or the first time that year, such as observing one of God's feasts, or being blessed to gather in a certain crop. (112)

Shemini Atzeret *sh'mee-NEE ah-TSAYR-et* • a term transliterated from Hebrew meaning "eighth day of assembly," the conclusion to the Feast of Tabernacles. (179-180)

Shevat *sh'-VAHT* • the post-exilic name of the eleventh biblical month. (21, 126)

shofar *shō-FAR* • a word transliterated from Hebrew, meaning a ram's horn which is hollowed out for use as a trumpet in biblical religious observances or to announce the **new moon.** Also once used in ancient Israel as a battle signal or alarm. (102, 106, 119-125, 127-129, 135, 150)

Simchat Torah *sim-ḥat to-RAH* • a term transliterated from Hebrew meaning (roughly) "rejoicing in the Torah" – a celebration of God's Word which is held at the conclusion of the Feast of Tabernacles. The Torah scroll is carried in processional, read aloud and rolled back to its beginning place at Genesis 1:1. (180-181)

Sivan *see-VAHN* • the post-exilic name of the third biblical month. (20, 23-24, 97, 99-101)

solar calendar • a calendar in which the first day of each year is determined by the cycle of the sun, and the months are then determined by dividing up the year into predetermined segments, without necessarily any particular regard for the lunar cycle.

Glossary and Index, *continued*

sukkah *soo-kah* • a word transliterated from Hebrew which literally means "thicket shelter" but is usually translated "booth" or "tabernacle." Plural *sukkot*. – a humble, impermanent shelter built in obedience to God's command, in order to remember God's miraculous provision for Israel during the exodus. Such structures are built by observant families and congregations during the Feast of **Sukkot** or **Tabernacles**. (165, 171-173, 175, 184, 186-187)

Sukkot *soo-KŌT* • a word transliterated from Hebrew meaning "booths" or "tabernacles" – a seven-day feast of the Lord held Tishri 15-21, followed by an additional eighth day of assembly on Tishri 22. A symbolic type of the coming thousand-year reign of Jesus, in which God's peace and prosperity will prevail worldwide. (21, 23, 25, 164-187, 195, 197-198)

Tabernacles, Feast of • See definition under **Sukkot**. (21-23, 25, 99, 164-187, 197-198)

Tammuz *tah-MOOZ* • the post-exilic name of the fourth biblical month. (20)

tefillah *t'-fih-lah* • a word transliterated from the Hebrew meaning "prayer." (149)

teshuvah *t'-shoo-vah* • a word transliterated from the Hebrew meaning "repentance." (149)

Tevet *tay-VAYT* • the post-exilic name of the tenth biblical month. (21)

Tishri or **Tishrei** *tish-ree* or *tish-ray* • the post-exilic name of the seventh biblical month. (23, 25, 119-120, 122, 125-126, 141-143, 147, 165, 172, 197-198)

torah *to-RAH* • a word transliterated from Hebrew with a literal meaning of "instruction, direction" but often mechanically translated "law." Broadly, *torah* is defined as all instruction given by God throughout Old and New Testaments. Narrowly, it can refer to a certain subset of His laws as defined in the first five books of Bible, or to the physical scrolls on which they may be hand scribed.

transliteration • a method of writing the pronunciation of a foreign word using the letters of one's own alphabet. For example, the Hebrew word שָׁלוֹם may be transliterated into the letters of English as "shalom."

Trumpets, Day of • also called "Feast of Trumpets" – an appointed time of the Lord held on Tishri 1. See full definition under **Yom Teruah**. (21-23, 25, 117-137)

tsedakah *ts'-dah-kah* • a word transliterated from Hebrew meaning "righteousness" or "righteous deeds." (149)

Unleavened Bread, Feast of • a seven-day feast of the Lord held Nisan 15-21. See also its Hebrew name, **Chag Ha Matzah**. Jesus was in the grave during this feast. (Note: "Unleavened Bread" is a term sometimes used interchangeably with the term "Passover" as a shorthand reference to the *general* time period in which all three appointed times of Nisan occur: *Passover, Unleavened Bread,* and *Firstfruits*.) (20, 22-23, 32-33, 49-61, 65-67, 70-72, 98, 100, 167)

Glossary and Index, *continued*

waxing crescent • according to modern astronomy, the first appearance of a slender crescent *after* the phase of the new moon, which is itself invisible. It was the *waxing crescent* which the ancient Israelites actually looked for to determine if a new moon had indeed occurred.

Weeks, Feast of • An appointed time of the LORD held on Sivan 6, exactly fifty days following Firstfruits (from which is derived its Greek name, **Pentecost**, "fifty"). According to Jewish tradition, Moses received the Torah on Mount Sinai on this exact date, and, according to the biblical accounts, Moses was indeed present on Mount Sinai over a period of days spanning the date of Sivan 6. The believers described in chapter 2 of the book of Acts received the indwelling Holy Spirit on this date. See also **Shavuot.** (20, 22-24, 65, 67, 72-74, 96-115)

western calendar • See also **Gregorian calendar.** (19)

Yeshua *yay-SHOO-ah* • an Old Testament Hebrew name (**Jeshua**), which is a short form of the Hebrew name *y'ho-SHOO-ah* (**Joshua**), which means "the LORD is salvation." Over time, this Hebrew name migrated from its Greek form, Ἰησοῦς *(ee-ay-ssooss)*, to its Latin form, **Iesus** *(yay-ssooss)*, to its English form, **Jesus**. After many centuries of usage in English, the name's initial consonant gradually evolved to a hard "j" sound as in "jar." "Yeshua" was the actual name that the first-century disciples (and Jesus' earthly family members) used when speaking to Him or about Him.

Yom Ha Bikkurim *yom hah bih-koo-REEM* • a term transliterated from Hebrew meaning "day of firstfruits" – an appointed time of the LORD held on Nisan 16. Jesus was resurrected on this date. See also **Firstfruits, Feast of.** (20, 23, 65-93)

Yom Kippur *yom kih-POOR* • a term transliterated from Hebrew meaning "the "day of atonement," but in the Bible appearing in the plural form "Yom Ha Kippurim" *(yom hah-kih-poo-REEM)* – an appointed time of the LORD held on Tishri 10, the most holy date of the biblical year and the only fast day in all of Scripture that is specifically commanded by God. Yom Kippur is a prophetic type of the future atonement of all Israel. See also **Atonement, Day of.** (21, 23, 127, 141-161)

Yom Teruah *yom t'-ROO-ah* • a term transliterated from Hebrew literally meaning "day of a shout" or (by extension) "day of a blast" (often roughly translated "day of a trumpet"). Commonly termed "The Feast of Trumpets," this appointed time of the LORD is held on Tishri 1 and is a prophetic type of the future translation of believers, also known as "the Rapture." See also **Trumpets, Day of.** (21, 23, 118-137, 149-150)

Ziv *zihv* • the pre-exilic name of the second biblical month. (20)

Index of Recipes

Apple Bundt Cake (for Day of Trumpets).. 136
Apple Matzah Cake (for Passover / Unleavened Bread) 61
Blintzes (for Feast of Weeks) 115
Charoset (for the Passover seder) 45
Matzah Balls (for soup; for Passover / Unleavened Bread) 61
Matzah Chocolate Layer Cake (for Passover / Unleavened Bread) 45

Index of Children's Crafts and Activities

Edible Sukkah (for Feast of Tabernacles) 187
Kids' Craft Lulav (for Feast of Tabernacles) 187
Omer Calendar (from Firstfruits to Weeks) 82
Paper Crown (for Day of Trumpets) 134
Paper Plate Empty Tomb with Angels (for Feast of Firstfruits) 78
Party Horn Shofar (for Day of Trumpets) 135
Tissue Paper Flower Garland (for Feast of Weeks) 114

Index of Songs and Liturgy

Adon Olam – Lord of the Universe / Eternal Lord (High Holidays) 133
Al Chet – For the Sin (Day of Atonement) 158
Aseret Ha Dibrot – The Ten Utterances (Feast of Weeks) 113
Avinu, Malkeinu – Our Father, Our King (High Holidays) 156
Bedikat Chametz – The Search for Leaven (Feast of Unleavened Bread) 60
Bread of Affliction, The (Passover) 43
Four Cups, The (Passover) 42
Kol Nidre – All Vows (Day of Atonement) 157
Lulav waving ceremony (Feast of Tabernacles) 185
Ma Nishtanah – The Four Questions (Passover) 44
Melech, Ozer – O King, O Helper (High Holidays) 132
Seder Plate Description and Narration (Passover) 41
S'firat Ha-Omer – Counting the Omer (Feast of Firstfruits / Weeks) 81
Shehecheyanu – Who has Granted us Life 112
To the Sukkah (Feast of Tabernacles) 184

Other Books
by James T. and Lisa M. Cummins

Messiah's Alphabet Book 1: A workbook for learning how to read, write and pronounce the letters of the Hebrew alphabet

The first book in the *Messiah's Alphabet* series introduces the Hebrew alphabet to those with no prior knowledge of Hebrew. The student is shown how to draw simple "stick figure" shapes for each letter, and then learns the sound and name of each letter in a fun and friendly manner. The book gradually introduces some of the most frequently used Hebrew words in the Bible, gently assisting the reader in learning to recognize and pronounce each one. Audio files of every lesson available.

Available now through online book retailers

Messiah's Alphabet Book 2:
Building a Biblical Vocabulary

The second book in the *Messiah's Alphabet* series, this workbook teaches basic Hebrew grammar on topics such as the definite article "the", the conjunction "and," plural nouns, adjectives and possessives for singular nouns. Guided readings of short Scripture passages are included throughout. Fun, simple exercises with all answers are provided. Puzzles, riddles and tear-out "flashcard" pages are included. Intended for students who have completed Book 1 or who have a solid working knowledge of the Hebrew alphabet and are able to phonetically "sound out" Hebrew words. Audio files of every lesson available.

Available now through online book retailers

Other Books by James T. and Lisa M. Cummins, *continued*

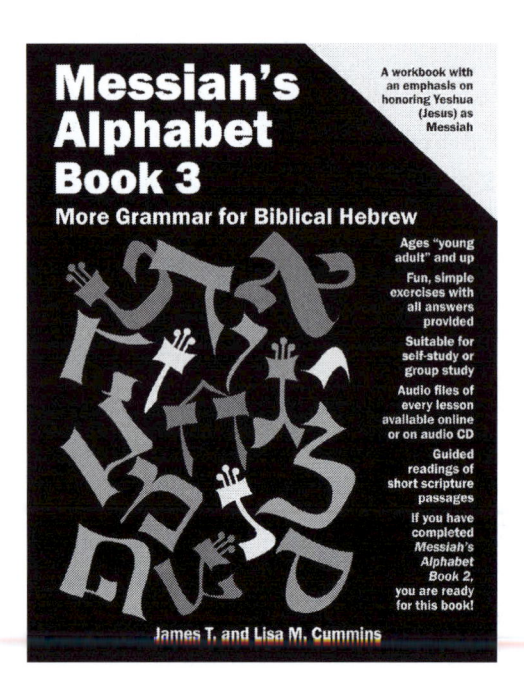

Messiah's Alphabet Book 3: More Grammar for Biblical Hebrew

The third book in the *Messiah's Alphabet* series covers topics such as participles, prepositions (standalone and inseparable), prepositions with pronominal suffixes, and construct chains (word pairs). Each lesson introduces plenty of new Biblical Hebrew vocabulary. Continuing in the same fun and friendly style as the other books in the series, the workbook contains cartoons, jokes, puzzles, flashcard pages, and answers to all exercises. Audio files of vocabulary from every lesson are available.

Available now through online book retailers

Messiah's Alphabet Book 4: Verbs and More Grammar for Biblical Hebrew

The fourth book in the *Messiah's Alphabet* series covers verbs (roots, past tense, future tense, imperative and infinitive), the direct object marker, possessive suffixes for plural nouns, and the reversing *vav*. Each lesson introduces new Biblical Hebrew vocabulary. Continuing in the same fun and friendly style as the other books in the series, the workbook contains cartoons, jokes, puzzles, flashcard pages, and answers to all exercises. The book also includes Verb Charts, which give conjugations of frequently used verbs. Audio files of all newly introduced vocabulary are available.

Available now through online book retailers

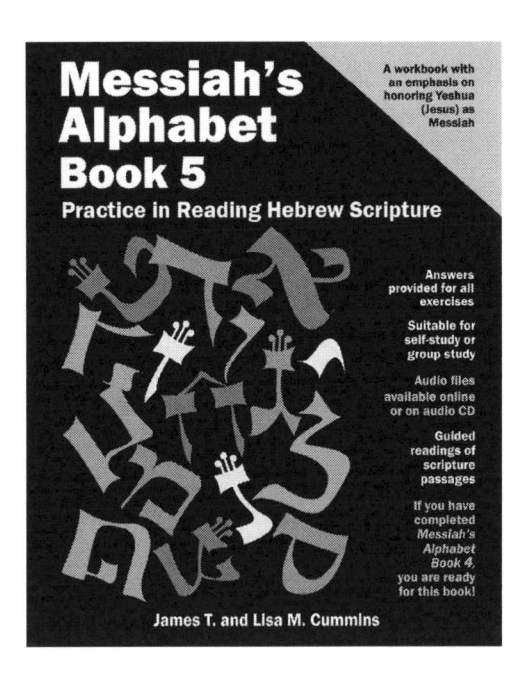

Other Books by James T. and Lisa M. Cummins, *continued*

Messiah's Alphabet Book 5: Practice in Reading Hebrew Scripture allows the student who has completed Books 1 through 4 of the series to spread his or her wings and practice reading entire passages of Scripture, using mostly the vocabulary already taught in the series. Some new vocabulary is taught in this book, too, including tear-out flashcard pages, verb charts and glossary. Comparison tables of Christian, traditional Jewish and Messianic translations for every passage are included. Intriguing discussion questions explore selected Hebrew phrases. Complete answer keys with grammatical notations included. Emphasis on Yeshua (Jesus) as Savior and Lord. Audio files of every lesson available.

Available now through online book retailers

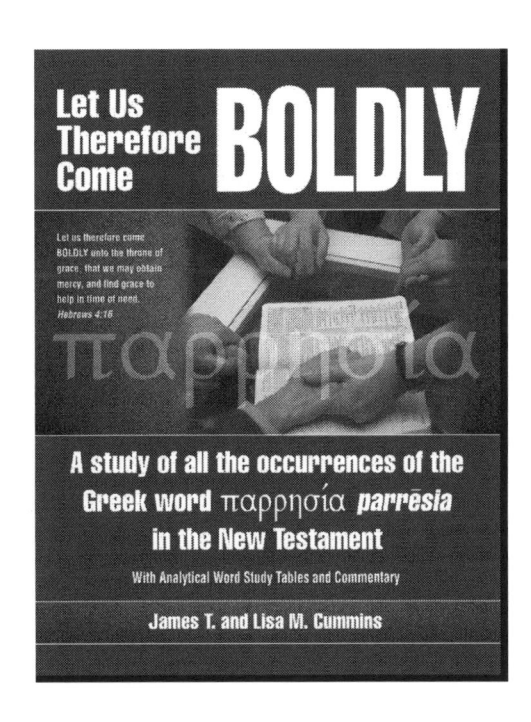

Let Us Therefore Come BOLDLY:
A study of all the occurrences of the Greek word parresia *in the New Testament*

This book leads the reader through all the occurrences of the Greek word for "boldness" in the New Testament. Throughout the study, the various meanings of this deep and wonderful Greek word are uncovered, along with practical applications for the believer's life. Graphic tables and insightful commentary make it easy for the student to understand the significance of every separate mention of the Greek word *parresia* – even if the student has no knowledge of the Greek language.

Available now through online book retailers

Other Books by James T. and Lisa M. Cummins, *continued*

Messiah's Alphabet: Names Have Meaning is an exploration into the actual Hebrew meanings of the names of certain people mentioned in the Bible. Surprising discoveries will unfold as you connect the true meaning of each Hebrew name with its prophetic significance and fulfillment in Scripture. The hidden Hebrew meanings underlying the names of New Testament people are also brought to light. While a basic knowledge of the Hebrew and Greek alphabets may be helpful, it is not necessary, as all pronunciations are provided in transliteration form using the letters of the English alphabet. All answers are provided in the text. Audio files of every lesson available.

Available now through online book retailers

Messiah's Alphabet: Places Have Meaning is an exploration into the actual Hebrew meanings of the names of certain places mentioned in the Bible. Surprising discoveries will unfold as you connect the true meaning of each Hebrew name with its prophetic significance and fulfillment in Scripture. The hidden Hebrew meanings underlying the names of New Testament places are also brought to light. While a basic knowledge of the Hebrew and Greek alphabets may be helpful, it is not necessary, as all pronunciations are provided in transliteration form using the letters of the English alphabet. All answers are provided in the text. Audio files of every lesson available.

Available now through online book retailers

OTHER BOOKS BY JAMES T. AND LISA M. CUMMINS | 215

God invented a calendar. Now, you can learn all about it!

Did any New Testament events align with God's special "appointed times" of the Old Testament?

How do God's Old Testament holy days act as prophetic "pictures" of future things to come?

How does knowing the order of the biblical months help clarify the order of events in the New Testament?

Did you know that certain historical events tend to recur during certain months in the biblical calendar – such as the destructions of *both* the first and second temples, which occurred more than 600 years apart, but on the *same date*?

Don't worry if you've never heard of a biblical calendar before... *Messiah's Calendar Book 1: Days, Weeks, Months and Years* offers a gentle introduction to the concepts of biblical timekeeping, God's calendar, and God's appointed times, with an emphasis on their ultimate fulfillment in Messiah Jesus (Yeshua). Learn about God's definitions of the day, the week, the month and the year. Get familiar with the order of the biblical months and see how it helps clarify the order of events in your New Testament. This book's educational illustrations and excellent graphics - packed with prophetic insights and historical information - make God's calendar easy to grasp. The writing style and choice of vocabulary are sensitive to both Jewish and Gentile readers, so this book is suitable for churches and Messianic congregations alike.

Other great features include:

- **Educational illustrations throughout**
- **Packed with biblical insights**
- **Listed scriptures are fully "typed out" for convenience in classroom study**
- **Brief descriptions of all feasts and fasts**
- **Easy explanations of any Hebrew or Greek terms, with simple phonetic pronunciations. (Prior knowledge of Hebrew or Greek is not necessary.)**
- **Additional resources in the back, including graphics, teachings and glossary/index**
- **Excellent for either group or individual study**

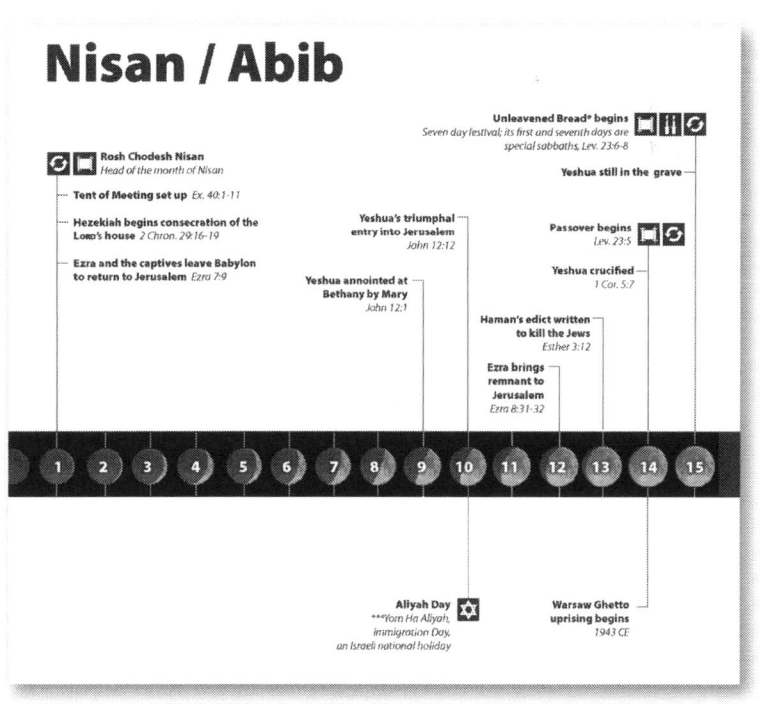

You'll enjoy the clear, easy to use graphics — portraying the date of every event mentioned in scripture... as well as the dates of key historical events which are not mentioned in the Bible.

Other Books by James T. and Lisa M. Cummins, *continued*

Phrase-By-Phrase Harmony of the Gospels – This is a visual, side-by-side arrangement of every phrase of the books of Matthew, Mark, Luke and John, in chronological order. Every phrase of every gospel is aligned side by side with the corresponding phrases in the other gospels, in table format. Each event includes its own geographical map and graphical timeline. Blended narrative contains every fact and detail of all four gospels, merged into a single, readable, chronological account.

Available now through online book retailers

Modular design: Focus your attention on one event per section.

Graphical Timeline on every section: Keep track of what happened before and what's coming up.

Phrase-By-Phrase Harmonized Table: Compare every phrase of scripture from all four gospels at a glance. Bolded and italicized typefaces indicate time and geography references.

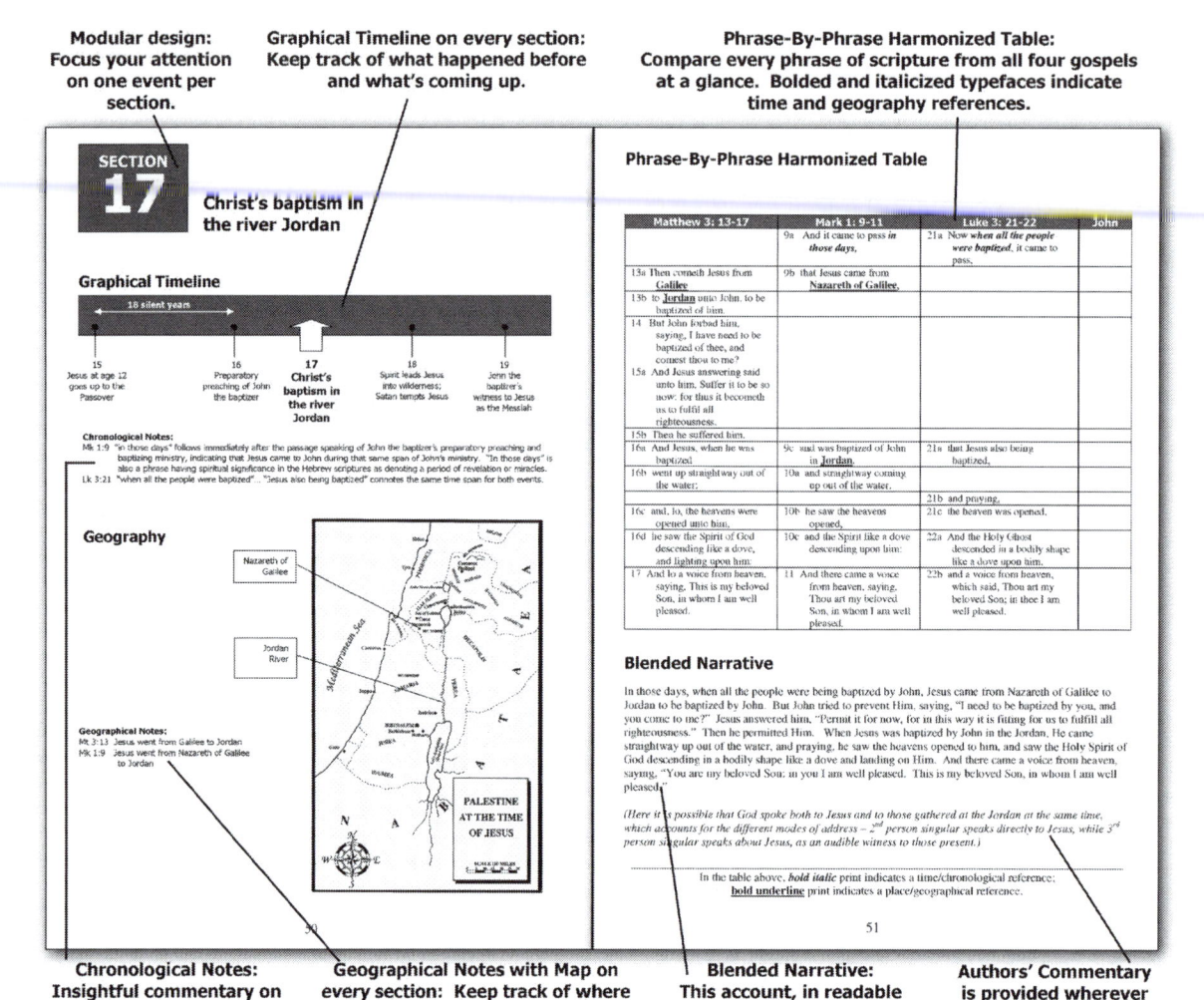

Chronological Notes: Insightful commentary on the historical or cultural significance of all time references.

Geographical Notes with Map on every section: Keep track of where each event occurs. Historical and archaeological notes are provided wherever applicable.

Blended Narrative: This account, in readable modern language, contains every factual detail of all four gospels, in chronological order.

Authors' Commentary is provided wherever clarification of difficult or problematic texts is necessary.

Other Books by James T. and Lisa M. Cummins, *continued*

Biblical Greek Book 1: A workbook for learning how to read, write and pronounce the letters of the Greek alphabet

The first book in the *Biblical Greek* series introduces the Greek alphabet to those with no prior knowledge of Greek. The student is shown how to draw simple "stick figure" shapes for each letter, and then learns the sound and name of each letter in a fun and friendly manner. The book gradually introduces some of the most frequently used Greek words in the Bible, gently assisting the reader in learning to recognize and pronounce each one. Audio files of every lesson available.

Available now through online book retailers

Biblical Greek Book 2: Nouns and Cases

The second book in the *Biblical Greek* series teaches about Greek nouns (singular and plural forms) and the five cases (nominative, genitive, dative, accusative and vocative), as well as the Greek article in all its forms. Book 2 expands upon the reader's basic knowledge of the "Top Twenty" most frequently used Greek nouns of the New Testament (whose nominative singular forms were taught in Book 1) while adding additional vocabulary. Handy charts, tables and lists are provided, as are tear-out flashcards and a glossary of all vocabulary. Enlarged graphics help the reader learn to recognize stem letters and case endings. Actual New Testament Scripture is used in the examples and exercises, for which complete answer keys are included.

Available now through online book retailers

Novels by James T. and Lisa M. Cummins

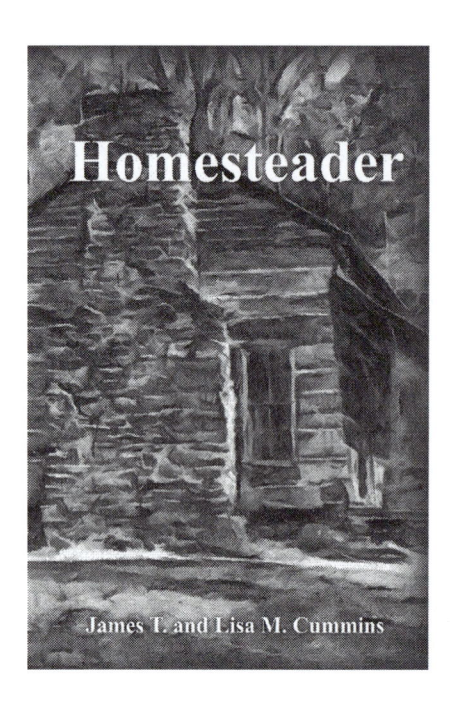

Homesteader

It's 1957, and thirteen-year-old Jimmy dreams of homesteading a piece of land just like he's seen the pioneers do on his favorite TV show. As soon as he finds the perfect spot to build a homestead, he gets caught trespassing on an old man's property. It's just the first of many hard lessons about the realities of life. After years of hard work and patience, Jimmy gradually begins to have some success. Throughout life's tragedies and triumphs, he learns the value of enduring friendship.

Available now through online book retailers

Orchard Hill

It is a time of economic desperation. When Raybun returns to the Kentucky homeplace after fighting in the Second World War, he is dismayed to discover the entire region suffering in extreme poverty resulting from economic changes beyond anyone's control. Now, Raybun must find a way to help his family and community. Through a series of small miracles and a growing, persistent faith, Raybun and his friends are able to bring restoration to the broken community, and find love along the way.

Available now through online book retailers under author names James T. and Lisa M. Cummins and pseudonyms Raybun and Penelope Bowland

Printed in Great Britain
by Amazon